To the Class of '68 at the University of Louisiana-Lafayette—
especially Michel Schexnayder, Stephen Webre, Edward Pratt,
Agnes Gauthier Mautner, and the late Eugene Morel

A Time
of Paradox

*America from the Cold War
to the Third Millennium,
1945–Present*

GLEN JEANSONNE

WITH DAVID LUHRSSEN

973
.92
J43

ROWMAN & LITTLEFIELD PUBLISHERS, INC.
Lanham • Boulder • New York • Toronto • Oxford

ROWMAN & LITTLEFIELD PUBLISHERS, INC.

Acquiring Editor: Niels Aaboe
Developmental Editor: Ann Grogg
Production Editor: Terry Fischer
Photo Editor: Andrew Boney
Typesetter: Andrea Reider

Published in the United States of America
by Rowman & Littlefield Publishers, Inc.
A wholly owned subsidiary of The Rowman & Littlefield Publishing Group, Inc.
4501 Forbes Boulevard, Suite 200, Lanham, Maryland 20706
www.rowmanlittlefield.com

PO Box 317
Oxford
OX2 9RU, UK

British Library Cataloguing in Publication Information Available

Library of Congress Cataloging-in-Publication Data

Jeansonne, Glen, 1946–
  A time of paradox : America from the cold war to the third millennium,
1945–present / Glen Jeansonne with David Luhrssen.
    p. cm.
  Includes bibliographical references and index.
  ISBN 10: 0-7425-3379-4 (pbk. : alk. paper) —
  ISBN 13: 978-0-7425-3379-0 (pbk. : alk. paper)
    1. United States—History—20th century. 2. United States—History—
20th century—Biography. 3. United States—Civilization—20th century.
I. Luhrssen, David. II. Title.
E741.J43 2005
973.91—dc22   2005029323

Printed in the United States of America

♾™ The paper used in this publication meets the minimum requirements of
American National Standard for Information Sciences—Permanence of Paper
for Printed Library Materials, ANSI/NISO Z39.48-1992.

Contents

Preface

A *Time of Paradox* has both a theme and a message. The theme derives from the inconsistencies and anomalies, some frustrating, some wonderful, in the human condition. The period covered in the book was a time of contradiction and irony, which I term paradox. I employ the word "paradox" in a metaphorical rather than in a literal sense. It is not a dictionary definition but can mean, in this context, irony, contradiction, a thing that seems to be what it is not, an unlikely event, or an oxymoron.

Each age has its share of paradoxes, in the metaphorical sense. Some are inherent to the march of civilization, with its relapses, and some are specific to the particular age. In the time covered here, the human condition never seemed more poignant; much was accomplished and much was lost. The term seems especially appropriate to this time because of the scope and dimension of both our successes and our failures. We dared greatly, and like all who dare greatly we sometimes failed greatly. Yet the period saw the unconquerable aspect of the human will emerge intact. What is even more striking is the acceleration of the pace of change, a term that combines speed and rate of increase in speed, finally producing a momentum that carries over unless it is blocked. While change is inevitable, it is neutral in itself, neither good nor evil. Change, even for good, can be painful, but what is more painful is resistance to change.

The message of *A Time of Paradox* is more complex and potentially more important. Yet, it cannot be summed up in a byte and might resonate differently with individual readers. This is no attempt to deliberately obscure but rather to grant each reader the right to his or her own interpretation. Inherently, people will read the book for different reasons, and find some parts more appropriate to their personal interests than others. But while *A Time of Paradox* is factual, it is more than a compendium of facts and illustrations. It is deliberately more personal, speculative, and provocative than the most textbooks, more imaginative than derivative, and it departs from some orthodox interpretations. It is succinct and jargon-free, yet it includes the essential facts as well as broad generalizations and original metaphors and examples. Unlike some similar books, it represents, for the most part, a single viewpoint. Although vulnerable to error of interpretation, the viewpoint is consistent, though it contains surprises. The author chose, for example, to devote more attention to such aspects of history as spirituality, technology, and sexuality, than comparable books. I hope to have done so in a manner that is open-minded and non-judgmental, yet take no offence to those who disagree. Errors of fact or interpretation can be mitigated by discussion and corrected in later editions.

For clues to the author's overall viewpoint, and the book's message, read carefully the prologue and the epilogue and, to a lesser extent, the prologues to the individual eras and the conclusions to the chapters within those eras. In general, I believe that such human traits as love and hate are not opposite emotions, but opposite extremes of the same emotion. And they can be transmuted.

Whether one reads *A Time of Paradox* as a scholar, a student, or a general reader, I hope it brings them pleasure as well as knowledge. The facts might be forgotten within a few years or submerged in the subconscious. The message in the metaphors might stick longer. Further, I have proceeded on the premise that history is a story about people much like ourselves and that when we read or write it we hold up a mirror to ourselves. People feel as well as think and *A Time of Paradox* is meant to appeal to feelings as well as to the intellect. The residue of the feelings will probably outlast the residue of the facts.

In addition, I believe the best guide to understanding history lies not in elaborate paradigms but in experience and common sense. There are definite patterns in history, but their origins and the way they emerge results from a mixture of factors, some obvious, some obscure, and some beyond human understanding. Though I believe things happen for a reason—otherwise there would be little point in studying or remembering them—I do not claim to know each specific reason. At best, I am an experienced guesser. Scholars should be careful about assuming that we are wiser than others. I have worked with fellow Ph.D.s my entire career, yet I suspect there are beggars on the streets of Calcutta with a potentially higher I.Q. than anyone at my university.

Another premise is that everything is connected. Thus I have tried to incorporate many varieties of history without purporting to be an expert in all of them. But appreciation of history requires not only an appreciation of its diversity but an understanding of how that diversity is connected. Albert Einstein believed that imagination is more important than knowledge in the study of physics. That is true in the study of history as well. After all, history tells us only the story of paths chosen. We do not know the results of where those not chosen might have led.

In analyzing the characters in our history books, I believe it is important to strike a balance between imposing the standards of our time on them, and viewing them in terms of what they knew at their time, and the realistic options they had. One surmises, for example, that General George Armstrong Custer might have reacted differently at Little Bighorn had he known of the Indians over the hill.

The organization of *A Time of Paradox* is related to its philosophical design and facilitates its use as a teaching tool, and as an escort through the past. The book is divided into eras, each with a theme. Each era is divided into six chapters that cover topically, within a rough chronological framework, the events of that era. The chapter themes relate to the theme of the era, which in turn connect to the overall theme of paradox. Each era includes three brief biographical profiles that illustrate a sub-theme of the period. The individuals are not selected for their significance, nor are they necessarily representative. In fact, most are secondary figures. Rather, they are chosen because of their illustration of the diversity of the era and the overall theme of paradox, as well as for their human interest.

The book includes a prologue and an epilogue, which interpret, summarize, and draw conclusions. Anyone wanting an overview might read these first. In addition, there is a separate prologue introducing each era, which provides an interpretive overview. There is a timeline for each era and a selective list of readings. The book is designed to be succinct, yet factually comprehensive and reasonably priced. Its relative brevity facilitates the use of complementary, more specialized studies. The provocative interpretations are intended to stimulate dialogue, whether in the classroom, in book clubs, or in the minds of individual readers.

In retrospect, what strikes me most about *A Time of Paradox* is its evolution in the direction of diversity and the breadth and breathtaking speed of change. The interconnections mentioned earlier include not only the interconnections of events to one another, but also the interconnections of America to other nations, perhaps, we will find, to other worlds. More important are the connections between individuals. All of these connections were necessary to arrive at the point we now stand.

We are mortal, in a narrow sense, yet each of us leaves behind an imprint on the planet earth. King Arthur is supposed to have told his aspiring knights that before he gave them a sword they must become a poet. The world needs poets and students, spiritual warriors and military warriors, scholars, and plumbers. It would not work if we were all one kind. I am proud to be a historian and consider it important. Yet I have never been summoned in the middle of the night to fix a history book that had suddenly burst open.

Acknowledgments

I EMBARK upon the prospect of thanking those who contributed to *A Time of Paradox* with trepidation. Because the genesis of the book is distant, and my memory is fallible, I might omit someone who rendered me valuable service. On the other hand, the help of some might be so subtle they may be surprised to be mentioned.

Bruce Borland, formally of HarperCollins, was crucial in accepting my idea for the book and more than any single editor believed in its trade potential. Mary Carpenter was largely responsible for bringing the book to Rowman & Littlefield. Laura Roberts Gottlieb of Rowman & Littlefield, the book's chief editor, exercised patience and coaxed out of me the best I could do. Andrew Boney was essential to the book's completion. Niels Aaboe is the final editor.

Over the course of a decade, about seventy-five referees read portions of the manuscript. However, only Ronald Snyder read the entire book and he wrote the most complete and thoughtful analysis. Of the readers who signed their reports, the most helpful were Leo Ribuffo, who, as usual, was intellectually honest, and Kari Frederickson, a former student, now a prominent historian.

David Luhrssen worked closely with me, especially in the book's final stages. He did the research and wrote the first draft of two of the chapters on cultural history. In addition, he helped with photograph selection, captions, and indexed the manuscript. I turned to Herbert M. Levine whenever I encountered a problem. An old teacher, colleague, and friend, Herb helped with photo and map research. He used his computer skills and strategic location near the Library of Congress to iron out numerous difficulties. I am grateful for the assistance of Michael Gauger, although he did not agree with the final version of the book.

I had a superb copy editor, Ann Grogg, who edited my previous book, *Transformation and Reaction*. Like most writers I incline to believe that the best strategy to altering my prose is benign neglect. Yet Ann improved it, while adhering to the principle: "If it ain't broke, don't fix it." Ann's husband Bob, who fact-checked, is one of the most meticulous historians I know. Meredith Vnuk checked facts and updated, as did Nick Katers, and Sarah Lager. Stacey Smith aided with photographic research, as did Mary Manion. Jacqueline Kelnhofer was my chief proofreader. Other proofreaders included David Luhrssen, Lori Lasky, Joan Hoss. Bruce Fetter, Neal Pease, and Lex Renda.

I owe major personal and professional debts to Joan Hoss. She literally lived with the book, typed the final manuscript, and prepared it for submission while I was away researching my next book on Herbert Hoover. Joan and John Kiekhaefer were my chief computer gurus. Though she is not a historian, Joan understands the book's underlying message better than anyone who has read it.

Greg Hoag is a wonderful teacher of non-academic truths and Sarah Sullivan, my personal trainer, kept my body intact. Milton Bates advised me on many aspects of the manuscript, including style, content, and publishing strategy, from its inception.

Some of my colleagues lent key support. Neal Pease, Jeffrey Merrick, Joe Rodriguez, and especially Lex Renda helped adjust my teaching schedule to my biorhythms. Among colleagues or former colleagues who suggested sources in their areas of expertise are Michael Gordon, Mark Bradley, Bruce Fetter, Victor Greene, David Hoeveler, and David Healy. No persons in the department were more essential to the book's completion than Louise Whitaker, Anita Cathey, and Teena Rawls.

The past and current directors of the Golda Meir Library provided access to its resources and all have been personal friends: Bill Roselle, Peter Watson-Boone, and Ewa Barczyk. My most important friend who navigated me through the labyrinths of library research is Ahmad Kramah, whose knowledge of recent American history is exceeded only by his generosity. Two of my colleagues on the University Library Committee, Winston Van Horne, and Mordecai Lee, have been particularly supportive.

There are several historians from whose work I have profited, some of whom are personal friends: Thomas C. Reeves, John Milton Cooper, William B. Pemberton, David Fromkin, James MacGregor Burns, Michael Beschloss, Dennis Dickerson, James W. Cortada, Thomas Schoonover, John Ehrman, and the late Stephen Ambrose.

I want to acknowledge some of the major influences in my life: my late father, Ryan J. Jeansonne, who knew the New Deal first-hand; the late

William Ivy Hair, who steered me through the shoals of graduate school and onto the dry land of an academic career; and Amos E. Simpson, a former teacher and mentor.

For providing the supportive environment that everyone needs, professionally and personally, I would like to thank Helena Pycior, Kathy Callahan, Vann Mobley, Patrick Steele, Stephen A. Webre, Edward F. Haas, Mathe Allain, Bill Pederson, Paul George, Dan Kohl, Michael Wynne, Eddie Lager, Richard Osborne, Irv Becker, Richard Pierce, Carl Brasseaux, William Warren Rogers, Lynnell Ransome, Bob and Bonnie Bruch, Michael Seeley, and Sharon Pace.

For inspiration, I had Leah and Hannah Jeansonne.

An Era of Uncertainty, 1945–1968

Prologue

EVEN AFTER winning World War II, Americans lived with uncertainty. They seemed to be fighting constantly, waging wars abroad in Korea and Vietnam and waging wars at home—one against poverty and, ultimately, one among themselves. The Cold War permeated these struggles, affecting domestic politics, culture, and international relations.

President Harry S Truman promoted the Marshall Plan and the Truman Doctrine, sent the United States into the Korean War, promised civil rights to minorities, and espoused a Fair Deal. But much of his domestic program faltered or fell short of expectations, and Truman, an upset winner in 1948, was a lame duck by 1952. Dwight Eisenhower, the World War II hero who succeeded Truman, took office determined to ensure enduring peace but had to settle for an inconclusive end to the Korean conflict and a continuation of the Cold War.

In the Cold War, America experienced instant fortunes, instant celebrities, and the specter of instant death. Americans had believed themselves secure, unchallenged with the might of the atomic bomb, until the Soviets acquired the power. Subversives within the federal government were helping prepare the country for a communist takeover, warned demagogic Senator Joseph McCarthy, who became a victim of his own excesses. Bigger bombs, greater radioactive fallout, multiple warheads, and ballistic missiles were to come. Despite it all, most Americans lived normal lives. More important than world events, especially in rural areas and small towns, were families, friends, jobs, and schools. Socially and economically, there were a host of ways to enjoy life during these affluent decades. Instead of shrinking from the Cold War, some moviemakers parodied it. Although the times were uncertain, Americans were concerned, perhaps saddened, but not hysterical.

If the bomb did not explode, the population did. From the mid-1940s to the mid-1960s, a baby boom occurred that affected the United States economically and politically, particularly in the 1960s. The initial wave of baby boomers, born in the year after World War II ended, entered college in 1964, the year of the Gulf of Tonkin Resolution, the Mississippi Freedom Summer, the Berkeley free speech movement, and the beginning of the urban riots. Television was the companion of the baby boomers, whose generation was the first to come of age under its influence. In 1950 only 8 percent of American families had TV sets; a decade later, only 10 percent did not have one. People watched Ozzie and Harriet, Lucille Ball, Milton Berle, the Kefauver Committee hearings, and the Army-McCarthy hearings. Other shows featured preachers Billy Graham, Norman Vincent Peale, and Bishop Fulton J. Sheen, popularizers who offered religion as a tonic. Elvis Presley, on the other hand, shook everyone up. To adult dismay, the boomers gyrated with him and tuned in to rock 'n' roll music, introducing a culture much as their elders embraced jazz.

Unlike the 1950s—a golden age, if one were white, male, and middle class—the 1960s were inhospitable to moderation. Bob Dylan, troubadour of the young, warned the older generation about the impending deluge of change. Again it seemed that successive decades were virtual mirror images. Yet the 1950s were more complex than they appeared, and the 1960s, for all their ferment, closed with nostalgia for the more peaceful 1950s. Under presidents John F. Kennedy and Lyndon B. Johnson, practically every social conflict erupted into the streets, overloading the national circuits with challenges, including an intensified civil rights movement, a feminist revival, protests against the Vietnam War, an unfinished War on Poverty, and a campus revolt. The war in Vietnam cast a pall over the United States, enraged the young, and toppled Johnson. The country learned a lesson in humility in the jungles of a distant land, where the marvels of American technology lost a war to ill-armed guerrillas. The assassinations of John Kennedy, Martin Luther King Jr., and Robert Kennedy rent the nation. Finally, a backlash carried Richard Nixon to the White House in 1969. "If you liked the 1950s, you will love the 1970s," a graduate student predicted in 1970.

In the meantime, the era that had produced successes began to cruelly undermine the American dream. Vietnam would fall to communists. The economy, affluent in the 1950s and approaching overdrive in the 1960s, weakened. With an aging infrastructure and industrial base, the United States lost ground to international competitors. The nation entered a postindustrial era, when job growth would lag and be limited primarily to the service sector, and a posturban era, when the suburbs would swell and the cities would dwindle, apparently a permanent trend. The nation changed in ways unanticipated. Like all changes, some embraced them, others bemoaned them, and still others denied them. More problems, more paradoxes awaited.

Time Line

An Era of Uncertainty, 1945–1968

March 12, 1947 Truman announces Truman Doctrine.

April 15, 1947 Jackie Robinson breaks color barrier in major-league baseball.

June 5, 1947 Marshall Plan proposed.

June 25, 1950 Communist North Korea invades South Korea.

February 27, 1951 Twenty-Second Amendment which limits a president to two terms ratified.

November 4, 1952 Dwight D. Eisenhower elected president.

May 17, 1954 Supreme Court outlaws school segregation in *Brown v. Board of Education.*

December 1, 1955 Bus boycott in Montgomery, Alabama.

January 5, 1957 Eisenhower promulgates Eisenhower Doctrine.

April 17, 1961 Bay of Pigs invasion.

August 13, 1961 Construction begins on Berlin Wall

February 20, 1962 John Glenn becomes first American to orbit Earth.

October 22 to November 20, 1962 Cuban Missile Crisis.

November 22, 1963 President John F. Kennedy is assassinated; Vice President Lyndon B. Johnson takes presidential oath.

August 7, 1964 Gulf of Tonkin Resolution.

July 2, 1964 Johnson signs Civil Rights Act.

November 3, 1964 Johnson defeats Barry Goldwater in presidential election.

July 30, 1965 Johnson signs legislation creating Medicare and Medicaid.

August 6, 1965 Johnson approves Voting Rights Act.

January 30, 1968 Tet Offensive.

March 31, 1968 Johnson announces withdrawal from presidential race.

April 4, 1968 The Reverend Martin Luther King Jr. is assassinated.

June 5, 1968 New York Senator Robert F. Kennedy is assassinated.

November 5, 1968 Richard M. Nixon defeats Democrat Hubert Humphrey in presidential race.

CHAPTER ONE

The Fair Deal
and the Cold War,
1945–1952

THE COLD War and an untested president brought open-ended dilemmas in foreign and domestic policy to the first administration of the Era of Uncertainty. Bluster and bluff were common on both sides of the canyon that divided communism and democratic capitalism. The wake of the war produced problems in the economy, in race relations, in gender roles, and in domestic politics. Paradoxically, the worst fears of Americans never materialized, but a host of smaller ones did.

Harry S Truman and the Postwar Economy

Throughout his White House years, Harry S Truman was haunted by the specter of Franklin D. Roosevelt. Roosevelt was imperial; Truman was ordinary. Roosevelt was eloquent; Truman was blunt. Roosevelt handled political problems with procrastination and finesse, whereas Truman carved up political opponents like a Thanksgiving turkey. Roosevelt battled for the top office four times. Truman did not want the presidency at all; it found him. He wanted to appear decisive, and to do so, he overcame self-doubt. He placed a sign on his desk that read: "The buck stops here."

Truman grew up in Independence, Missouri, where he graduated from high school yet never attended college. A World War I vet, he worked as a bank clerk, a farmer, and a clothing store proprietor. Entering politics late, he won an administrative post—county judge—with the assistance of the notorious Democratic Kansas City machine masterminded by Thomas J. Pendergast. He married his high school sweetheart, Bess Wallace, and settled in as a minor local official. In 1934, Truman was elected to the U.S.

Senate at Pendergast's initiative because the machine needed a veteran with a reputation for honesty. In 1944, after Vice President Henry A. Wallace was dropped for alienating conservatives, Truman was the compromise choice for second place on the ticket. The ticket won, Roosevelt died, and Truman became president.

World War II had unthrottled the economy and ended the depression. Postwar economic problems focused on shortages, reconversion to consumer production, readjustment of the labor force, and inflation. Despite fears of its resurrection, the depression was dead. Consumer demand, suppressed by the war, rushed to fill appetites for homes, automobiles, refrigerators, and other items. Congress enacted the G.I. Bill of Rights which furnished funds for former servicemen to go to college, obtain a technical education, or buy a house. Unemployment fell to 2 percent in 1945.

Still, the national debt had soared into the stratosphere, from $34 billion in 1940 to $248 billion in 1945. The nation spent more to defeat the Axis than in all the previous history of the republic. Inflation, held under control by the Office of Price Administration, leaped when the office was phased out. The Korean War, beginning in 1950, brought increased military spending, which stimulated the economy.

Inflation triggered demands from labor for higher wages. When these were unmet, unions struck, just as they had done in a similar situation in 1919. The strikes started with important industries such as steel and meatpacking in 1946, compounded by even more vexing strikes by railroad workers and coal miners in 1946. Truman ended the railroad strike by threatening to draft recalcitrant workers into the army. John L. Lewis, leader of the United Mine Workers, was the last holdout, but ultimately the strike was settled under government pressure.

Truman lost patience with some labor leaders, yet when Republicans sought to trim their sails via the Taft-Hartley Bill of 1947, he vetoed it, only to have his veto overridden. The Republican Congress elected in 1946, led by Ohio Senator Robert Taft, an arch-conservative, passed the bill over protests of the unions and the president. Designed to define unfair practices for labor as the Wagner Act of 1935 had outlawed certain practices for business, it outlawed the closed shop (requiring a worker to join a union as a condition of employment), and barred union contributions to political campaigns. Eighty-days notice must be given before major strikes, followed by negotiations. During the Korean War, strikes by telephone and telegraph workers and an imminent strike by steelworkers disrupted the war effort. After Truman threatened to seize facilities facing impending strikes, the Supreme Court declared such a seizure unconstitutional. A seven-week steel strike followed, costly to the country and Truman's reputation as an evenhanded chief executive.

Truman's first major address to Congress in 1945 produced a basket stuffed with liberal legislative proposals. Among them were national health insurance, a higher minimum wage, regional developments similar to the Tennessee Valley Authority, a permanent Fair Employment Practices Committee, and restrictions on business. His program was dead on arrival. The country was weary and wanted bounty, not social experimentation. Truman's popularity plummeted. People missed Roosevelt. The new president wanted to clamp a lid on economic expansion rather than let prosperity flourish. He lacked the ability to control inflation. He tried to bully unions. The Republican motto in the 1946 congressional campaigns summed up the nation's mood: "Had Enough?" The short answer was "yes." The GOP won control of both Houses of Congress for the first time since the Hoover administration.

Two significant acts were nonetheless passed regarding the presidency. The Presidential Succession Act placed the House Speaker and Senate president pro tem ahead of the cabinet in the line of succession after the vice president. Truman believed elected officials should be first in line. The Twenty-Second Amendment, ratified in 1951, limited the president to two terms. Meanwhile, Truman faced a divided country and party for his reelection bid in 1948. The cupboard was full of ambitious domestic proposals but practically barren of achievements. Truman proved more decisive internationally, but his foreign policy was not expected to help him much. At the time of the election Allied planes were airlifting sustenance to beleaguered West Berlin, blockaded by the communists.

Truman selected Kentucky Senator Alben Barkley as his running mate. The Republicans believed they had a winner by nominating New York Governor Thomas E. Dewey, pairing him with California Governor Earl Warren. Not only did this ticket provide ideological and regional balance; it coupled the two most populous states. Dewey had run before. In 1944 he had lost to Roosevelt, yet had done better than previous challengers. Moreover, Truman was no Roosevelt and the voters were restless.

So restless were the Democrats that their party cracked apart at their convention. The southerners defected over a prointegration civil rights plank, and created the States' Rights Democratic Party, dubbed the Dixiecrats. They nominated two southern governors: J. Strom Thurmond of South Carolina and Fielding Wright of Mississippi. Further splintering, Henry Wallace stole radicals and some liberals, running as the nominee of the Progressive Party. The Progressives received some support from communists, while the

Dixiecrats robbed the Democrats of some southern regional support. All that was left was the center, but that is where the votes were.

The Republicans wrote a liberal platform proposing a list of progressive reforms. Truman called their bluff by summoning Congress into special session and offering them the opportunity for the Republican-dominated branch to enact their program. When they failed to do so, he denounced them as hypocrites. Now the Missourian had his issue. He would run against the Republican Congress. Ignoring the fact that he was part of the government, he ran as an outsider. Moreover, he reached out to the common people, trekking cross-country by train to "Give 'em hell," as one supporter suggested. Dewey was overconfident. He remained dignified and avoided commitment on some issues in order to have a free hand when elected. All the polls said he would win.

But Dewey did not win. Nonetheless, the anti-Truman *Chicago Tribune*, which had gone to press before the late returns were in, ran a banner headline the next morning, "Dewey Defeats Truman." That morning a reporter snapped a photo of Truman brandishing the headline. Naturally he was grinning. The result was the presidential upset of the century. Truman won 24.1 million popular votes and 303 electoral votes to 21.9 million and 189

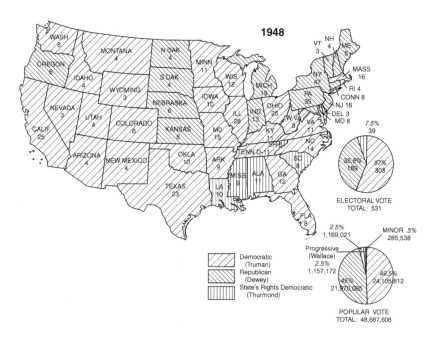

Election of 1948

for Dewey. Thurmond gained about 1 million popular votes and 39 electoral votes; Wallace also won about 1 million popular votes but no electoral votes. Dewey was decimated. What had gone wrong?

First, the polls stopped polling too early and used questionable methods, such as employing telephone books and automobile registrations to obtain lists of potential subjects to question. Many Truman voters were too poor to have either. The polls failed to account for the undecided vote, which shifted to Truman in the weeks after they ceased polling. Also, Truman was more down-to-earth and likeable than Dewey. Truman's aggressive campaign made Dewey resemble a stuffed shirt. Truman set a domestic agenda that attracted groups of Roosevelt's coalition, even though it did not pass. And his decisiveness in foreign policy did count. Finally, one cannot discount the factor that many of Truman's constituents identified with the underdog.

The Fair Deal

In his 1949 State of the Union address Truman used the term "Fair Deal" to describe his program. Truman wanted to expand social services, enact civil rights, and regulate business. In this session Congress agreed to his proposals for public housing, increased minimum wages, and extended Social Security coverage. Yet it remained opposed to national health insurance and the president's plan to wean farmers from price supports. Under plans developed by a commission led by former President Herbert Hoover, appointed by Truman, Congress reorganized the executive branch, consolidating departments and simplifying chains of command.

Truman was ahead of congressional and public opinion in seeking betterment for minorities. The first major presidential candidate to publicly solicit African American votes, he could not deliver major civil rights legislation. He did, however, take steps by executive orders. Truman continued the desegregation of the armed forces and sought an end to discrimination in interstate transportation, educational inequality, the poll tax, and lynching. Although progress occurred slowly or not at all in some areas, the president from Missouri set a liberal racial agenda that would, for the most part, reach fruition. There were symbolic and substantial gains for African Americans, such as Jackie Robinson's breaking of the color barrier with the Brooklyn Dodgers in 1947. Once the skill of black athletes was established, colleges and professional teams raced to recruit them.

The reality for most African Americans, in the rural South and in northern city ghettos, was grinding poverty, inadequate education, and public humiliation. They and other minorities made economic gains during the war, yet, they remained an underclass. In the South, racial segregation was

★ JACKIE ROBINSON: CHAMPION ★

His struggle predated the emergence of "the first black who"
in many areas of the American society.

—DAVE ANDERSON

CROSSING THE COLOR LINE
Integrating baseball as depicted
by Hollywood in *The Jackie
Robinson Story.*
(Library of Congress)

H E COULD HIT. He could vacuum up ground balls. He was the most daring base runner of his time. His skills alone merit his place in the Baseball Hall of Fame. Yet Jackie Robinson was much more than a baseball player. In the Era of Uncertainty he was a pioneer in race relations, a businessman, a fund-raiser for charities, and a civil rights activist. When his mentor, Branch Rickey, sounded the trumpet to sign Robinson to a Major League contract, the walls of segregation in professional baseball came tumbling down. Baseball lay at the heart of American culture, and Robinson's breakthrough was followed by a series of victories for African Americans, among them the 1954 Supreme Court decision ordering school desegregation and the sweeping 1964 Civil Rights Act.

In 1947, when Robinson joined the Brooklyn Dodgers, most white people believed that black athletes lacked the intelligence or skills to compete with white players. Desegregating the Major Leagues took someone who was more than a talented player. It took a person who was disciplined, who would not fight back when taunted, spiked, booed, or hit with a beanball. Asked at his first news conference what he would do if a white pitcher threw at his head, Robinson replied, diplomatically, that he would duck. But the restraint that he demonstrated in his early Major League years did not come easily for this angry man. "I had to fight hard against loneliness, abuse and the knowledge that any mistake I made would be magnified because I was the only black man out there," Robinson said. He chafed at being confined to segregated hotels and restaurants on the road and, once established, showed more of his fiercely competitive nature, arguing with umpires and tongue-lashing players who harassed him.

It is often overlooked that Robinson might have failed. If he had, it would have seriously jeopardized the ability of African Americans at that time to shatter the barrier of racial inferiority. He had to excel as a player before he could succeed as a racial trailblazer, and at both, he performed beyond expectations. "We were riding his shoulders right out from under the worst part of that white power lie," Roy Wilkins wrote. "Every time Jack got a hit, stole a base or made a great play in the field, he was telling them for all of us, 'It's a lie!'" Robinson was National League Rookie of the Year in 1947, when he led Brooklyn to the pennant. During his ten-year career, he was often among the league leaders in batting, stolen bases, and fielding. He was chosen the

Most Valuable Player in the league in 1949, when he led the circuit in batting average and base stealing. The most versatile Dodgers player, he started at first base, second base, third base, and in the outfield. With Robinson, the Dodgers dominated the National League, although they won only one World Series title, in 1955, his last season. He was elected to the Baseball Hall of Fame in 1962, his first year of eligibility.

Robinson retired before the 1957 season because age and injuries had eroded his skills. He then invested and worked in businesses, wrote a newspaper column, was a popular public speaker, and campaigned for politicians such as Nelson Rockefeller and Hubert Humphrey. He supported integration and quarreled with black nationalists. Robinson lived through profound changes in lifestyles. His son, Jackie, was wounded while serving in Vietnam, became addicted to drugs there, and died in a car accident the year before the elder Robinson died in 1972, at fifty-three. He had earned a place as one of the most respected men in the United States. But the paradox did not escape him that although he had opened the way for African Americans with superior skills, equal opportunity for ordinary African Americans remained incomplete. There was one more paradox: it was his sense of feeling alone that fired his will to achieve the feats that won him the hearts of millions. "You are Jackie Robinson, who is consumed by rage and pride," sports columnist Jimmy Cannon wrote. "You're a complicated man, persecuted by slanderous myths, using anger as a confederate. No athlete of any time has been assaulted by such an aching loneliness which created your personality and shaped your genuine greatness."

Sources: The best book on Robinson is Arnold Rampersad, *Jackie Robinson: A Biography* (1997). Also see Richard Scott, *Jackie Robinson* (1987), and Joseph Dorinson and Joram Warmund, *Jackie Robinson: Race, Sports, and the American Dream* (1998).

pervasive. African Americans could not attend white public schools, drink at segregated fountains, vote in most elections, attend most state colleges, or be considered for anything other than menial jobs. Health care was poor, and there was little opportunity for upward mobility, and the password was despair. Blacks in the North continued to vote Democrat, as they had since the 1936 election landslide for Franklin Roosevelt, but even the chance to vote could not ease despair.

Native Americans, too, were impoverished, underemployed, and largely ignored. Disease was endemic, including alcoholism. After John Collier resigned as federal Indian affairs commissioner in 1945, the government created a commission to compensate Indians for land seized. This action foreshadowed the policy of termination that became official in 1953, whereby the United States would sever its relations with tribes.

By 1950, when the Korean War broke out, the Fair Deal had run its course. Major legislation was lost; some minor measures passed. Truman was overly ambitious in announcing goals and lacked finesse in implementing them. Extensions of the New Deal were introduced in a climate less favorable than the Great Depression or the World War II, when public sacrifice for the common good seemed essential. There was no crisis but, rather prosperity. Many wanted to slim down the federal bureaucracy rather than expand it, to consolidate gains. Even Roosevelt had experienced a legislative roadblock to domestic reform by 1938. Truman could push proposals in one end of Congress but he could not pull them out the other. He lacked patience with politicians and even with music critics. When a journalist criticized Margaret's efforts at professional singing, Truman threatened to punch him in the eye. The president, like Margaret Truman, seemed out of tune with the times.

A host of minor furies nipped at the president's heels. His friend, military aide Harry Vaughn, accepted kickbacks for favors. Corruption emerged in the Reconstruction Finance Corporation and the Internal Revenue Service. Truman was usually loyal to his cronies, regardless of their dishonesty. Even his own party seemed bent on self-destruction. Tennessee Senator Estes Kefauver held televised hearings on organized crime and connected many of the criminal bosses to urban Democratic machines. The hearings were an early omen of the political potency of television and made a national reputation for Kefauver.

From World War to Cold War

Following World War II, War Crimes Trials were conducted in Nuremberg and Tokyo. Surprisingly, many were tried under provisions defined in the Kellogg-Briand Treaty, which meant something after all. The most grisly testimony related to the Holocaust in Europe and to Japanese treatment of prisoners of war. The testimony relating to the Holocaust, in particular, revealed an insidious underside of the Third Reich, the callous cruelty of its leaders. It also drove a nail into the coffin of the idea of racism, which would persist, but would never again be respectable. And sympathy for the chief victims of the Nazi atrocities, the Jews of Europe, helped survivors gain a foothold for a homeland in Israel.

Like Woodrow Wilson, FDR and his predecessors had cobbled together an international organization designed to confine war to the past. The United Nations, headquartered in New York, was much like the League of Nations. A major exception was that the United States, rather than remain aloof, would assume leadership. An eleven-member Security Council was charged with preserving the peace by collective action if necessary. The machinery was cumbrous, however. Each of the five permanent

READY
FOR WAR
U.S. Army tests
the atom bomb
in Nevada, 1952.
(National
Archives)

members: the United States, Britain, France, China, and the Soviet Union, could veto actions. The General Assembly, which included most of the world's countries, was a glorified debating society. Increasingly it engaged in rhetorical debate related to the protagonists in the Cold War.

The most uncertain facet of the Era of Uncertainty was the Cold War. Heaped on both sides were mountains of munitions, many of them nuclear bombs. Yet, paradoxically, it was not a war in the usual sense. It was characterized more by fear of war than actual war. There was fighting between proxies of the principals, limited wars, propaganda wars, and psychological wars. But, in a tribute to common sense on both sides, the big bombs were never launched or dropped. Never before had humanity possessed the opportunity to completely destroy itself. And humanity passed up the opportunity.

Some efforts were made to ensure international supervision of atomic weapons. Not surprisingly, since communists and capitalists distrusted each other and tried to stack proposals to favor their side, nothing substantial was accomplished. The arms race galloped out of the gates. In 1949 the Soviets detonated an atomic bomb, ending the American monopoly. There followed an American hydrogen bomb, far more powerful than atomic bombs, in 1952, and a Soviet hydrogen bomb in 1953. Bombs tested were so potent they had no practical value except to overawe the adversary.

Some factors in the Cold War were territorial and ideological. Communist ideology, as refined by V. I. Lenin and Joseph Stalin, was expansionist and driven to dominate. Its objective was, first, consolidation where it existed and, ultimately, world control. Highly motivated, it became the most messianic secular ideology of the twentieth century. Unlike fascism, it made converts as well as conquests. Based on the idea of loyalty to the working class rather than a nation, communism, in all its major manifestations, was in fact led by nationalists. It imposed a command economy, prohibited religion, banned free speech and free elections, and taught ferocious pride in competition with the West from fields as diverse as tractor production to the space race to the Olympic Games.

Capitalism was equally competitive and equally self-righteous. It, too, was expansionist; it needed trade to sustain prosperity. Yet it was not so regimented. Capitalism was compatible with democracy. A command economy, with its centralized government and productive plan, was incompatible with democracy. Capitalism boasted of the wonders of private property, which communism prohibited. And the West practiced, for the most part, freedom of religion and of the press and held competitive elections. Initially it appeared the discipline of communism gave it an advantage. A dictated economy could concentrate resources in one area, such as military might, or education, and excel, even while sacrificing other areas.

The Cold War made each side nervous because its outcome seemed uncertain. Soviets hoped to sustain moral superiority by pointing to industrial and military accomplishments. Americans, they said, wallowed in ease. Each side counted armies and courted Allies. Yet each side claimed, probably truthfully, that it wanted to win by peaceful competition.

When World War II ended Europe was already divided. Stalin's armies occupied the East, including Poland, with the dividing line drawn through Germany. Stalin could not and would not be ousted from these nations, which came to be called the Soviet bloc. Their economies were integrated and their governments were Soviet puppets. In a speech on February 9, 1946, Stalin declared capitalism and communism incompatible and vowed that communism would prevail. Winston Churchill also addressed the contest near its beginning, declaring memorably a month later that an "Iron Curtain" had descended across Europe.

Britain, America's most constant ally, was financially and emotionally exhausted after the war. It handed off its responsibilities in Greece and Turkey to the United States. In Greece, a civil war between monarchists and communists raged. In Turkey, the Soviets pressed for access to the Mediterranean Sea through Turkish-controlled straits. Truman requested $300 million to arm Greece and $100 million to aid Turkey, which Congress approved. More important, he issued a promise to spread the umbrella of American defense to protect any nation threatened internally or externally with communist takeover. This commitment, known as the Truman Doctrine, was a complement of the Marshall Plan, announced by Secretary of State George Marshall in June 1947, to give economic aid to rebuild Europe, making it less vulnerable to communist appeals. The Marshall Plan became the greatest success of the Truman administration. For a modest investment, the United States obtained trading partners and Allies. It was not entirely unselfish, yet it was mutually beneficial. Western Europe not only revived; it became an economic powerhouse.

Probing for a strategy to counter Stalin's, an American Russian expert, George Kennan, in a "long telegram" and in an article in *Foreign Affairs*, proposed the idea of "containment." The United States would meet force with counterforce and contain the Soviet bloc within its existing borders. Later applied to Asia as well as Europe, virtually every American president, whatever their rhetoric, practiced containment. The Cold War thus became a war of attrition.

Reforms helped improve the readiness of the military and intelligence organizations. The 1947 National Security Act combined the War and Navy departments in the Defense Department. The air force became independent of the army. The Central Intelligence Agency (CIA) centralized intelligence gathering, and the National Security Council (NSC) was created to advise the president on foreign policy. A memorandum issued by the National Security Council, NSC-68, called for a massive arms buildup. The memorandum was never approved, yet many of its recommendations were implemented with the outbreak of the Korean War. The United States was now prepared to confront communism on a variety of fronts.

Military challenges came with a flurry. In February 1948, a Soviet-instigated coup in Czechoslovakia enveloped another nation behind the Iron Curtain. America reauthorized the draft. Four months later, the Soviets blockaded access to West Berlin, a free outpost in the sea of East Germany.

After the war, Germany had been partitioned. The United States, France, and Britain occupied the western half, which became a capitalist democracy. East Germany, occupied by the Soviets, became a Soviet satellite. Berlin, the prewar German capital, was also partitioned into eastern and western sectors, though it was surrounded by East German territory. West Berlin was an avenue of escape to the West and a beacon of democracy, evidence of the productive power of capitalism.

Truman feared that forcing his way through the blockades on the ground might result in war with the Soviet Union. Therefore he ordered an airlift to send all necessary materials to West Berlin. The first shot, if one were to be fired, would come from the Soviet side.

The Berlin airlift strained the capacity of American cargo planes and the resources of West Berliners. Nonetheless, the communists were losing the struggle for world opinion. In May 1949, they lifted the blockade. The same year, two nations were carved out of prewar Germany: West Germany, with its capital in Bonn, and East Germany, with its capital in East Berlin. Significantly, the Berlin blockade inspired the North Atlantic Treaty Organization (NATO), binding American with Northern and Western Europe, Canada, and other anticommunist nations. Intended as a deterrent to communist aggression, NATO was the first permanent, peacetime alliance in American history. In response, the Soviets created the Warsaw Pact, a counteralliance of communist nations.

Containment in Asia, War in Korea

Some politicians and intellectuals argued that by focusing containment on Europe, the United States neglected a more populous, more dynamic, and more vulnerable part of the world—Asia. The "Asia First" group focused on China, Korea, and Indochina, all of which became Cold War battlegrounds. In China, where nationalists and communists competed for supremacy, Truman had dispatched Marshall in 1945 in a fruitless, yearlong quest to reconcile the foes. Washington continued to arm and equip the Nationalist leader, Jiang Jieshe (Chiang Kaishek), but the forces of communist chief Mao Zedong (Mao Tse-tung) drove the demoralized forces of Jiang's corrupt government off the mainland and onto the island of Taiwan (Formosa) in 1949. The United States refused to recognize communist China diplomatically, and Republicans charged Truman and Marshall with "losing" China. Mao's government proved no less repressive than Jiang's. He aligned it with the Soviet Union and made China a military state, but the newly cemented alliance began to crack before it dried, for both giants competed for leadership of the communist movement.

East of China, the Korean peninsula was divided at the 38th parallel. The North was a communist state under Dictator Kim Il Sung, who was anxious to conquer the South, led by Syngman Rhee. Rhee, on the other hand, was ambitious to take North Korea, so the United States denied him offensive weapons. Less inhibited, Moscow sent tanks to Kim, who was tempted further when the last American troops were withdrawn from the region in June 1949. Then, Secretary of State Dean Acheson excluded

Korea from the American defense perimeter in June 1950. After consulting with Stalin, Kim launched an invasion on June 25, 1950, that routed the South Koreans. Acheson persuaded the UN Security Council to brand North Korea an aggressor. The council voted to defend the South, thanks to a boycott by the Soviets who were protesting the council's refusal to seat communist China instead of Taiwan on the Security Council, and were thus unable to exercise their veto.

Truman authorized use of American naval and air forces in the conflict, then sent ground troops under General Douglas MacArthur. After stabilizing the minuscule perimeter around the southern port city of Pusan, MacArthur launched an audacious, amphibious attack at Inchon, a port near Seoul, the South Korean capital. North Korean troops were driven back above the 38th parallel, where they war had begun. Now Truman and the UN authorized MacArthur to cross the boundary and unite Korea under a noncommunist government. MacArthur drove almost to the Yalu River, the boundary between Korea and China. Undetected, Chinese troops massed at the border, and Chinese leaders had indirectly warned they might intervene if UN forces approached their border. The Chinese did intervene en masse, sending the surprised, outnumbered American troops into a retreat that ultimately stabilized at the 38th parallel.

So far, the war was a draw. The North could not conquer the South; the South could not capture the North. MacArthur found the stalemate humiliating. He proposed plans to threaten the use of atomic weapons, blockade the Chinese coast, and use Jiang's troops for a diversionary attack on the Chinese mainland. Like most good generals, MacArthur was assertive and desired total victory. Truman feared such a plan might precipitate a third world war, and ordered MacArthur to clear his statements with Washington. Instead, MacArthur offered to negotiate with Chinese generals personally and proclaimed, "There is no substitute for victory."

Whatever the merits of tactics, MacArthur had been insubordinate, he had violated the chain of command. Truman, who did not like MacArthur's imperious personality, fired him, with relish.

MacArthur returned to a hero's welcome in America, ticker tape parades and a moving address before a joint session of Congress. A gifted orator, he brought some to tears, especially when he concluded that "Old soldiers never die, they just fade away." Surprisingly, MacArthur did fade away, although he would have liked the Republican presidential nomination in 1952. The verdict of history has been less kind than his contemporary Americans to MacArthur's generalship in Korea. Active generals are supposed to carry out policy made by civilians, not make it themselves. Nonetheless, the general who succeeded Truman, Dwight Eisenhower, repeated MacArthur's threat to use nuclear weapons rather than tolerate indefinitely a static front. Possibly this was one factor in breaking the log-jam over truce negotiations at the village of Panmunjom.

While trying to extricate itself from a bloody war in Asia, the United States backed into another in Vietnam, a former French colony that Japan occupied in World War II. Ho Chi Minh, the leader of the communist-nationalist Vietminh, had been seeking the liberation of his country since the 1919 Versailles Peace Conference. On September 2, 1945, Vietnam pro-claimed its independence, but the French decided to reimpose colonial rule. Ho rebelled. The French refused to collaborate with American plans for defending Western Europe unless the United States supported them in Vietnam. Because the Vietminh were communists, Washington viewed the French presence in Vietnam as a deterrent to communism. In 1950 Congress approved $10 million to aid Bao Dai, the French-installed emperor.

Politics were interpreted through the Cold War lens in the volatile Middle East. The major issue in the region, a Jewish state, had simmered since the nineteenth century, when Zionists sought such a homeland, preferably in Palestine. Controlling Palestine under mandates from the League of Nations and the United Nations, the British limited Jewish immigration, but Jews smuggled in immigrants beyond the quotas; Arabs opposed the influx and violence raged. In mid-1947 Britain announced that it would relinquish its mandate. A UN commission recommended the partition of Palestine into Jewish and Arab states. On May 14, 1948, Jews in Palestine declared the independence of Israel, repelling attacks from five Arab nations. Seven hundred thousand Palestinians fled to the West Bank of the Jordan River and the Gaza Strip, a part of Egypt. Eleven minutes after independence was declared, Truman extended diplomatic recognition to Israel, beating the Soviets. The next year, the warring parties signed an armistice, yet a permanent peace remained elusive. The United States sup-ported Israel, while the Soviet Union armed the Arabs.

Iran also became a Cold War battleground. During the world war, Allied troops had occupied the nation to prevent a Nazi invasion, promis-ing to withdraw within six months after the end of the conflict. The United States and Britain evacuated their forces, but Soviet soldiers remained and began agitating a civil war between the Iranian government and separatist rebels. Only after Truman threatened to defend Iran with force did the Soviets pull out.

Pursuing friendship in Latin America, the United States signed the Inter-American Treaty of Reciprocal Assistance, a mutual defense pact, in 1947 and helped establish the Organization of American States in 1948. The United States set about dismantling its small empire. In 1946, the Philippines became independent and the United States gave Puerto Rico increased authority. The island would govern internal affairs, with Washington making foreign policy and providing defense. Two Puerto Ricans favoring independence tried to shoot their way into Blair House, Truman's temporary residence while the White House was being refurbished, to assassinate the president. One gunman was killed, and the other was wounded and captured.

The Cold War at Home

The Cold War not only dominated international affairs; it affected politics, culture, and the media in America. Free speech was compromised in the quest to silence communist sympathizers. The government grew in proportion to the perceived threat, yet some complained that large government constituted creeping communism. Tolerance of those who favored radical ideologies nosedived.

To be sure, there were real communists in America, and some spy rings. For the most part they were annoyances rather than threats. Moreover, to conclude that the nation was gripped by "hysteria" is rhetorical overkill. Most people led their daily lives as usual. Yet a few celebrated cases raised concern. In 1945, federal agents found secret government documents in the files of *Amerasia*, a magazine with a procommunist slant. In 1946, a Canadian spy ring was uncovered that had passed American military and nuclear information to the Soviets in World War II. The Truman administration imposed a background check on federal employees from 1947 to 1951 and established loyalty review procedures. Loyalty Boards fired three hundred, and three thousand resigned. Some cities, states, universities, and labor unions required loyalty oaths without considering whether anyone who was actually a spy would hesitate to lie about it.

In the courts, several cases captured the public's attention. During the 1948 presidential campaign, leaders of the Communist Party of the United States were convicted of advocating the violent overthrow of the government, a violation of the 1940 Smith Act. The Supreme Court upheld the convictions in *Dennis v. U.S.* (1951). The Alger Hiss case was even more polarizing. Hiss, a former State Department official, a polished Ivy Leaguer, and liberal intellectual, was accused by Whittaker Chambers, a former communist, of being part of his spy cell in the 1930s. Chambers alleged that Hiss had stolen diplomatic, not military or atomic secrets, for the Soviet Union. Hiss seemed the more credible of the two; he was better dressed and eloquent and had high-ranking friends in the Democratic Party. The affair degenerated into a morality play equating liberalism with communism and the Democratic Party with treason. Yet partisan motives did not mean that Hiss was innocent. Hiss and Chambers were questioned by the House Un-American Activities Committee (HUAC), then, in response to a challenge from Hiss, Chambers repeated the charges publicly. Hiss sued for slander; whichever man was lying was guilty of perjury. After the introduction of some convincing circumstantial evidence against Hiss, some of it produced by Congressman Richard Nixon, Hiss was convicted of perjury early in 1950 and sentenced to five years in prison. He never relented protesting his innocence.

More serious was the case of Julius and Ethel Rosenberg, a couple accused of stealing atomic secrets for the Soviets. The Rosenbergs were implicated by Klaus Fuchs, a German-born scientist living in Britain, who had worked on the Manhattan Project. Fuchs confessed to spying and identified four Americans, including the Rosenbergs, as collaborators. The Rosenbergs were convicted in March 1951, chiefly on testimony by their alleged collaborators, and sentenced to death. Protesting their innocence, the Rosenbergs claimed persecution because they were Jews and liberals. They refused offers of clemency if they would identify other spies and were executed on June 19, 1953.

The chief mischief-maker in the anticommunist crusade, because most of the communists he pursued were of his own invention, was Senator Joseph R. McCarthy of Wisconsin. More than any politician of his time, he gave some credibility to the impression that Americans were running from ghosts. Yet he never uncovered a real communist, although he garnered loads of publicity; initially, the publicity was mostly good. On February 9, 1950, McCarthy delivered a speech in which he claimed to possess a list of 205 communists working in the State Department. He never explained who had given him the list or showed it to anyone. Each time he was asked to pin down his accusations, he instead produced additional ones. He raced to stay ahead of the newspaper headlines, which piled up. A maestro at manipulating the press, he became one of the best-known politicians in the country.

McCarthy's shenanigans resulted in little tangible legislation. Not so with one of his political allies, Democratic Senator Patrick McCarran of Nevada, who helped steer through Congress the 1950 McCarran Internal Security Act. The act required that communists register with the attorney general and barred them from working for the government or in defense industries. The 1952 McCarran-Walter Immigration and Nationality Act prohibited communists from immigrating to the United States. McCarran's Senate Internal Security Committee held hearings in 1951 that blamed China experts, known as the "China hands" for the "loss" of China to communism. Some were discharged from their positions in the State Department.

DRIVING TO VICTORY
Dwight D. Eisenhower on the campaign trail, 1952.
(Dwight D. Eisenhower Presidential Library)

HUAC held hearings in 1947 on communist influence in Hollywood. Some suspected that Hollywood deliberately shaded movies to make communism appear attractive. The Hollywood Ten, a group of screenwriters, directors, and producers, refused to testify, citing the Fifth Amendment's protection against self-incrimination. They were fined, imprisoned briefly, and worse yet, denied employment.

"I Like Ike"

As the 1952 presidential campaign loomed, polls showed Truman to be one of the most unpopular incumbents in history. The Democrats therefore drafted Illinois Governor Adlai Stevenson, a respected liberal, an eloquent speaker, considered an intellectual by his supporters. For vice president the Democrats chose a segregationist, Alabama Senator John Sparkman. Candid and witty, Stevenson, told that he had the votes of all the thinking people in the country, replied that this was not enough; he needed a majority.

The Republican candidate was not an eloquent speaker, but neither did he talk down to the American people. Best, Dwight D. Eisenhower was a war hero, less controversial than MacArthur, who was waiting for a call from his party that never came. Eisenhower had common sense and an ingratiating grin as well as toughness, discipline, and a midas touch with the masses. He promised, if elected, to go to Korea, implying he would end the war. He did both. More important than his political principles was his temperamental stability; he was a harmonizer who inspired trust, and as he managed a vast bureaucracy during World War II, he was thought to be able to manage the Cold War. For his vice presidential running mate, Eisenhower tapped California Senator Richard M. Nixon, who had made a reputation as a member of HUAC by pursuing Alger Hiss. "Ike" never warmed to Nixon, yet Nixon was a professional politician with connections to his party's hierarchy. Eisenhower thought of asking Nixon to quit the ticket after newspapers reported that California businessmen had contributed a secret "slush fund" for him, but the senator saved himself with a televised speech that swayed viewers. The "Checkers" speech, so named because Nixon told of the cocker spaniel puppy his daughters had received as a gift from a supporter, marked a pioneering use of television to influence public opinion.

The Eisenhower-Nixon team won a comfortable victory, 33.9 million popular votes (55.1 percent) and 442 electoral votes to 27.3 million popular votes (44.4 percent) and 89 electoral votes for the Democrats. The GOP also won narrow control of Congress.

Although Truman's popularity lay at low tide when he left office, historians have judged him less harshly. In domestic affairs he proposed a progressive agenda, although he did not achieve it. In foreign affairs, his decisive actions might have saved Western Europe, Berlin, and Korea. After tumultuous times, though, Americans were ready for an aging former general who, they believed, would soothe the nation's nerves.

CHAPTER TWO

Peace and Peril, 1953–1960

IN THE Age of Uncertainty, the 1950s were an interlude of peace and prosperity. Paradoxically, the age was less stable, and more dangerous than it seemed. Prosperity was incomplete, and America feared for its security when the Soviet Union, a nuclear power, appeared to gain the lead in the space and missile race.

Dwight D. Eisenhower

The staid public image of the Eisenhower administration and the seeming colorlessness of its supporters prompted some to label the 1950s a period of "the bland leading the bland," a generalization that obscured the great paradox of the decade: calm at home and danger internationally from the Cold War. Nor were the politics and the generation bland; they were simply conservative in what was an ordinary period compared with the Great Depression and World War II. Befitting the time, Dwight D. Eisenhower was a man of paradox. He was raised in a pacifist family and became a man of war, commander of the Allied effort in Europe that helped end the greatest conflict to engulf the planet and, later, military leader of the North Atlantic Treaty Organization (NATO). His country looked to him to preserve peace. Despite his military background, he pared the defense establishment and warned the nation about the power of a military-industrial complex.

Born in Denison, Texas, Eisenhower grew up in Abilene, Kansas, and graduated from the United States Military Academy. He began in the Army in 1915, remaining stateside as a tank instructor during World War I and advancing slowly in the postwar Army, becoming a brigadier general in 1941. When World War II started in Europe, Eisenhower was assigned

WEATHERING THE COLD WAR
Eisenhower with Secretary of State John Foster Dulles.
(Dwight D. Eisenhower Presidential Library)

to work with General George C. Marshall, the Army chief of staff, who promoted him over senior officers to lead the invasions of North Africa, Sicily, Italy, and Normandy. A planner, not a bold field commander, Eisenhower kept peace among the fractious Allies and their temperamental generals. After the war, Eisenhower served as military governor of the American zone in Germany and wrote *Crusade in Europe* (1948), a book about the war that made him wealthy. He served briefly as president of Columbia University, and then was commander for NATO, a job he left to seek the GOP nomination.

To the public, "Ike" seemed friendly, yet he could be a hard, unsentimental man, thanks to his years in the military. He had never been religious, but he joined the Presbyterian Church to set an example for observance. Bright if not brilliant, a precise writer if a poor speaker, he delegated work so he could avoid details. The former general led by indirection, which spared him blame and denied him praise. With Mamie Eisenhower, he had a conventional marriage. Eisenhower's most influential cabinet member was an international lawyer, Secretary of State John Foster Dulles, a rigid anticommunist and moralist.

Eisenhower had his greatest domestic success in economic prosperity, sustained because of the baby boom, business expansion, and technology. He came to office promising to slow the growth of the federal government, although spending by state and local governments compensated. Welfare expenditures rose, and defense consumed more than half the U.S. budget each year during his term. The last was a source of concern, for Eisenhower believed that the country might spend itself into weakness with too much defense.

Among consumers, credit purchases soared. Most expensive items were bought on installment and prosperity was fueled by advertising, yearly automobile style changes, and cheap gasoline. Yet there were weaknesses. Poverty was endemic in city centers, the rural South, Appalachia, and declining New England mill towns. Recessions occurred in 1954 and 1958. During the first, the deficit grew to $12.1 billion, the largest since 1946, and unemployment rose to 6.4 percent, at which it stayed until the second. In the major downturn of 1958, corporate profits fell more than 25 percent and the government ran another deficit. The Achilles' heel of the economy was agriculture, as farmers overproduced and remained in business only with federal subsidies. The president planned to reduce but did not end the subsidies. He advocated a soil bank program to remove acreage from production and devote it to ungrazed grass, forest, or reservoirs. Thwarted when Democrats added amendments for higher payments to farmers, Eisenhower vetoed the bill. The economy faltered near the close of the decade.

The most significant domestic legislation enacted during Eisenhower's presidency was the Interstate Highway Act of 1956. A large undertaking, the bill was sold to Congress partly as a Cold War measure. The highways would enable cities to evacuate during a nuclear attack. New four-lane federal highways superseded the state-built two-lane roads that connected most cities. The interstate system changed society by expediting the transfer of traffic from railroads to highways. On water, transportation was upgraded when Congress passed legislation in 1954 allowing for construction of the St. Lawrence Seaway in cooperation with Canada. Connecting the Great Lakes with the St. Lawrence River, the seaway became a major transportation system upon completion in 1959.

Despite his antipathy to the growth of government, Eisenhower signed legislation expanding Social Security coverage to 7.5 million people, among them farmers, physicians, and clergy. He approved an increase in the minimum wage from 75 cents to $1 per hour and agreed to the Federal

Housing Act of 1954, which liberalized lending for home construction. But broad school construction bills foundered over inclusion of parochial schools and use of federal money as a wedge to accelerate school desegregation. Prospects for other significant Republican domestic measures were dampened in the 1954 elections, as the GOP lost control of Congress. Democrats retained a majority for the rest of the administration.

Senator Joe McCarthy continued his crusade against communism after winning a second term from Wisconsin voters in 1952. Eisenhower disliked McCarthy but did not want to criticize him openly. The administration had its own anticommunist agenda. In 1954, for instance, a security clearance was denied for atomic scientist J. Robert Oppenheimer, and the Communist Control Act stripped citizenship from those who sought the violent overthrow of the government. But McCarthy persisted. He excoriated the Voice of America, a radio network broadcasting U.S. views to communist countries in Eastern Europe, because it quoted from the works of controversial writers. And he agitated for the United States Information Agency to remove books by communists and their sympathizers from libraries abroad. The investigations that accompanied these crusades proved embarrassments.

If Eisenhower miscalculated his ability to deflect attention from McCarthy, he was right in one assessment: the senator's downfall would come at his own hand. In 1954, incensed that an Army dentist was promoted from captain to major despite failing to sign a loyalty oath, McCarthy charged that the Army was soft on communism. McCarthy was vulnerable because his chief aide on his Senate investigations panel, Roy Cohn, had demanded that the Army grant special favors to draftee David Schine, who had parlayed a superficial knowledge of communism into an unpaid consultancy to the committee. The senator thought Cohn went too far, yet did not restrain him. Stung by McCarthy's allegations, the Army made public Cohn's threats. The Senate panel launched an inquiry into the matter. The televised Army-McCarthy hearings from April to June 1954 were the denouement of the communist hunter's career. Interrupting the proceedings and browbeating witnesses, McCarthy appeared a rude bully, short of credibility. The worst waited until Joseph Welch, the chief Army counsel, seized upon a miscue by his adversary. McCarthy had pledged not to mention that Fred Fisher, a young lawyer in Welch's firm who was not involved in the hearings, once belonged to a communist front organization. But when Welch baited Cohn, McCarthy lost his temper. The Wisconsin senator interrupted and disclosed the Fisher association. Welch accused McCarthy of cruelly smearing the young man, damaging his career. "Have you no sense of decency, sir, at long last? Have you no sense of decency?" Welch asked.

The verdict of the investigating committee was split, faulting McCarthy and the Army. The public and the Senate were tiring of the senator's baseless accusations and publicity seeking. A recall effort against McCarthy in Wisconsin failed in 1954, but on December 2, 1954, the Senate condemned him for verbally abusing colleagues. (Condemnation was the least severe penalty, below expulsion or censure.) From that point he declined into depression and alcoholism, and three years after the rebuke, McCarthy died at age forty-eight of liver failure.

The Warren Court and the Judicial Revolution

Another paradox of the 1950s was that Eisenhower, who disliked federal activism, appointed the most activist chief justice of the century. In 1953, he nominated Earl Warren, a three-term governor of California and the GOP vice presidential nominee in 1948. Warren's career, too, revealed paradoxes: he championed civil rights and federally mandated reapportionment, yet as California attorney general he had advocated internment of Japanese Americans during World War II and opposed legislative reapportionment. Before ascending to the chief justiceship he had never been a judge, but he united and guided what had been a divided Supreme Court. His Court led public opinion and set more precedents than did the Court of the great John Marshall. The Court issued landmark pronouncements on civil rights, on procedural safeguards for those accused of crimes, on extension of the Bill of Rights to the states; and on freedom of speech, the press, and religion. Liberals applauded the Court's activism. Conservatives objected that the justices were making law, not interpreting it.

Arguably the most critical decision of the century was *Brown v. Board of Education* (1954), wherein Warren persuaded a unanimous court to repudiate the "separate but equal" doctrine accepted in the 1896 *Plessy v. Ferguson* case. "Separate educational facilities are inherently unequal," the court declared. Henceforth, America was not to be the land of opportunity for white people only. A constitutional logjam that had frustrated Congress was broken, yet it was simpler to change law than to alter attitudes.

Many white people, including Eisenhower, who criticized the court privately and refused to endorse the decision publicly, felt the justices were proceeding too quickly. White southerners dug in for "massive resistance," involving delay and intimidation of pro-integrationists, and demanded Warren's impeachment. Their legislators in Congress, denouncing northern attempts to implement a "Second Reconstruction," signed a "Southern Manifesto" designed to circumvent desegregation by legal yet devious methods. The Ku Klux Klan and other groups attracted militants who linked integration to communism, racial intermarriage, and the weakening of the white race. More respectable leaders, lawyers, and businessmen joined White Citizens Councils to oppose integration. White families fled public schools for suburban, private, and religious schools.

Except for law and graduate schools, higher education did not begin to desegregate until the 1960s in the Deep South, according to most histories. Yet the first Deep South University to desegregate was actually Southwestern Louisiana Institute (SLI), now known as the University of Louisiana, Lafayette (ULL). It is notable for several reasons: first, because it has been neglected by historians; second, because virtually no violence occurred; and third, because of the large number of black students involved. Although integration that occurred at such better-known universities as Alabama and Ole Miss involved only a handful of students, sometimes only one or two, eighty black students enrolled in 1954 at SLI. Possibly because the opposition was limited to verbal abuse, it might have seemed less newsworthy. Yet it might have been more typical than the massive resistance at Ole Miss.

The 1955 murder of Emmett Till, a black teen from Chicago visiting Mississippi, although it involved only one person, showed the charged racial atmosphere. Till flirted with a white woman, whose husband and half-brother killed him. The slayers, who later confessed to a journalist, were acquitted by an all-white jury.

Brown spurred the civil rights movement from the top down. At the grassroots level, the Montgomery bus boycott of 1955–1956 was a catalyst. African Americans mounted a successful protest against public buses after a seamstress, Rosa Parks, was convicted of violating a law requiring segregated seating. The Supreme Court struck down the statue. The boycott demonstrated the power of defiance against an unjust law and produced the major civil rights leader of the era, the Reverend Martin Luther King Jr. A Baptist pastor, he was selected to lead the boycott because he was new to the city and had few enemies. The ministry was one of the few professions open to educated African Americans who filled leadership roles in the fight against discrimination; their churches furnished networks for communicating resistance. Southern black people were willing to endure punishment to call attention to inequities. King borrowed his doctrine of civil disobedience from the teachings of Henry David Thoreau, Reinhold Niebuhr, and Mohandas Gandhi.

King instructed his followers to love their oppressors, emulating Jesus. The justice of his appeal and the long-suffering dignity of his followers brought widespread sympathy. King institutionalized his efforts by founding the Southern Christian Leadership Conference (SCLC) in 1957. In his brief lifetime the Nobel Peace Prize recognized his work; after his death, his birthday became a national holiday.

The accomplishments of King and his disciples did not occur in isolation, for the tides of history were flowing in their direction, part of a worldwide uprising of oppressed peoples that dismantled European colonialism in the 1950s and 1960s. Even the Eisenhower administration was swept up in the current. With White House backing, albeit lukewarm, Congress passed the first civil rights law since Reconstruction, the Civil Rights Act of 1957. Weaker than originally proposed, the measure created a Civil Rights Division in the Justice Department and empowered an assistant attorney general to investigate complaints regarding voting rights violations. In a test of the *Brown* ruling in 1957, Arkansas Governor Orval Faubus summoned the National Guard to block the integration of Little Rock's Central High School. Eisenhower federalized the Guard and dispatched one thousand paratroopers to maintain order and protect African American students. Presidential intervention came belatedly, yet demonstrated that *Brown* would be enforced.

CLAIMING THEIR RIGHTS
African Americans sit-in at a segregated lunch counter
in Greensboro, North Carolina.
(Bettman/Corbis)

Black students from North Carolina Agricultural and Technical University ignited the next confrontation, sitting down at a Woolworth's lunch counter in Greensboro in 1960 and refusing to leave until they were served. Complemented by boycotts and demonstrations, the sit-ins grew, and six months later, white businessmen integrated restaurants. Sit-ins spread throughout the South, a tactic favored by the Student Nonviolent Coordinating Committee (SNCC), more aggressive than King's passive resistance. Launched in the early 1950s, the movement's momentum was reflected in the Civil Rights Act of 1960. The law empowered federal courts to protect voting rights and made it a federal crime to obstruct court orders by intimidation. Considering where it started, the push for equal rights made important progress in the 1950s.

With other groups, the story was similar. Lives of Asian Americans slowly improved in the 1940s and 1950s. Native Americans were a virtually invisible minority, numbering just 343,000 in 1950 and 523,000 in 1960. Congress decided Indians were to succeed or fail on their own, subject to the same rights and responsibilities as other Americans. Federal termination policy let Indians assimilate into white society divorced from public aid, a policy that some Indians and white people said constituted neglect. Several tribes agreed to the plan in 1954, but by the middle of the decade, termination had lost momentum, although it remained in effect until 1969. Meanwhile, in 1954 responsibility for Indian health care was transferred from the Bureau of Indian Affairs to the Public Health Service, which served it better.

In mid-decade, the only developments detracting from an overall upbeat American mood were the fears of communism and Eisenhower's heart attack on September 24, 1955, in Denver. Luckily, no crisis arose while the president recovered and Vice President Nixon, Eisenhower's chief of staff, Sherman Adams, and the cabinet ran the country. Any doubts about Eisenhower seeking reelection in 1956 were dispelled when friends and advisers persuaded him that he was the only Republican who could win. His doctors cleared him medically. Ileitis, an inflammation of the small intestine, felled him in June 1956, but surgery brought him relief and Eisenhower remained a candidate.

For the Democratic nomination, the chief contenders were ex-Illinois Governor Adlai Stevenson and Estes Kefauver, who won the New Hampshire primary only to lose large, critical states. Nominated on the first ballot, Stevenson left the vice presidential nomination to the convention, and Kefauver won a close contest with Massachusetts Senator John F. Kennedy.

Campaigning less than he had in 1952, Eisenhower made enough speeches to assure the public of his fitness. His record of a booming economy and peace was formidable. Troubles abroad—the Soviets were suppressing a revolution in Hungary, and Israel, Britain, and France had invaded Egypt for seizing the Suez Canal—encouraged voters to trust in Eisenhower's steady hand. Eisenhower prevailed with almost 35.6 million popular votes and 457 electoral votes to Stevenson's 26 million and 73.

Peace—And a Tie—In Korea

Soon after his election in 1952, Eisenhower redeemed his campaign promise to go to Korea. During seventy-two hours on the peninsula, he traveled to the battlefield, met troops, visited wounded soldiers, conferred with South Korean leader Syngman Rhee, and decided that the United States could not incur more casualties along a static front. Since 1951 peace talks had stalled over the issue of prisoners of war. Many North Korean soldiers wished to remain in the South, rebelling against leader Kim Il Sung's insistence on repatriation. In 1953, however, North Korea agreed to American terms, following Eisenhower's threat to use nuclear weapons and expand the war. North Korea accepted voluntary repatriation, with the proviso that its officers be permitted to try to persuade prisoners to return. Rhee, who wanted to unify the Koreas on his terms, tried to sabotage the talks by releasing twenty-five thousand prisoners into the countryside. Eisenhower checked him by vowing to discontinue support for additional offensive maneuvers against the North. Rhee would be on his own if he attempted to resume the war. Yet if he cooperated in a settlement, the United States would sign a mutual security pact with South Korea. In July 1953 an armistice was signed at the village of Panmunjom, dividing Korea roughly at the 38th parallel, where the line had been drawn before the war. The truce (which fell short of a treaty) committed the two sides to negotiations leading to reunification, which never produced a united nation. The battles had cost the lives of thirty-three thousand Americans and of more than 1 million from the Koreas and China.

There were no victory celebrations, no cheering crowds to welcome American troops home. Like the War of 1812, the Korean conflict ended in a tie. The war, nevertheless, saved South Korea from communist conquest and led to a 1954 accord in which Washington extended protection to Taiwan. Notwithstanding the lack of enthusiasm at home, the Korean armistice was one of Eisenhower's main achievements. He stopped the fighting six months after taking office.

Fulfilling another 1952 campaign pledge about foreign policy was more difficult. The Republican administration, Dulles said, would take a more vigorous Cold War position than containment. If the United States fought to prevent communism from expanding without trying to uproot it, the best the Free World could hope for was a stalemate. Under Eisenhower, containment in Eastern Europe would be replaced with "liberation of these captive peoples," Dulles said. But when the Soviets crushed workers' demonstrations in East Germany in June 1953, protests fueled in part by American radio broadcasts in West Berlin, the administration failed to help them. Even a mere promise to liberate people from the yoke of communism might require a bigger military, confounding GOP promises to cut expenses and balance the budget. Defense spending, amounting to 60 percent of Truman's last budget, would have to be slashed, confronting Eisenhower and Dulles with the problem of providing more military muscle at less cost.

In 1954 Dulles announced a solution, the policy of massive retaliation. America would respond to any international threat with nuclear bombs that provided "more bang for the buck" because, relative to their destructive power, they were cheaper than a conventional army. Eisenhower would be able to pursue a "New Look" defense program relying primarily on the Strategic Air Command. A policy based on nuclear bombs, however, amounted to a one-dimensional defense incapable of fighting limited wars.

Into the breach stepped Dulles, arguing that the important factor was not whether a country used nuclear weapons but whether its antagonists took the threat seriously. The more credibility the American deterrent inspired, the less chance it would have to be used. To prevent war, the United States had to be willing to go to the brink of war. Brinkmanship, liberation, and massive retaliation made up the tripod of Eisenhower's defense program. Dulles claimed that he used brinkmanship to avert war in Indochina and over Quemoy and Matsu, islands claimed by Jiang and shelled by Mao. It is doubtful that the doctrine made a positive contribution. In practice, containment remained American policy, as reflected in Dulles's forging of mutual defense pacts with forty-three countries to encircle the USSR.

Another foreign policy challenge pitted the administration against fellow Republicans. Ohio Senator John Bricker thought the Constitution should prohibit executive agreements on diplomacy such as the "sellouts" that FDR had made at Yalta. In 1954, with strong GOP support in the Senate, he proposed an amendment providing that international agreements other than treaties could not become law in the United States unless Congress approved. Eisenhower opposed the plan, and in the upper house it failed by just one vote to gain the two-thirds needed to pass a constitutional amendment. Congress exhibited a paradoxical mind-set a few years later, practically giving Eisenhower carte blanche to mobilize military forces for intervention in crises over Quemoy, Matsu, and the Middle East.

Dominoes in Vietnam

American-Soviet relations thawed slightly after Joseph Stalin's death in 1953. Nikita Khrushchev emerged as leader after a period of collective rule. Taking command of an empire that was overextended and losing direction, Khrushchev had to impose Stalinist repression on Soviet satellites or relax his grip. In the spring of 1956 he seemed to choose the latter, delivering a speech to a secret Communist Party congress in which he attacked the brutality of Stalin's regime and promised that the Stalinist dictatorship was over. The Soviet Union could coexist with the United States. But the road to de-Stalinization was fraught with peril. Khrushchev wanted to allow more freedoms, although not to the point of losing his satellites. Once begun, de-Stalinization careened out of control. In June, riots erupted in Poland, where demonstrators demanded the removal of Stalinists, and Wladislaw Gomulka, who proclaimed that there were many roads to socialism, took power. Khrushchev threatened a crackdown, then retreated when Gomulka pledged to rally the Poles against it.

Rebellion went further in Hungary. Students marched on October 23, 1956, to demand that an anti-Stalinist, Imre Nagy, be returned to power. When secret police tried to crush the uprising, workers struck, Nagy seized power, and Hungary withdrew from the Warsaw Pact. Fearing that all of Eastern Europe might follow Hungary, Khrushchev sent in 200,000 troops and 4,000 tanks, killing 40,000 Hungarians and sending 150,000 fleeing. Violating a pledge of safe conduct to Nagy, the Soviets seized him, tried him covertly, and executed him. The repression of popular uprisings damaged the communists, who could maintain power only through force. Americans did not escape criticism, however, because after Radio Free Europe broadcast messages encouraging revolts, Washington did nothing to support them. "Liberation" was false hope.

With fallout from atomic tests intensifying global fear of the arms race, Eisenhower was more serious about nuclear arms control than about liberation. He proposed an "atoms for peace" program under which Washington and Moscow would contribute fissionable material to a United Nations agency for industrial use, as well as an "open skies" plan allowing the United States and the Soviet Union to inspect each other's defense installations from the air. Nothing came of these proposals, or of a 1955 Geneva summit that brought Eisenhower and Khrushchev face to face.

Three years later, without a formal agreement, both countries halted atmospheric nuclear tests for the rest of the Eisenhower administration.

The Cold War spilled over to Asia, where the superpowers battled through local proxies. Khrushchev vowed to wage "wars of national liberation" in Asia and Africa. Loath to have American forces wage a ground war in Asia, Eisenhower worried about an incremental communist takeover, starting in Vietnam. "You have a row of dominoes set up, and you knock over the first one, and what will happen to the last one is the certainty that it will go over very quickly." Therefore, the United States had to prevent the first domino from falling, even if it meant supporting a corrupt, unpopular government. The chief American objective focused on maintaining stability more than on encouraging democracy.

Seeking to reimpose colonialism, the French were frustrated by their inability to destroy Ho Chi Minh's Vietminh and to defeat the guerrillas' hit-and-run tactics. In 1954 they hoped to lure the Vietminh to Dien Bien Phu, a heavily fortified outpost along the Laotian border where they could trap the rebel army. But it was the French who were trapped. Twelve thousand troops discovered themselves surrounded by Vietminh and several Chinese divisions occupying high ground above the outpost. France erroneously believed that the Vietminh would never be able to get their artillery or enough ammunition to the isolated Dien Bien Phu. With the guerrillas encircling the area, though, the French were unable to rescue their soldiers without American intervention. The Pentagon devised a plan whereby bombers and carrier jets, possibly carrying nuclear weapons, would end the siege, but Eisenhower rejected it, unwilling to act without support from the British and the Congress. The French conceded that nuclear weapons would kill their troops as well as the Vietminh. Eisenhower disliked colonialism and urged France to grant Vietnam independence, but he needed support from Paris in the fight against communism in Europe, especially for German rearmament. He supported the French in Vietnam without giving them all they wanted.

On May 7, 1954, Dien Bien Phu fell. A new government committed to withdrawal took power in Paris. Meanwhile, a British- and Soviet-sponsored conference met at Geneva to consider Far Eastern problems, resulting in a treaty that the American delegation, participating as observers only, did not sign. A cease-fire was declared; the French were to withdraw; Vietnam was divided at the 17th parallel into a communist North under Ho and a capitalist South under former emperor Bao Dai. Reunification elections were to be held in 1956. With the settlement, the French passed the baton to the United States. America created the Southeast Asia Treaty Organization, binding Washington, France, Britain, Australia, New Zealand, the Philippines, Pakistan, and Thailand to consult in a crisis and to defend South Vietnam, Laos, and Cambodia. Washington could hardly have found a land less auspicious for nation building. The United States would be drawn in to defend a decrepit southern dictatorship against a brutal, militaristic northern one. Weapons and tactics adequate to defeat a determined jungle enemy, the Japanese, in World War II, would falter before an equally determined jungle foe, the communist Vietcong. In a contest of patience, nerve, and attrition, the Americans would fall short in all three.

Americans might have terminated their involvement by yielding an almost-certain victory to Ho's communists in the reunification elections, which they realized would probably mean the end of free votes. In the competitive context of the Cold War, this option was not seriously considered. The United States staked its hopes on Ngo Dinh Diem, who arrived from exile in America to defeat Bao Dai and become president of South Vietnam, with the help of the Americans and the Central Intelligence Agency (CIA), in 1955. A proud, principled nationalist who hated the French he formerly served, Diem was a devout Catholic who antagonized the largely Buddhist population. Defying world opinion, with backing from Washington, Diem set conditions for the reunification elections he hoped the North would not accept: it must permit international inspections of the polling. Ho was even less a democrat than Diem. Never elected, he had come to power through a series of coups. Then he liquidated political opponents to consolidate his dictatorship. The North was less corrupt, more purposeful, and more disciplined, but it was a regimented society which lacked religious freedom, censored the press and had a backward economy.

The United States proceeded to train a large South Vietnamese army and organized a force to assassinate Vietcong officials. Growing opposition to Diem in the South prompted the North to organize the National Liberation Front, composed of communist foes of Diem. Diem rejected American recommendations to implement reforms. Eisenhower's successor was to face the bleak choice of withdrawing or of expanding the American role.

Elsewhere in the region, Eisenhower had to avoid war between China and Taiwan over the offshore island chains of Quemoy and Matsu. The nationalists, who occupied the chains, and the communists both claimed the islands, considering them potential stepping-stones to invasion of the other side. In September 1954 the communists began shelling the islands. A mutual defense treaty that Dulles negotiated with Taiwan in December omitted Quemoy and Matsu. The next month, China attacked the Tachen Islands, also claimed by Taiwan, prompting Congress to pass the Formosa

Resolution which empowered the president to use force to prevent the conquest of Taiwan, the Pescadores, and other unspecified islands. This was the first time that Congress had given a president the advance authorization to engage in war at a time and place of his choosing. Eisenhower, who believed that the Soviets were behind all the trouble, and Dulles affirmed that if war broke out the United States would use nuclear weapons. In May 1955 the Chinese initiated talks aimed at resolving the crisis and stopped shelling.

Three years later, after the nationalists had increased their forces on the islands, China resumed bombardment of Quemoy and Matsu, then blockaded the islands. Eisenhower, who wanted neither appeasement nor war, sent Dulles to Taiwan to extract a pledge from Jiang Jieshe not to use his military to regain the mainland. China responded with a brief ceasefire, then an announcement that it would shell the islands only on odd-numbered days of the month, permitting resupply on even days. The crisis, Eisenhower said, had degenerated into a Gilbert and Sullivan comic opera. Subsequently, Jiang reduced his garrison and the communists ceased shelling. Eisenhower realized his objectives of avoiding war and preserving Taiwan's independence.

Uncertainty in the Middle East and Latin America

In the Era of Uncertainty, no region was as uncertain as the Middle East, where Cold War rivalries, Arab-Israeli enmity, and Western hunger for oil made a troublesome mix. One hot spot was President Gamal Abdel Nasser's Egypt, which illustrated the paradoxes of the Cold War. Eisenhower believed the nationalist Nasser was leaning toward alignment with the communist camp. The United States was firmly allied with Britain and France, yet their interests in the Middle East were not always compatible. Finally, in Egypt, America was asked to give financial support to a nation that was committed to the destruction of Israel, a country that counted on Washington's protection.

The United States agreed to finance the Aswan Dam on the upper Nile to produce hydroelectric power. Many Americans opposed the loan because Nasser recognized communist China, purchased arms from Czechoslovakia, and was stockpiling weapons to attack Israel. Eisenhower worried that Egypt would be unable to repay the money. Egypt countered with a repayment plan that was unacceptable to the administration. Eisenhower placed conditions on the loan that Egypt rejected, and the president canceled the financing. Nasser nationalized the Suez Canal, through which more than half the British and French oil supplies flowed, vowing he would pay for the dam with canal tolls. Israel, concerned that Nasser would acquire too much power, invaded Egypt in October 1956, and Britain and France did likewise in two days, ostensibly to protect the canal. In addition, the three nations also wanted to overthrow Nasser. Washington risked the loss of critical Arab nations if it sided with its traditional allies. Opposing nationalization of the canal but thinking his allies had overreacted, Eisenhower backed a UN withdrawal resolution. Ike organized an embargo of Latin American oil to Britain and France, and put American air forces on emergency alert to discourage Khrushchev from launching air strikes against the invaders. These actions led Israel, Britain, and France to announce early in November that they would leave Egypt.

In a matter of weeks, Eisenhower had weathered two international crises, over Egypt and Hungary, won reelection, and eased some global tensions. There were long-term effects to the Egyptian affair, however. Soviet influence grew in the region, with Khrushchev agreeing to finance the dam and send arms to Syria. The United States supplanted Britain and France as the leading Western power in the area, assuming responsibility for curbing communist influence in the Middle East and guaranteeing that the West would have access to oil. Following the crisis, in 1957 Congress adopted the Eisenhower Doctrine, a resolution authorizing the president to use force in the area to halt communist aggression. Twice in the next year Eisenhower invoked this power. First, he backed Britain, which sent troops to Jordan to protect King Hussein from pro-Nasser forces. Second, he dispatched fourteen thousand Marines to Lebanon to safeguard President Camille Chamoun from Muslim militias that the administration believed were communist inspired. No fighting resulted, but Eisenhower deterred the Soviets again.

An earlier Middle Eastern trouble spot, Iran, was the scene of a different type of American action: use of the CIA under director Allen Dulles, younger brother of the secretary of state. Eisenhower feared that Iran, containing vital oil deposits and bordering the Soviet Union, might fall into the Soviet orbit. Leftist Prime Minister Muhammad Mussadegh had nationalized the Anglo-Iranian oil company and accepted communist support. The administration found an alternative in Mohammad Reza Shah Pahlavi, who had ascended to the throne during World War II when the British deposed his father, a Nazi collaborator. If the Iranian people were forced to choose between the shah and Mussadegh, who shared power in a constitutional monarchy, they would side with royalty, Washington predicted. Learning that the shah planned to overthrow him, Mussadegh seized complete power in the summer of 1953. The shah fled to Rome. Then a pro-shah, American-hired mob filled the streets and backed the military when, with CIA assistance, it arrested Mussadegh. The shah returned and took control. Iran stayed in the Western camp under the shah, who grew arrogant and corrupt, as Americans would regret, painfully, two decades later. The United States masterminded, but to avoid alienating Egypt did not join, the Baghdad Pact, a defense treaty linking Iran, Britain, Turkey, Iraq, and Pakistan. Also, Washington negotiated a consortium of Western companies, in which Americans held a 40 percent stake, to develop Iranian oil.

Employment of the CIA cloaked American involvement in Iran; in Vietnam; in 1953 Philippine elections, as agency meddling led to the installation of a government favorable to Washington; and in 1954 in Guatemala. Another left-leaning leader, Guatemalan President Jacobo Arbenz Guzman, alarmed the administration by nationalizing land owned by the American United Fruit Company and by purchasing arms from Czechoslovakia. Further, the CIA claimed he was planning to establish a communist base in Central America from which to export revolution. The agency supplied and trained forces loyal to Carlos Enrique Castillo Armas to stage a military coup that drove Arbenz from power. Armas led a military dictatorship that returned the United Fruit property, yet became one of the most abusive Latin American dictators. Tyranny, though, seemed of less concern to the CIA than the downfall of leftist regimes that might destabilize the hemisphere. Apparent CIA successes prompted the United States to rely increasingly on the spy organization. In 1958 the agency unsuccessfully attempted to overthrow the Indonesian government; in 1959 it helped install a pro-Western regime in Laos. Eisenhower evidently did not know it, but the CIA also plotted to assassinate leaders Fidel Castro of Cuba and Patrice Lumumba of Congo.

Latin America harbored hostility toward the giant of the north, as evidenced in 1958, when Eisenhower sent Nixon on a tour there. In Peru and Venezuela crowds heckled, jeered, egged, and spat on him. Yet the spectacle paled before the threat of a communist outpost in Cuba, as Fidel Castro came to power in 1959, overthrowing the reactionary autocrat Fulgencio Batista. Castro nationalized American oil and sugar refineries without compensation, repressed religious expression, conducted show trials and executions of Batista's followers, and turned to the Soviets for a long-term trade pact. Refugees fled Cuba for south Florida, becoming an influential political faction and a potential exile army dedicated to ousting Castro. Before the end of Eisenhower's second term, the CIA was training such a force in Guatemala. In 1961 America severed diplomatic relations with Havana. The new communist outpost became a Cold War flash point where an error could trigger a nuclear exchange.

Anxiety from Above:
Satellites, Missiles, and Spy Planes

Long a dream of humanity, space exploration became a reality in the 1950s, although entwined with the nuclear nightmare. Rocket development became urgent, not because of the prospect of searching the heavens but because rockets could carry atomic warheads. Americans, therefore, were shocked when the Soviet Union launched a 184-pound satellite, *Sputnik*, on October 4, 1957. *Sputnik II* lifted off in November, weighing 1,100 pounds and bearing a live dog for medical monitoring. The United States had expected to launch the first satellite late in 1957 during observance of the International Geophysical Year, when scientific explorations of the Earth and space were emphasized. Yet it was not until January 31, 1958, that the Army, sandwiched between two failed navy projects, sent the eighteen-pound *Explorer I* into orbit. Even though American satellite launches soon became routine, Soviet satellites were heavier and boosted into orbit with rockets of greater thrust.

A major propaganda victory for Moscow in the Cold War, *Sputnik* shook the confidence of Americans, making them worry that Soviet technological prowess might prompt neutral nations to cast their lots with communists. Americans succumbed to self-doubt. The harshest complaints fell on the educational system, thought to lack some of the toughness and discipline of Soviet schooling. A book entitled *Why Johnny Can't Read* (1955) became a best seller. Eisenhower, too, was criticized. If he spent the same amount of time on the satellite program as on his golf game, detractors argued, the United States would be leading the space and missile race. In the interest of keeping defense spending down, Eisenhower tried to ignore the clamor for additional funds for missile research. He also rejected the report of a presidential panel that urged stronger defense and bomb shelters. Research and spending, nevertheless, were accelerated. Defense was cited to justify not only highway construction but also the 1958 National Defense Education Act, providing low-interest loans for college students who would teach math, science, and foreign languages in public schools, and for graduate students who would become college instructors. On July 29, the Congress created the National Aeronautics and Space Administration (NASA), and in 1959 the agency initiated Project Mercury, the manned space program. Accustomed to reaching for the stars, Americans aimed for the moon.

Communism prompted more than three hundred thousand East Germans every year to flee to the West via Berlin. The Berlin exodus depleted the East of skilled workers and embarrassed communism. In November 1958, Khrushchev warned that if the United States did not withdraw from Berlin in six months, he would turn over access to the city to the East German government, which was hostile to the American presence and which Washington did not recognize. Eisenhower said he was prepared to negotiate over Berlin only on the basis of German reunification.

As months elapsed and the Soviets did not act on their threats, tensions cooled. Eisenhower and Khrushchev scheduled a summit for May 1960 in Paris, to be preceded by an American tour by the Soviet leader. Eisenhower, in turn, would visit the USSR. Talks on Berlin were on the summit agenda, although the president hoped to achieve more: an arms control agreement that would be the big step toward ending the Cold War. The international climate was favorable. Both superpowers had declared voluntary moratoriums on nuclear testing in 1958. Khrushchev seemed ready to conclude a treaty, and during his American trip he and Eisenhower had promising discussions at Camp David, the presidential retreat in Maryland.

Even while the leaders chatted, American U-2 spy planes continued to overfly Soviet airspace and photograph military installations. Usually the U-2s flew too high for Soviet antiaircraft missiles, but Francis Gary Powers's plane had engine trouble, dropped to a lower altitude, and was shot down over Soviet territory in May 1960. Powers ejected, was captured, and confessed. When the Soviets announced the downing of the jet, on the eve of the Paris summit, the United States, assuming that Powers was dead and the wreckage dispersed, said the aircraft was a weather plane that strayed off course. Khrushchev next revealed that Powers had been captured, catching Washington in a lie and jeopardizing the summit. Khrushchev demanded that Eisenhower halt the flights, which the president did, and apologize, which Ike did not. The summit broke up without an arms deal and Eisenhower's trip to the Soviet Union was canceled. Still, it was doubtful that any political resolution could have been found to satisfy both sides. Future presidents negotiated deals but lacked sufficient determination or political clout to end the arms race.

1960: Running for TV Cameras

The aborted attempt to strike an arms control deal was the biggest in a number of disappointments and losses that, for Eisenhower, overshadowed his second term. In November 1957 he suffered a minor stroke from which he recovered, but it was clear to him and to his inner circle that the stress of the Oval Office was taking its toll. In each of the next two years, he lost

THE WORLD
WATCHES
A contemporary
cartoon of the
Kennedy-Nixon
presidential
debate.
(Library of
Congress)

an important member of his administration. A minor scandal led to
Adams's resignation before the 1958 congressional elections. Adams had
accepted a coat, a rug, and hotel expenses from a textile manufacturer
under federal investigation, raising the question of influence peddling. The
Adams scandal contributed to an election beating that made Eisenhower
the first president to have to deal with three successive Congresses dominated by the other party. Then in 1959, John Foster Dulles died of cancer,
taking from Eisenhower his major partner in diplomacy. Under Dulles's
successor, former Massachusetts Governor Christian Herter, Eisenhower's
chief diplomatic activity was to make international trips to encourage peace.

Political setbacks at home seemed to weigh on Eisenhower. After the
1958 elections, he spent the rest of his term combating what he perceived
as a spendthrift Congress eager to earmark more for defense, education,
and social programs. Democrats had always been big, irresponsible
spenders, he thought, but now, so, too, were members of his own party.

Looking to the 1960 presidential election, he was gloomy, worried that the GOP nominee would match his Democratic foe promise for promise, repudiating all that Eisenhower had done over two terms.

Nixon preempted his only strong rival for the nomination, New York Governor Nelson Rockefeller, by committing himself to a stronger national defense and more liberal positions on domestic issues. The promise discouraged the still-popular Eisenhower, who never warmed completely to Nixon and running mate Henry Cabot Lodge, from giving Nixon the rousing endorsement he sought, though he disliked the Democratic ticket of Kennedy and Texas Senator Lyndon Johnson. Perhaps the ambivalence of the Eisenhower-Nixon relationship damaged the vice president most when the president, asked about the administration decisions in which Nixon had participated, said: "If you give me a week, I might think of one."

Young, charismatic, handsome, and a World War II hero, Kennedy came from a wealthy family that lavishly financed his campaign. He faced potential liabilities in that he was in ill health and he was Catholic, a target of religious prejudice. But Kennedy and his well-oiled campaign machine deftly defused the religious issue and rolled into the general election to "get the nation moving again." Kennedy aimed to inspire Americans with the

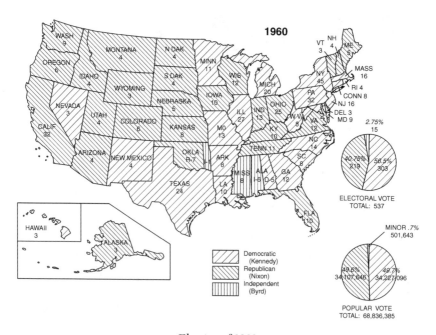

Election of 1960

noble purpose of winning the Cold War. Further symbolizing the dawning era of media-centered politics, Kennedy mastered television, outshining Nixon decisively in at least the first of three televised debates, based more on style than on substance. Kennedy won the closest popular election of the century, with only .01 of 1 percent more than Nixon, a margin of fewer than 120,000 votes, 34.2 million to 34.1 million, although the electoral margin was 303 to 219, and there were allegations of vote fraud in the key states of Illinois and Texas. The Democrat was the first Catholic elected president and, at age forty-three, the youngest man elected president.

Days before leaving office, Eisenhower delivered a nationally televised farewell address. Remembered most is the old general's admonition that "In the councils of government, we must guard against the acquisition of unwarranted influence, whether sought or unsought by the military-industrial complex." Even as he urged caution, his successor was planning the expansion of the military and an increase in defense spending. The changes sprang from a generation of leadership more aggressive than its predecessor.

In domestic and foreign affairs the president left the United States in only marginally better shape than he found it. On civil rights, progress was slow and Eisenhower provided little leadership; he was also reticent about confronting McCarthy. In diplomacy, the administration stuck to an outmoded China policy, failed to appreciate the urgency of nationalism, set dangerous examples of military and CIA involvement, showed poor judgment with the U-2 flights, and failed to curb the arms race.

Paradoxically, Eisenhower could take the most pride in what did not happen. He prevented major wars and limited defense spending. The Era of Uncertainty experienced a relatively stable decade while he was at the helm. If he did not inspire, neither did he panic. He kept the economy humming and treated his foreign adversaries with respect. After the Korean War, which he ended, not a gun was fired in anger on his watch. The next decade would not be so lucky.

CHAPTER THREE

The Affluent Society

MATERIAL RICHES were abundant in the Era of Uncertainty, yet peace of mind was elusive. Among the paradoxes was the mixture of rebellion, inertia, and spiritual seeking. Economic growth shaped American life in the quarter century following World War II, which ended the Great Depression. The 1950s were prosperous and stable. The following decade was turbulent yet even more prosperous, though inflation climbed toward the end and poverty persisted in spots. Minorities, farmers, and Appalachia lagged. At center stage in the Era of Uncertainty, under Dwight D. Eisenhower and Lyndon Baines Johnson, was a continuation of the debate over the size, power, and purpose of the federal government. Having begun under Theodore Roosevelt and waxed during the New Deal era, Americans asked of the Great Society: Was it an idea whose time had come?

The 1950s and 1960s

Scripture states: "The poor ye will always have with you." Americans set out to disprove that ancient adage, whether by prosperity wrought by free enterprise in the 1950s or by government action in the 1960s. Neglected groups, such as minorities and women, demanded to share the wealth. The baby boom generation, the most prosperous to date, raised its expectations more rapidly than they could be sated.

Americans were unified by the national purpose of winning the Cold War, and by the fear of losing it. In this materialistic period, interest in religion rose to new heights. In the 1950s religion was an ally of conformity; in the 1960s religious seekers made it an instrument of breaking away. Racial progress, too, advanced on the wheels of moral fervor, yet ultimately dissipated, another victim of unmet expectations. Science and medicine

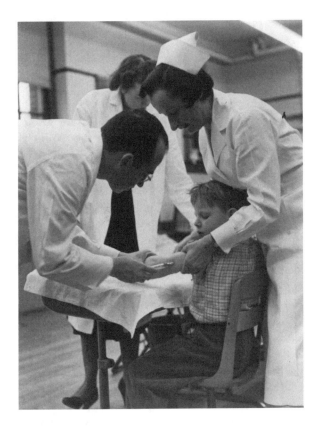

WIPING OUT
POLIO
Dr. Jonas Salk innoc-
ulates a child, 1954.
(Library of Congress)

produced marvels and medical miracles, lifted spirits, spurred the economy, and saved lives. The most irrepressible of revolutions, the sexual revolution, marched on.

The 1950s were politically conservative, yet politics does not dictate social mores. The 1960s seemed more adventurous. Conservatives and liberals argued throughout the era whether the government was doing too much too soon, or too little too late. In the end, the period reaffirmed that the only certain method of progress is trial and error. Remarkable changes occurred in politics, society, foreign policy, race and gender relations, and more. Yet change and progress are not synonymous, and the period included cataclysmic changes following assassinations. Like the 1920s, an effervescent decade punctured by the stock market crash, the 1950s had some qualities of a fool's paradise. As the 1960s closed, however, no one would have referred to the decade as a paradise, for fools or anyone else.

The Economy

America had the highest standard of living of any major nation during the Era of Uncertainty. Without realizing it, Americans were winning the Cold War with their mighty economy. Accounting for only 7 percent of the human population, America generated 40 percent of world income, nearly half the electricity and large shares of steel, copper, and coal on the globe, and more automobiles and domestic appliances than any other country. Farmers, too, outproduced their foreign counterparts, even though just 8 percent of Americans labored in agriculture by 1960, down from almost 63 percent a century earlier. Production boosts were rapid, without increases in labor, because of improved machinery, herbicides, and insecticides. Southern agriculture benefited from the development of a mechanical cotton picker, but this meant the loss of manual work, much of it performed by African Americans.

Women played a major role in prosperity; their number in the workforce jumped 44 percent from 1947 to 1962. The number of jobs traditionally held by women, such as nursing, clerical work, and teaching, grew because of the growth in the service sector of the economy. The consequences of increased numbers of working women affected families: parents were together less and divorced more, charities lacked volunteers, and office friends replaced neighborhood friends.

In the decades after World War II, many Americans realized their ambitions of home ownership. The proportion of families paying mortgages rose from 55 percent to 60 percent during the 1950s. Developers who employed thousands of construction workers could make fortunes in the crowded market of suburban housing. Notable were William Levitt, a skilled salesman, and his brother, Alfred, an architect, who teamed up to erect tracts of houses on Long Island, one of the first mass-produced subdivisions. The Levitts could complete a home every seventeen minutes and sell their houses immediately. Customers lined up for the homes the night before they went on sale. Each small, virtually identical house featured a bookcase, a fireplace, and a television. Eventually, seventeen thousand homes housed eighty thousand people. Air conditioning made homes more comfortable, especially in the South, which became a tourist mecca.

Tourists and others could drive to their destinations in more powerful, fancier automobiles. Cars, produced as new models annually, featured tail fins, chrome, radios, power steering and brakes, and automatic transmissions. General Motors, with its best-selling Chevrolet, became the world's largest corporation. Chain motels opened to serve motorists, beginning in the 1950s with the Holiday Inn. Kemmons Wilson, a Memphis builder, produced a simple, standardized design including a swimming pool, air conditioning, and television sets, which he franchised. By the end of the decade Wilson had fifteen hundred motels, with a new one going up every two and a half days. Mass-produced, standardized products that sold reasonably were applied to the food industry as well, notably with the McDonald's hamburger chain, which became ubiquitous. Dick and Maurice McDonald, who produced hamburgers by assembly line and limited the menu to that item, were bought out by Ray Kroc, who expanded nationwide, then worldwide. McDonald's helped initiate a mania for fast-food—the ten-minute lunch with no tipping.

The government contributed to the general prosperity with a strategic tax cut during the Kennedy administration, and increased spending during the Johnson administration. From 1963 to 1966 the gross national product increased at a virtually unprecedented 5 percent. Unemployment dropped from over 5 percent to around 3.5 percent. Still, the combined spending for the Vietnam War and the War on Poverty propelled the economy into overdrive and set the stage for the economic problems of the 1970s. The economy began to weaken in the late 1960s as many realized that American plenty was finite. Michael Harrington's *The Other America* (1962) inspired government programs to vanquish poverty, yet poverty persisted, though mitigated. The latecomers to the middle-class job market, especially minorities, women, and immigrants, continued to lag. A college education became a prerequisite for work previously requiring a high school or grade school education. The chain food, motel, and other service industries generated millions of jobs, but they were menial and low paying.

The origins of immigrants changed in the 1960s as immigration regulations placed more emphasis on uniting families than on job skills. Political refugees from communism were accepted from nations that had undergone revolutions, such as Cuba and Hungary. In 1965, the Immigration and Nationality Act changed immigration priorities, lifting some restrictions on Asian and African immigrants. Yet it capped immigration from the Western Hemisphere, at 120,000 annually, for the first time. New ethnic groups turned increasingly to religion, especially Catholicism, as a source of cultural identity. Ethnic and religious politics peaked in 1960 with the election of John F. Kennedy, an Irish Catholic. Kennedy received 80 percent of the Catholic and Jewish vote, but only 37 percent of the Protestant vote, in edging the Quaker Nixon.

Organized labor emerged from World War II bigger and stronger; the AFL at 10 million members and the CIO at 4.5 million. Workers rejected revolutionary schemes and supported mainstream unions. They won yearly cost-of-living increases and benefits such as medical care and vacations. Some leaders, notably Walter Reuther of the CIO, viewed political activity as embracing economic reform, civil rights, and equality for women. Labor remained liberal and a supporter of the Democratic Party, but there were rank-and-file defections to conservative George Wallace in the 1964 primaries and in the 1968 general election.

By the mid-1950s the AFL and CIO had evolved from rivals to confederates and in 1955 they merged as the AFL-CIO with 16 million members. Reuther and George Meany, the presidents of the combined union, believed that the future lay in the organization of white-collar workers, who by 1956 outnumbered blue-collar toilers. Union growth included the public sector, such as teachers and postal workers. Once more paradox was present: the percentage of union members in the workforce diminished in the 1950s. Labor was weakened by its failure to recruit African Americans and Hispanics aggressively. The decline in industrial jobs and increase in white-collar workers, many of them committed not to strike, restricted the pool of potential members. Prosperity also made workers reluctant to strike.

A catalyst to economic growth, science produced a wonderland of consumer products and millions of jobs. There were: electric clothes dryers, blenders, and frying pans; automatic garbage disposals; the Polaroid camera; and the long-playing record. Jet planes and rockets emerged from defense research, as did the computer. From early, slow, bulky computers developed during World War II, the computer went on to revolutionize transportation, industry, business, and education. Some consider it the most significant scientific development of the second half of the twentieth century.

Medicine developed in quantum leaps. Jonas Salk developed a vaccine for the crippling polio virus in 1955 and it was followed by an oral vaccine developed by Albert Sabin in 1962. There was a vaccine for measles, and there were hundreds of new drugs and antibiotics to combat rheumatoid arthritis and asthma; tranquilizers relieved some mental pain. An oral contraceptive, "the pill," appeared in 1960, a new weapon in the arsenal of the sexual revolution. In 1964, an ally in birth control, the intrauterine contraceptive device, reached the market. Gains were made against two killers: smoking and heart disease. In 1967 the first heart transplant was performed in South Africa.

Heart disease and lung cancer were linked to smoking in the 1960s, when 52 percent of men and one-third of women smoked. Ashtrays were ubiquitous. Athletes and physicians marketed cigarettes. Fraternities and sororities held "smokers" for pledges. But in 1966, two years after the surgeon general reported the health consequences of smoking, packages were required to carry warnings. In 1972 cigarette ads were banned from radio and television. Increasingly, people quit.

Suburbia, Migration, and the Baby Boomers

In the nineteenth and early twentieth centuries, Americans had moved from farms to cities, yet in the affluent decades, the migration was from cities to suburbs. Starting in 1950 and continuing for thirty years, eighteen of the twenty-five largest cities in the country lost population and the suburbs gained 60 million people. Urban critics disparaged suburbs as bland places of tasteless conformity in their dwellings and people. The criticism was overstated; suburban homes were no more alike than high-rise city apartments. The most basic motive for moving outward was that people wanted to own homes with lawns and gardens, as they could not in the crowded, expensive city. Suburbs offered excellent schools, wholesome places to raise children, dependable fire and police protection, and green, open space. The suburbs of the 1950s and 1960s were almost exclusively white. In some cases, developers refused to sell to minorities; in others, price was the chief barrier.

Although suburbs continue to be largely white and socially stratified, their diversity is increasing as they evolve, paradoxically, into small towns reminiscent of an earlier America. It would be a mistake to idealize either

THE SPREAD OF SUBURBIA
Tract housing and the postwar landscape.
(Library of Congress)

cities or suburbs, or to judge demographic trends in moral terms, as was done early in the twentieth century when rural Americans moved to cities. Places do not define individuals, nor do they dictate individual lifestyles, although they do influence them.

For better or worse, Americans by the twenty-first century are living in a post-urban society. Since 1950 more than 90 percent of metropolitan growth has taken place in suburbs. By January 2005 more than two out of three persons in the nation's urban areas lived in suburbs. Still, less densely populated cities, although experiencing problems, also offer opportunities to serve better the population that remains.

As the demographic landscape evolves, the pain that accompanies change cannot be denied. The rich are relocating into downtown condominiums paying a premium for access to cultural offerings. The poor cluster in inner cities, which lag in job opportunities as high-tech jobs follow skilled workers to the suburbs. Big-city education constitutes a failure in some respects. Schools that were virtually all-white in the 1950s have evolved into virtually all-minority, undermined by truancy, drugs, and low graduation rates. A sense of hopelessness, however, is offset by a determination to reform schools and inspire students. Some of the simplest reforms might be the most effective: reducing class size, and reading a daily newspaper at home, with parents, starting in elementary school. Newspapers, which are cheaper than television sets, should be read for enjoyment, outside of school. By college age these students might be literate, inquisitive, reasonably well-informed, and less bored.

Cities also continue to erode in stability because the downtown areas, appealing to rich, often childless couples, or older, highly successful executives, lack middle-class families with children. This is less a governmental problem than a demographic one. Most people did not flee cities because of bad government and good government will not necessarily bring them back.

Suburbs expanded from childbirths as well as flight from cities. From 1946 to 1964 some 75.9 million Americans were born, a "baby boom" that produced two-fifths of the national population. The baby boomers were the largest, richest, and best-educated generation in U.S. history and created a bulge in the population pipeline at each stage of their development. First they crowded into elementary school classrooms, leading to teacher shortages. Next they generated enormous growth in higher education, opposed the Vietnam War, led the sexual revolution, experimented with recreational drugs, and injected idealism into politics, only to retreat into disillusionment. In the 1980s many became young urban professionals, "yuppies." As the generation approached retirement questions arose over whether Social Security could sustain its numbers.

If there was a central paradox of baby boomers, it was their complexity, leading them in a variety of directions. Theirs was the most idealistic and altruistic generation—and the most selfish and narcissistic. Labeled bland as middle school students in the 1950s, they were called hedonists as college students in the 1960s, though they were often the same people. As they aged they became interested in jobs, families, and annuities, and many settled into conventional lifestyles they once ridiculed. The simplest explanation for the contradictions is that the generation changed its mind repeatedly as it evolved. The baby boomers stand out not because they were more fickle, but rather because there were so many of them and they thus had a wide impact. In fact, many of the changes sometimes attributed to politics and economics can probably be linked at least partly to demographics. For example, violent crime, frequently associated with the young, increased as the boomers reached their teens and beyond. By the time the boomers attained middle age, violent offenses decreased and white-collar transgressions increased.

Boomers and their families also moved southward and westward to the Sunbelt, seeking better jobs and climates. California was the prime destination. Its population increased by 5 million, 20 percent of national population growth, during the 1950s. California became the largest state in 1963. Low taxes and labor costs attracted industry and the region outgrew the North and East. In time the Republican Party dominated the Sunbelt. Though neglected by government studies and urban planners, small towns remained an alternative to cities and suburbs, offering a sense of history and community, self-sufficiency, cohesiveness, and the absence of traffic jams. Almost unnoticed, they were a "third way," hospitable, in particular, to retirees, extended families, and small businesses.

The Sexual Revolution

In the decades after World War II, sexuality exploded and sexual themes permeated popular culture. Sex became recreational as well as a means of producing families, an evolution that had begun a hundred years earlier. The war was a catalyst for change, introducing servicemen to cultures with more relaxed sexual standards and encouraging wartime dalliances, arising partly from loneliness, at home. Teenagers grew up more quickly and had sex at earlier ages. Babies were born to younger women, many of them unmarried. The sexual revolution was liberating, yet its dark side contributed to the paradox and uncertainty of the era: some perceived sex as gratification without cost, and such a view is seldom realistic. Although monogamy might or might not be natural, freer sex sometimes came at the cost of guilt or, at least, divided loyalties. The melting pot of popular culture encouraged the decoupling of sex from its traditional link to love. As one psychologist said, "Sometimes it's love and sometimes it's just sex." The profound power of sex, detached from moral strictures, made it difficult to determine whether lovers loved one another or merely loved having sex.

The sexual revolution had roots beyond the libido. The second feminist movement sprang largely from writers, marchers, and academicians, to whom sexual equality could be interpreted in terms that were physical, social, economic, psychological, and identity affirming. Most influential was Betty Friedan's 1963 book, *The Feminine Mystique*. Bright, highly educated, Friedan felt unfilled by motherhood alone. "The problem that has no name," as she called it, was essentially boredom. She wanted to be a writer and became one of the most significant ones of her time. Her book and activism helped stimulate creation of the National Organization for Women in 1966. In 1972 Gloria Steinem, ironically once a Playboy bunny, founded *Ms.* magazine, a major feminist periodical. The second feminist movement espoused the same sexual standards for women that society had taken for granted for men: women should be as free to take a variety of partners, families should not inhibit either gender sexually. Part of the sexual liberation that did not involve intercourse did involve fathers sharing in child care and housekeeping, freeing women to work, enjoy hobbies, and relax. Some feminists opposed pornography as an exploitation of women's bodies, but others considered it a matter of free speech. Some women "dressed" down, scorning heels, makeup, and other accoutrements that made them "objects" of men. Simultaneously, women had the right to take the initiative in calling a man, asking him for a date, approaching him in a bar, or proposing marriage. On the other hand, women who did not marry should be respected, not denigrated as "old maids." The thrust of the argument was that a woman did not have to find her self-value in a man. Feminists opened career opportunities for women and often considered women without careers inferior.

Feminists were a minority, yet a disproportionately influential one. Women who had careers in academia, publishing, government, or wrote in the new field of women's studies were rarely nonfeminists, but feminists, of course, did not represent all women. Some women chose to lead conventional lives as homemakers and enjoyed pursuing men by wearing the fashionable clothing feminists scorned. The debate also involved men. Some nonfeminists believed feminists were disrespectful of men, even those who were essentially well-meaning. No one dared ask the question openly, but at least in some male locker rooms men asked if they ought to have a

ONE MAN'S
SEXUAL
REVOLUTION
Publisher Hugh
Hefner with
Playmates of
the Month.
(Library of
Congress)

voice in whether their pregnant wife or lover had a baby or an abortion. Even by removing judgmentalism from the dialogue, it is clear that sexuality, in all of its manifestations from boardroom to bedroom, is perhaps the most complex paradox of the century and the most uncertain aspect of the Era of Uncertainty.

Sex was everywhere: movies, music, photo magazines, and celebrity lifestyles. Female Hollywood stars dressed provocatively and changed lovers and husbands like the weather, drawing more people to their films, perhaps to experience these lifestyles vicariously. Revealing dress percolated down to high school students and some college students. Drugs and alcohol loosened inhibitions, on the silver screen and small screen as well as at parties and on dates. If Americans had ever been prudes, they were prudes no more. The most popular genre was the romantic comedy, and many suggestive movies, rated PG-13, were considered acceptable for children. Because Hollywood movies were sexy did not necessarily mean that they were crude, artless, or unfit for consumption. Still, anyone who lived through the 1950s and 1960s cannot help but wonder at the rapid pace of sexual influence in everyday life. In 1953 Hugh Hefner launched the highly profitable *Playboy* featuring a seminude female centerfold. Next came the Playboy philosophy of sex for the moment, and Playboy clubs to serve rich white males, their drinks delivered by curvaceous female "bunnies."

Books such as Grace Metalious's *Peyton Place* (1956) depicting a small New Hampshire town as a hotbed of sexual intrigue, sold millions of copies, and spawned a radio and television series. Jacqueline Susann's *Valley of the Dolls* (1966), an account of a sexually active, unmarried professional woman, became one of the best-selling books of all times. The books appeared while the Supreme Court was creating a more permissive legal atmosphere. Spanning the 1950s and the 1960s, justices ruled on a series of cases that opened a window to obscenity. "A book cannot be persecuted unless it is found to be utterly without redeeming social value," the Court stated. Rock 'n' roll's premier pioneer, Elvis Presley, gyrated his hips suggestively while he strummed his guitar and sang. Presley had started as a gospel singer, and the mixture of sexuality and religion remained a staple of the musical industry, its performers, and its followers. In the 1980s the world-known evangelist Jimmy Swaggart, a piano pounding partisan of Christian music, was seen as a sexual libertine, and other examples followed. Sex, religion, motion pictures, and music had a common root in that they worked on the emotions and loosened inhibitions. The counterculture of the late 1960s produced musical festivals, such as Woodstock, famous for good music and good sex. The connection of music, sex, and dance was the intertwining of beat, rhythm, lyrics, and movement. The connection was historic, but the scope was revolutionary.

Science and academia to some degree supported liberalized sexual expression. Sigmund Freud had approved sex as an antidote to mental illness in the late nineteenth and early twentieth century. Anthropologist Margaret Mead concluded that Polynesian Island children were happier than American children, possibly because their lifestyle was less inhibited. Sex researcher Alfred Kinsey produced two pathbreaking books, *Sexual Behavior in the Human Male* (1948) and *Sexual Behavior in the Human Female* (1953). Kinsey began as a researcher of insects at the University of Indiana, then developed an interest in human sexuality, at that time almost a virgin discipline. Taking large samples of sexual histories, he interviewed his subjects in depth and filmed sexual activities. His research rocked the supposedly staid 1950s. Kinsey showed that a sexual revolution had long been underway, underground. Premarital sex, masturbation, adultery, and gay and lesbian sex were more frequent than most Americans realized. He tried to free sex from the inhibitions of dogma, and, more questionably, from love and emotion, trivializing it, some complained, as a mechanical act. On the one hand, Kinsey lit the fuse that ignited women's and gay and lesbian liberation movements in the 1960s. On the other hand, he had darker, more self-serving motives, advancing an agenda that at worst became another variety of dogma. As time passed, some researchers claimed that Kinsey's research was flawed because, although his sample was large, it was not representative of the general population, omitting, for example, highly religious individuals. Kinsey, nonetheless, helped legitimize human sexuality as a field of research.

Whatever the motives and influence of Kinsey, a gay and lesbian revolution burst forth in the late 1960s. The focal point was the "Stonewall riot" of 1969, in which gays and lesbians fought New York police who raided a gay bar. The theme of gay rights would have a major impact in succeeding decades as society became more tolerant in matters of sexual orientation. Yet criticism, some of it religious, surfaced again in the 1980s with the appearance of AIDS (acquired immune deficiency syndrome), which appeared first in large numbers in the gay community. Eventually, such celebrities as the actor Rock Hudson and the basketball star "Magic" Johnson contracted the disease. By the time Johnson was infected the virus had moved into the heterosexual community and included drug users who shared contaminated needles.

The highest leaders of the land shared in the sexual revolution. Indeed, some were promiscuous. John Kennedy, Lyndon Johnson, Bill Clinton, and Martin Luther King had adulterous affairs. The great basketball center Wilt Chamberlain claimed he had slept with a thousand women. In Hollywood, on Broadway, among aspiring models and starlets, even in the news industry, sleeping with the boss was a way to get ahead. Powerful men and women, political leaders, and celebrities, were sought after as lovers. Henry Kissinger, Nixon's national security adviser and secretary of state, explained: "Power is the ultimate aphrodisiac." By the end of the baby boomer rein of the youth corps, the sexual revolution had gained the momentum of a locomotive roaring downhill. Like all-powerful impulses that move fast, it changed America, and the locomotive roars on.

A Spiritual Barometer

Religious interest in the 1950s often has been dismissed as superficial, and that of the 1960s has been described as waning. Always central to American life, religion had a prominent place in the affluent decades. In 1950 some 57 percent of Americans belonged to a church or synagogue; in 1959 that figure was 69 percent. No other Western culture equaled that of the United States in the percentage of population associated with a religious institution. Americans are seekers whose journey frequently involves religion, a trait that did not bypass the baby boomers, perhaps the biggest cohort of religious searchers ever.

In the context of the 1950s organized religion was prominent. Yet religion was something to do, rather than something to be. Usually it was found between the walls of religious institutions rather than in solitary reflection. Public prayer was more of a ritual than private prayer. Reflecting the sunny prosperity of the decade, religion offered an uplifting message that was largely responsible for the optimistic outlook of the era despite potential nuclear holocaust. The interest in religion was manifest by the popularity of such books as Henry Morton Robinson's *The Cardinal* (1950) and Catherine Marshall's *A Man Called Peter* (1951), both the basis of hit films. In 1956 *The Ten Commandments* became the top-grossing movie to that time, and children were released from school to see it.

In the Eisenhower years patriotism included an element of Christianity, sometimes called civil religion, but more appropriately, civic religion. The central idea, which had long been a part of the concept of American exceptionalism, was that America was God's chosen nation, set apart to be an example for the world. Yet the Soviets, whose official philosophy was atheism, also felt that destiny was moving in their direction, their victory inevitable. Just to make sure, both built bigger and better bombs.

Eisenhower rarely attended church before reaching the White House, but became a churchgoer to set an example for the nation. During Ike's administration Congress added "under God" to the Pledge of Allegiance in 1954 and "In God We Trust" to coins in 1956. Eisenhower was president during an age of religious popularizers and was friends with some of them. Protestant minister Norman Vincent Peale's 1952 book, *The Power of Positive Thinking*, sold millions of copies. Peale explained that faith in God and oneself were the keys to success. Modern psychiatry has used similar techniques to treat depression and other mental illnesses, with the caveat that if one has a happy outlook, success is not important. Evangelist Billy Graham, a North Carolina Baptist, filled stadiums to hear his sermons and made converts by the thousands. Later, his crusades, which he took worldwide, were a mainstay of television. Graham was no simpleton but his message was simple: faith in God was more important than rules. Salvation was a gift; it did not have to be earned. Graham became the friend of presidents, including some who exploited his friendship, as well as the civil rights leader and fellow Baptist Martin Luther King Jr.

RALLYING FOR RELIGION Evangelist Billy Graham preaches a sermon to 40,000 people attending the annual Reformation Day held in New York City, 1957. (AP/Wide World Photos)

King's role as a civil rights leader is the stuff of legend; his role as a religious leader is sometimes obscure. From the beginning, King and other civil right leaders used the black churches as a fulcrum of the movement. The churches provided a moral basis for direct action, furnished biblical foundations as the moral rationale for equality, and pointed out white hypocrisy. An interconnected network of dedicated believers, African Americans themselves found sustenance in biblical arguments for their crusade, at least in the early years. King learned from Gandhi and the Bible that love could overcome hate, though it would not be easy, and that those who rely on love must suffer and exercise patience. Like the conservative Graham, King's oratorical ability was a potent weapon in his arsenal. And he did overcome.

Popular religion overshadowed formal theology during the Age of Uncertainty, yet there were profound theologians who thought creatively and wrote inspiring prose. Reinhold Niebuhr was the best-known theologian, merging theology and activism, accepting imperfection, and striving for social justice. Yet his brother, Richard, might have been the most profound and systematic theologian of the era. Eschewing the popular journalism and lecture circuit in which Reinhold thrived, Richard led a comparatively quiet career, avoiding the increasing tendency to link secularism and religion. Emulating Richard Niebuhr, Paul Tillich, an inspiration to King, dismissed the connection between theology and nationalism.

For Catholics, the era produced a renaissance. Most important were the reforms of Pope John XXIII, especially those of Vatican II, a council convened by the pope from 1962 to 1965. For the first time the pope made an effort to embrace the ecumenical movement to unite all Christians. The council liberalized the Mass by approving the use of the vernacular and by giving the laity a greater role in the service.

Women, however, did not have much of a voice in Vatican II or in the other debates affecting religious institutions. At the grass roots they were active in denominations, attending services more often than men, dominating religious education, and doing most of the volunteer work. They seldom made policy and still were barred from entering the priesthood. Much the same could be said for gays and lesbians. They fought valiantly, with slow progress, to be ordained or even to have their lifestyle accepted. In the twenty-first century the issue continued to animate debates.

In the 1960s Americans turned inward. Some turned away from organized religion altogether or merged spirituality with meditation and a variety of philosophies, some of which, such as Marxism, excluded God. Religion motivated some to work to eradicate poverty, to volunteer for the Peace Corps, and to bring solid food as well as spiritual manna to the needy. Religion motivated some participants in the Vietnam antiwar movement, and elements of the counterculture crept into religious services, such as use of guitars, folk music, circling to hold hands and acknowledge the participants as spiritual partners, and criticism of materialism and the government.

The most important spinoff from the counterculture undercurrent was the rise of New Age philosophy and religion, which had no prescription for practice and for which any summary will oversimplify. Some turned to Eastern philosophies and religion such as Buddhism (including the Tibetan variety), Daoism, and Confucianism. Many took lessons in martial arts of the East; others were inspired by spiritual dance. A spate of books poured out, including self-help books exploring the connections between sex and spirituality and dismissing of the idea that God had a human form of the male gender. The seekers, who continued their quest in the twenty-first century, mixed astrology, alternative medicine, noncompetitive exercise, and the teaching of a spiritual lifestyle to their children. The New Age seekers continue to experiment with herbal medicine, acupuncture, and the Indian belief that energy centers called *chakras* influence one's physical and mental health. There was, and is among New Age practitioners, a strong strain of beliefs in psychic phenomena, including mind-body medicine and mental telepathy. Stress reduction techniques include massage, unblocking of energy, and communing with nature, surrounded by greenery, alone or in groups. Many believe in reincarnation, that humans have lessons to learn in every lifetime until they complete their journey and merge with the One Force. Some view God as a source of intelligent energy that dominates the universe, less like the Christian God than like the "Force" of the popular motion picture series *Star Wars*. In fact, notable movies of the period, especially those by George Lucas and Steven Spielberg, carry undertones with spiritual messages, and can be watched on several levels by adults and children. In some circles of young people, the departing words were not "Good-bye," but "May the Force be with you."

New Entitlements

Once upon a time in America, "rights," were protections for individuals against aggressions threatening personal safety or status. Most of the Constitution's amendments, most notably the first ten, protect individuals. This understanding began to change with the rise of group consciousness in the 1960s, particularly inspired by the civil rights movement and feminism. The list soon expanded to other groups defined by age, ethnicity, education, even neighborhood or region. Rights became something owed to a group by the government, and in part, Lyndon Johnson's Great Society and War on Poverty addressed these concerns. There was nothing inherently wrong with the concepts of group rights, or even their evolution into "entitlements"—benefits owed by the government. Yet there were practical problems. As opposed to most traditional rights, "entitlements" required resources, namely money. Once enacted, it was almost impossible to remove them from the federal budget, which rose automatically every year. Groups competed for entitlements, especially when there did not seem enough to go around. The concept polarized politics and political parties, which upped the ante to outpromise the opposition. Parties and politicians who refused to play the game were often defeated at the polls.

In the short run, especially while the Great Society was operating at full throttle, the concept did much good. But the idea of entitlements raised expectations and weakened economic incentives. LBJ did not deliberately encourage the notion; he believed in education and job training to enable people to better their lives. Yet over time this idea was translated into the idea that the government owed not opportunity but results. While many of the early antipoverty programs aimed to place trainees in jobs, over time the program came to imply the promise of a job and, eventually, a "decent job." Yet even if the government were to become the employer of last resort, there had to be something useful for the employees to do, they had to have the skills to do it, and there had to be money to pay them. When the resources could not be found to do all these things, the resentment contributed to the sour mood that closed the 1960s, producing, in the waning days of his term, the irony of poor people demonstrating on the Mall against Lyndon Johnson, of all people.

Though entitlements were not a hot subject of debate and there was much sympathy for groups that had suffered discrimination, who were denied an education, or whose job description stopped with "secretary," as demands increased and resources dwindled, a reaction set in. The backlash first arose among conservatives who believed the white middle-class and blue-collar workers had been demonized, patronized, and squeezed out in the scramble. They were expected to feel guilty for not being poor or for the possible sins of their forefathers. A good many were committed to social uplift, yet resented being scapegoats. If their complaints had not contained an element of truth, they would not have resonated. Some former liberals, termed neoconservatives, joined the march to the right. Journalists and scholars such as Daniel Patrick Moynihan, Nathan Glazer, Irving Kristol, and Norman Podhoretz took to the pages of *Commentary* and *The Public Interest* to challenge the prevailing liberal orthodoxy. Doubting the competence and compassion of big government, they wanted a government that served individuals, not groups. Although group identity had its place, in the long run, they believed, one's individual identity was the only thing no one could take away. If the government fed all the hungry with all the caviar they could gorge, it would not necessarily make them happy. White Christians joined neoconservatives in deploring the counterculture, drug use, lack of discipline, and a decline in self-reliance. They advocated sexual restraint, traditional families, and less glamorizing of unconventional lifestyles. By the late 1960s these conservatives were poised to take over politics.

The affluent decades were a failure only in the sense that they were not an absolute success. The 1960s ended not with a total rejection of the decade's values, nor of its predecessor's. The political dialogue was healthy, motivated less by mean spirits than by competing interests, and the best way to create a society that would not only be great, but good, moral, secure, and satisfying. A time of paradox indeed.

CHAPTER FOUR

Cultural Dissent

THE ERA OF Uncertainty culminated in the youth rebellion of the 1960s, which destabilized the nation yet left a host of lessons. First, there is nothing wrong with uncertainty because progress means taking a chance. Second, if one wants space, he or she must allow others to have it. Finally, accept change, but do not try to force it. If it happens at all, it will happen at a pace influenced by historical circumstance, as an idea whose time has come.

Culture both shaped and reflected the times. The decade of the 1950s was mislabeled "placid," for the dissent and unconventional lifestyles of the 1960s could already be seen in the acting of Marlon Brando and James Dean, the rock 'n' roll of Elvis Presley, and the writing of the Beat authors Jack Kerouac and Allen Ginsberg.

Hollywood: A Star-Crossed City

Hollywood turned a dark face to the dilemmas of the 1950s, including the Cold War, the McCarthy era, and the nuclear nightmare. Films depicted labor corruption, prison violence, and racism. Nuclear testing prompted the genre of monster films that titillated and frightened young audiences, like an amusement park ride where the danger is illusional but the thrill is real. One film that achieved cult status later, partly because it resembled a caricature of the horror film genre, was *Invasion of the Body Snatchers* (1956), in which aliens took over human bodies.

Westerns were popular on the silver screen, as they were on television. John Wayne, the most popular actor, also played military heroes. Westerns helped satisfy the craving of Americans for a romantic view of the mythic past. The plots focused on the heroism of white male cowboys who were brave, pure, and deadeye gunslingers. Indians symbolized roadblocks to the advance of civilization. Nonetheless, as movies gained sophistication,

HOLLYWOOD'S IMAGE OF DESIRE
Movie Star Marilyn Monroe appearing with the
USO Camp Show, "Anything Goes," 1954.
(National Archives)

they grew more realistic in their depiction of cowboys and Indians alike. Delmer Dave's *Broken Arrow* (1950) was an early attempt to show the past from an Native American perspective. Fred Zimmerman's *High Noon* (1952) depicted a frontier town shadowed by fear and cowardice, with one man alone left to uphold its honor.

If the Western emphasized American triumphalism, *The Wild One* (1953) introduced a subculture of brawling bikers as the mouthpiece for criticism of the status quo, conveyed in a format that was physical as well as psychological. Marlon Brando represented a biker rebelling against the middle-class lifestyle others were trying to attain. Asked what he was rebelling against, Brando responded, "What've you got?" James Dean, too, was a rebel, though more nuanced, embodying the uncertainties of the first wave of baby boomers as they came of age.

Hollywood films became sexier and more daring, dealing with taboo subjects to outflank television. To do so, Hollywood had to circumvent its own code of self-censorship. Usually the public gets what it demands in the field of entertainment. What it wanted was actresses such as Marilyn Monroe, once a *Playboy* pinup, who combined sexuality, superficial innocence, and an undercurrent of sophistication. Her name on the marquee guaranteed an audience. The philosophy of the insatiability of the male libido was parodied in Billy Wilder's *The Apartment* (1960). Violence splattered the silver screen in Alfred Hitchcock's thriller *Psycho* (1960). A brilliant director, Hitchcock combined mystery, sexuality, humor, and plot with clever use of camera angles, a vivid imagination, special effects advanced for the era, and a deft touch.

In the 1960s Hollywood's self-censorship was stretched until broken. Stanley Kubrick's adaptation of Vladimir Nabokov's novel *Lolita* (1962) depicted a middle-aged professor's sexual encounter with a pubescent girl. Kubrick pushed Hollywood politically with *Dr. Strangelove; Or, How I Learned to Stop Worrying and Love the Bomb* (1964), a brutal satire about enthusiasm for nuclear war. Late in the decade Hollywood glamorized outlaws in *Bonnie and Clyde* (1967), a pair of depression-era bank robbers resurrected as beautiful people. *Easy Rider* (1969) harked back to the world of rebellious bikers in more complex terms than the 1950s films.

TV: Home Entertainment in a Box

Hollywood soon lost its near monopoly on the American imagination. Cinema entertainment lost ground rapidly following the war and fell behind the new medium of television. The small screen could be viewed with family, friends, or children in one's living room. Unlike the cinema, one could change channels if one did not like the show. Increasingly, there was more variety and higher quality. Let in as a friendly guest, television threatened to take over the home, eating up time for family meals, outdoor activities, parties, homework, and conversation. Teenagers seemed to flit between television and telephone. In the end, Americans became addicted, though this was not necessarily technological determinism. There was some truth in the idea that television inspired antisocial behavior, but this appraisal also carries an element of an alibi, or at least an evasion of individual responsibility. After all, one could simply turn it off. Early shows were largely all white and middle class. Though racism was a factor, marketing was a more important one. Television thrived on advertising and aimed at an audience that could buy Chevrolets and refrigerators, or, better yet, Cadillacs and mansions in Malibu.

Television was not all about actors and directors, prejudice and advertisers. As a technological catalyst for change in the Time of Paradox it ranks

★ CHARLES VAN DOREN: THE MAN FOR THE ROLE ★

I've learned a lot about good and evil.
They are not always what they appear to be.
—CHARLES VAN DOREN

QUIZ SHOW WITH A CHEAT SHEET
Contestant Charles Van Doren
on the quiz show *Twenty-one*.
(Library of Congress)

CHARLES VAN DOREN was perfect, decided the producers of *Twenty-One*, one of the quiz shows that had become a television fad in the 1950s. He was young, handsome, unassuming, and an English instructor studying for his Ph.D. at Columbia University. His father was a famous professor and writer at Columbia and his mother and uncle won acclaim as authors. The producers wanted to rig the show to make him their new champion. Initially Van Doren was reluctant, not seeking public glory. However, they persuaded him with the argument that his success would inspire teachers and students—and with the prospect of winning up to $100,000. And perhaps Van Doren thought it would be his chance to impress his family. "I've been acting a role for ten or fifteen years, maybe all my life," he admitted later. "It's a role of thinking that I've done far more than I've done, accomplished more than I've accomplished, produced more than I've produced." That *Twenty-One* was "fixed" to make the show dramatic and entertaining, that Van Doren would be coached and given the answers, did not matter.

So Van Doren said yes to the producers and became king of the NBC-TV show when the reigning champion, Herbert Stempel, "took a dive" by deliberately answering a question wrong. For weeks, from late 1956 into 1957, Van Doren kept winning, adding to his money total (which would reach $129,000), and receiving hundreds of letters daily from people thanking him for his contribution to intellectual life. Offers poured in to write, to lecture, to appear in movies. NBC promised him a job as a $50,000-a-year commentator on the *Today* show. He was a folk hero who magazines called "the new All-American boy." Still, Van Doren was tormented by guilt and begged the producers to be defeated. "I felt like a bullfighter in a bull ring with thousands and thousands of people cheering me on, and all I wanted to do was get out of there," he admitted. When he learned that he would finally lose to lawyer Vivienne Nearing, his reaction was, "Thank God!"

Van Doren went on to complete his doctorate and take a professorship at Columbia, in addition to his *Today* duties. His comfortable world, however, was shattered in 1958, when Stempel, angered that he missed out on the fame garnered by the more telegenic Van Doren, revealed publicly that *Twenty-One* was fixed. There were other reports of dishonest quiz shows, and a New York grand jury began investigating. Many who had been involved with the shows, Van Doren among them, said they knew nothing of wrongdoing, but the grand jury was skeptical, and a House of Representatives subcommittee held hearings. In the fall of 1959, Van Doren was subpoenaed, appeared before the lawmakers, and read a long statement of confession. "I would give almost anything I have to reverse the course of my life in the last three years," he said. "I was involved, deeply involved, in a deception. The fact that I, too, was very much deceived cannot keep me from being the principal victim of that deception, because I was its principal symbol. There may be a kind of justice in that." Cheap fame was expensive.

Soon after his statement, NBC fired Van Doren and Columbia accepted his resignation. His admission shocked a number of commentators, who wondered how such a bright man with so much to offer could have been involved in something so tawdry, and whether the quiz show scandals were symptoms of a sick society. Nevertheless, there was great sympathy for Van Doren. Letters to NBC protested his firing. Columbia students rallied in opposition to his dismissal from the university. Newspapers and magazines reported that a majority of people believed he had been punished enough and deserved another job. Several universities expressed interest in hiring him.

But Van Doren retreated from the public eye, moving from the East to Chicago, where he lived quietly, worked as an editor for *Encyclopedia Britannica*, and edited significant collections of literature. Having carved out considerable, genuine accomplishments on his own, he never again spoke openly of his part on *Twenty-One*. The paradox of what Van Doren seemed to be and the reality beneath the veneer, as well as the juxtaposition of his rapid rise and dramatic fall, make him an apt symbol for the Era of Uncertainty.

Sources: For book-length treatments of Charles Van Doren and the quiz show scandals, see Kent Anderson, *Television Fraud: The History and Implications of the Quiz Show Scandals* (1978), and Joseph Stone and Tim Yohn, *Prime Time and Misdemeanors: Investigating the 1950s TV Quiz Scandal—A D.A.'s Account* (1992). For useful and well-written short treatments, see Eric F. Goldman, *The Crucial Decade—and After: America, 1945–1960* (1960); Erik Barnouw, *Tube of Plenty: The Evolution of American Television* (rev. ed, 1990); and David Halberstam, *The Fifties* (1993).

with the automobile, the computer, antibiotics and vaccines, space exploration, and atomic energy. Few innovations made their impact so rapidly. In 1946 there were only six thousand TV sets in the country, more than half of them in New York City. By 1950, there were 12 million. By 1970 there were 70 million sets, 38 percent of them color. Among scholars, TV's negative effects seemed apparent. It pulled families apart or drew them together without communicating. They went out less, and the new diversion dulled minds and dimmed imaginations because the activity was passive. Yet television also brought news into homes as no previous medium. It shaped attitudes, generating emotional as well as intellectual reactions. It showed the graphic violence of the Vietnam War and the conflicts of the civil rights movement. Without television, Elvis Presley and the Beatles, who appeared on the *Ed Sullivan Show*, would not have become international celebrities.

Many of the formulas for television programs were borrowed from radio. These included soap operas, variety shows, police dramas, situation comedies, and, increasingly, athletic contests. Detective and police stories included *The Untouchables, Dragnet,* and *77 Sunset Strip.* Even more numerous were Westerns. In 1959 there were twenty-nine Westerns on the fall schedule of NBC, CBS, and ABC. Live dramas were a high point of television in the 1950s, yet live dramas were forced into extinction because of their cost and fear of making a mistake. Exposure of quiz show cheating in 1959 nearly destroyed the genre, discredited networks, and wrecked careers. The wages of network sin were public outrage, channel switching, and the virtual demise of the big-payoff quiz shows. Other formulas involved science fiction, sometimes combined with the mystique of the supernatural, as in Rod Serling's *Twilight Zone. Star Trek,* a science fiction adventure, had limited appeal in its first run, but it developed a cult following and was spun off into television sequels, books, and memorabilia.

Federal Communications Commission Chair Newton Minow in 1961 dismissed television as a "vast wasteland." Vast it was, and vaster it became. Yet viewers could be selective. Television brought news, sometimes live, into American homes with immediacy. Edward R. Murrow's CBS program *See It Now,* inspired hard-hitting documentaries in the 1950s. The middle 1960s were a golden age of national news anchors such as the trusted Walter Cronkite of CBS and the erudite David Brinkley and Chet Huntley of NBC. Their newscasts expanded from fifteen minutes at the dawn of the medium to thirty minutes in the 1960s. The trend culminated in *60 Minutes,* a CBS investigative news program that premiered in 1968. Television news also contributed to the decline of daily newspapers as many learned to take their information from sound bytes. Television changed politics. Time for advertising was expensive. Candidates often paid more attention to the background and setting needed to attract news cameras than to their abbreviated message. People watched televised conventions but paid less attention to written platforms.

Rockin' to New Rhythms

If teenagers were addicted to television, to a large extent they dictated choices in popular music. If a single word could encapsulate popular music, it was "variety." As often in America, changes in taste were affected by technology. For the buying public, except performers, sheet music was of little concern. The period saw the growing popularity of durable vinyl sound recordings and high-fidelity record players. Amplifiers no larger than suitcases were stacked as high as buildings at the end of the 1960s. Radio broadcasted recorded, rather than live music. The electric guitar became more prominent, and tape began to change the way recordings were made.

SHAKING ALL OVER
The first rock star: Elvis Presley, 1956. (Library of Congress)

★ JANIS JOPLIN: A TURBULENT LIFE FOR TURBULENT TIMES ★

Freedom's just another word for nothing left to lose.
—KRIS KRISTOFFERSON, "ME AND BOBBY MCGEE"

A PIECE OF HER HEART
Janis Joplin lived her songs.
(AP/Wide World Photos)

JANIS JOPLIN'S life was a paradox of artistic triumph and self-destructiveness. Like other musicians who came of age in the Era of Uncertainty, she was drawn into the deep end of rock, in which the volume level had become earsplitting and the electronic distortions were meant to simulate the sensory-bending experience of LSD. Also like her peers, she grounded her foray into the unknown on one of America's oldest forms of musical expression, the blues. Her hard-driving delivery reinvented the jubilance of such African American forebearers as Bessie Smith, called "the Empress of the Blues" in the 1920s.

By the time of Joplin's 1966 arrival in San Francisco, the mecca of music and the emergent counterculture, some white male vocalists had already immersed themselves in the blues. It was part of a search for authenticity in a culture that increasingly appeared artificial—plastic. Joplin was seen as a woman playing a man's game in the largely white, male-dominated rock scene of the 1960s.

Joplin waged a revolt against the conventional symbols of female beauty and celebrity. An ugly duckling by the standards of the previous generation, she was reincarnated as a swan on her own terms, with her frizzy hair and peacock frocks helping to broaden definitions of beauty and fashion. Her membership in and later leadership of a succession of all-male bands reinforced this image. With her first hit song, "Piece of My Heart" (1967), she set an image for herself of vulnerability beneath a swaggering exterior.

Joplin's performances and raw sexuality were an example of music's role in the sexual revolution of the 1960s. Symbolic of a hedonistic pursuit of pleasure, she was embraced by the counterculture for her refusal to submit to limits. It was this refusal to acknowledge limits that led to a succession of drug-related deaths among leading rock stars in the Era of Uncertainty, including Jim Morrison, Jimi Hendrix, and Joplin, killed by a heroin overdose in 1970 at twenty-seven. Joplin's biggest hit was posthumous, her recording of Kris Kristofferson's "Me and Bobby McGee," a low-key country ballad whose pensiveness stands at odds with earlier recordings and raises intriguing questions about the artist she might have become.

Equally intriguing, and more ironic, was the incorporation of the musical rebellion of the 1960s and its stars into the mainstream capitalism economy. "They're paying me $50,000 a year to be like me!" Joplin exclaimed. Fifty thousand dollars was big money in the 1960s, especially for a counterculture that prided itself on disdaining wealth. For an unpopular teen from Port Arthur, Texas, being encouraged to be herself might have seemed victory enough. To be paid handsomely for it struck Joplin as the most paradoxical turn of all.

Freedom means many things. To the rebels of the 1960s it often meant pushing the limits of conventional society, moving to a rock beat, flaunting sexuality, experimenting with drugs, taunting presidents, and living in communes. To Janis Joplin, freedom meant simply being her uninhibited self because she had "nothing left to lose."

Sources: Studies of Joplin include David Dalton, *Janis* (1971); Deborah Landau, *Janis Joplin: Her Life and Times* (1971); Dynise Balcavage, *Janis Joplin* (2000); Myra Friedman, *Janis Joplin and Buried Alive* (1999); and John Cooke, *Janis, Performance Diary, 1966–1970* (1997).

Electric guitarist and recording engineer Les Paul contributed the technique of "overdubbing," separately recorded layers of instruments and voices.

As the form of music changed, so did its content. African and European influences had cross-pollinated to create distinctly American music since the previous century, but black music acquired greater prominence after World War II. Frank Sinatra brought Tin Pan Alley to a pinnacle during the 1950s. Yet his old-style pop music was giving way to a defiant black sound that changed music worldwide. Jazz lost popularity, despite innovations. Saxophonist Charlie Parker and trumpeter Dizzy Gillespie pioneered a harmonically daring genre called bebop. Trumpeter Miles Davis inaugurated the emotionally restrained version, cool jazz. Popular audiences did not warm to these undanceable forms, and many of the popular dance bands disbanded. As for "serious music," it had grown entirely too serious for most audiences.

African Americans embraced a new music, rhythm and blues, which maintained the dance beat of big-band jazz in a small combo format featuring electric guitar. The sound was accepted in the South, where black and white people had always appreciated each other's music. Presley and other young southern whites enjoyed greater access to black popular culture than their northern peers, and they would take the lead during the

1950s in the mix of white and black music called rock 'n' roll. Even in country music, a traditional white genre, important artists such as Hank Williams and Bill Monroe acknowledged their black musical roots.

In the 1960s, rhythm and blues evolved into soul, derived partly from black gospel music. Berry Gordy founded Motown Records to promote the new sound and found buyers. Small recording companies nurtured rock, especially Sun Records, which released Presley's debut recording, "That's All Right (Mama)" in 1954. A year later Presley's music moved beyond the South when RCA signed him to a contract. Not until he appeared on television in 1956 did he become a national figure. The former Memphis gospel singer reeled off hits: "Hound Dog," "Jailhouse Rock," and "Heartbreak Hotel." At one point Presley recorded fourteen consecutive records selling more than a million copies each. Women found him seductive, although in private he was shy, and his chief loyalty was to his mother. Not even the payola scandals of 1959, in which disc jockeys admitted they had accepted bribes to promote records, retarded the rise of rock. It was already "All Shook Up."

Rock contributed to the generation gap that opened in the 1950s and yawned into a chasm during the late 1960s. Among the contributors to the youth musical rebellion were Chuck Berry, a black man nearing thirty when rock took hold, and Bob Dylan, a white man. Dylan began his career as a folk singer renowned for protest songs such as "Blowin' in the Wind," and "The Times They Are A-Changin'." He progressed from an acoustic to an electric guitar and a rock band. Across the Atlantic, British teenagers embraced rock. Like Presley, the Beatles achieved instant stardom after appearances on American television. A "British Invasion" followed that included the Rolling Stones.

As the antiestablishment counterculture developed, rock flirted with psychedelia, music that stimulated the experience of hallucinogenic drugs. Psychedelia brought in groups like the Doors, whose singer, Jim Morrison, drew from Near Eastern melodies and Brazilian rhythms. Eventually the mainstream turned from battling the counterculture to preempting it. A leading corporation advertised near the end of the decade, "The Revolution is on CBS."

History and Literature after the Guns of World War

Americans, proud of the victory in the world's greatest war, celebrated their heritage in a triumphalist spirit in the first years of the Era of Uncertainty. Magisterial narrative histories attempted to explain the American accomplishments and describe their heroic leaders. One of the first, and best, was

Arthur M. Schlesinger Jr.'s *The Age of Jackson* (1945). In fast-paced prose, the Harvard historian depicted the hero of New Orleans as a representative of American virtues such as adventure, ambition, rebelliousness, and gloves-off politics. In Schlesinger's mind, Jackson resembled a greater hero he was to chronicle, Franklin D. Roosevelt. Richard Hofstadter focused on themes such as interest group competition reflected in political leadership in *The American Political Tradition and the Men Who Made It* (1948). Hofstadter won Pulitzer Prizes for *The Age of Reform* (1956), a provocative look at populism, progressivism, and the New Deal, and for *Anti-Intellectualism in American Life* (1963). Another historian, who wrote chiefly about the South, C. Vann Woodward, a giant in the profession, wrote *Origins of the New South, 1877–1913* (1951) and *The Strange Career of Jim Crow* (1955).

As early as the 1950s, American intellectuals began to doubt whether their society worked as well as had been claimed. William H. Whyte Jr. criticized suburbia and large bureaucracies in *The Organization Man* (1956). C. Wright Mills's *White Collar* (1951) and *The Power Elite* (1956) portrayed the middle class as lacking purpose. In *The Lonely Crowd* (1950), David Riesman questioned whether middle-class Americans were as alienated as Mills believed and if it made sense to belittle the satisfaction many workers derived from rising into white-collar jobs.

Popular books helped energize social movements and inform debate in the Era of Uncertainty. Rachel Carson's *Silent Spring* (1962) drew attention to the pollution of natural resources and helped inspire the environmental movement. Ralph Nader's *Unsafe at Any Speed* (1965) questioned automobile safety and encouraged a consumer revolt. Penetrating analysis complemented the activism of the civil rights movement. Alex Haley assisted Nation of Islam leader Malcolm X in writing *The Autobiography of Malcolm X* (1965). James Baldwin's essays were arguably as influential as his novels; his *Notes of a Native Son* (1955) shared perceptive insights into the black community, its failures, and its relations with white America. Philosophy, considered esoteric by most Americans, soldiered on in academia, as Sidney Hook continued to unravel the implications of John Dewey's pragmatism in *The Quest for Being* (1961).

The most striking literary rebellion occurred among the Beats, who emphasized spontaneity, sexuality, illicit drug use, and spirituality. Allen Ginsberg's poem "Howl" (1956) and Jack Kerouac's novel *On the Road* (1957) invited young people to reject "square" society. Kerouac characterized it as "rows of well-to-do houses with lawns and television sets in each living room with everybody looking at the same thing and thinking the same thing at the same time." Critics countered that although the Beats fled convention, their destination was unclear. "We gotta go and never stop going till we get there," a character said in *On the Road*. When another character asked, "Where we going, man?" the answer was, "I don't know, but we gotta go."

Some authors who came of age after World War II grappled with the meaning of their place in society. Norman Mailer's *The Naked and the Dead* (1948), drawn from his service in the Pacific, and Kurt Vonnegut's *Mother Night* (1962) and *Slaughterhouse-Five* (1969) depicted World War II as a drama of the absurd. In *Catch-22* (1961), Joseph Heller went further, describing army policies as insane. If one were insane, he could be excused from flying missions. Yet if he asked to be excused, that would prove his sanity and he would have to fly them. Of course if he did not ask, he would have to fly them anyway. Another aspect of insanity was the subject of a 1962 classic, Ken Kesey's *One Flew over the Cuckoo's Nest*, which depicted a mental institution where the patients were saner than the doctors and nurses.

James Michener wrote historical novels on a grand scale. His best sellers included *The Bridges of Toko-ri* (1953) and *Hawaii* (1959). Michener's novels were long and intricately descriptive. Sloan Wilson's *The Man in the Gray Flannel Suit* (1955), a story of conformity among white-collar workers, was one of the few popular novels by a new writer to interpret the decade. In the 1960s Gore Vidal produced historical novels such as *Washington, D.C.* (1967) and a story of Hollywood transvestitism, *Myra Breckenridge* (1968). Like Mailer, Vidal became a highly publicized public personality, appearing on television and frequently quoted in newspapers and magazines.

As the center of the American publishing industry, New York remained a mecca for writers and a popular setting for fiction. *New Yorker* magazine nurtured the talents of writers whose short stories delighted in emotional nuance rather than conventional plots. One such writer, J. D. Salinger, reached an enormous audience with *The Catcher in the Rye* (1951), one of the handful of great American novels because it deftly appealed to shared human experiences. The protagonist, young Holden Caulfield, reflects on the hypocrisies and inconsistencies of the adult world and their betrayal of their own ideals. Ralph Ellison's intricately plotted *Invisible Man* (1952) also ranks as one of the great American novels. Like Caulfield, it involves a search for identity, in this case, a black youth coming of age in white America. Again like Caulfield, his journey ends with a mixture of disillusionment and acceptance. The nameless protagonist feels betrayed by white society and also by those who want to overturn that society.

Reflective, philosophical, and quintessentially southern, Walker Percy, in novels such as a *The Moviegoer* (1961) and *The Last Gentleman* (1966), wrote in a the cultural context of his native region. He depicted the South as becoming homogenized and estranged from its own history.

Poetry scattered in many directions after the war and produced no giants of the status of Robert Frost or Carl Sandburg. Social and political alienation were the themes of the Beat poets.

During the 1960s, many writers, such as Bob Dylan, who would probably have been poets in earlier times, turned to songwriting as a more effective way to reach a mass audience, due to the shrinking marketplace for poetry.

On Stage and Canvas

The end of the war ushered in a new generation of playwrights. Of the leaders of the post–World War I era, only Eugene O'Neill still enjoyed a fruitful career, with such psychological masterworks as *The Iceman Cometh* (1946) and *Long Day's Journey into Night* produced in 1956. The first major post–World War II playwrights, Tennessee Williams and Arthur Miller, like O'Neill, probed the unspoken feelings and recriminations of troubled families. Williams's *A Streetcar Named Desire* (1947) and *Cat on a Hot Tin Roof* (1955) visited sweaty southern settings, peopled by colorful characters, seething sexuality. Miller wrote one of the most important American plays, *Death of a Salesman* (1949), which featured an unforgettable character, Willy Loman, a traveling salesman ruined by capitalistic competition and his own ego, "never anything but a hard-working drummer who landed in the ash can like the rest of them!" exclaimed Loman's son, Biff.

The introduction of television and the growing popularity of home entertainment displaced Broadway from the center of culture. However, the theater remained an important training ground for actors, writers, and directors who moved on to Hollywood. Paddy Chayefsky's *Middle of the Night* (1956) was an adaptation of his well-received TV play, *Marty*, a story of lonely hearts who find each other in an insensitive world. *Marty* also became a successful movie. Neil Simon began as a writer for television comedian Jackie Gleason and went on to pen such Broadway comedy hits as *The Odd Couple* (1956), which was adapted into a movie and a popular TV series. Among the most popular and lucrative plays were Broadway musicals such as Frederick Lowe and Alan Jay Lerner's *Brigadoon* (1947), Richard Rodgers and Oscar Hammerstein's *South Pacific* (1949), and Frank Loesser's *Guys and Dolls* (1949). Departing from this upbeat tone, Stephen Sondheim and Leonard Bernstein's *West Side Story* (1958) was a contemporary tragedy about lovers and racial animosity modeled on *Romeo and Juliet*.

The stage took small steps in the direction of racial diversity, especially after the box office success of Lorraine Hansberry's *A Raisin in the Sun* (1959), about a black family whose mother's powerful love held them together against social deprivation. Yet most innovations in theater occurred "Off Broadway," districts in New York where performance spaces were cheaper and financial risks lower and where theater emulated the European avant garde more than Broadway. Off Broadway produced new plays on the cutting edge of culture. One such drama was *Hair* (1968), a musical popular for its then-shocking treatment of drugs, sex, and nudity.

New York also spawned a new movement in visual art, abstract expressionism, in which the object disappeared and only arrangements of color remained. Slinging paint onto canvases on the floor of his studio, Jackson Pollock became the most celebrated figure of abstract expressionism; Robert Rauschenberg assembled "combines" from objects he found on the streets of Manhattan, including mirrors, cardboard, postcards, and broken umbrellas. Rauschenberg's greatest influence was his idea that virtually anything is art if the artist says it is.

The rise of pop art in the 1950s delineated a change in intellectuals' attitude about culture. Modern art had been defined as avant garde, and as highbrow. Its supporters had felt threatened by the rise of popular culture. Pop art resulted from a generation of artists, many of working-class origins, who studied on the G.I. Bill and whose perceptions were shaped by popular culture. The most famous pop artist, Andy Warhol, adopted Rauschenberg's idea that the artist defines art. Beginning his career as a commercial artist, Warhol turned to commercial objects, such as his Campell's Soup can (1966). He and others attracted attention to genres such as rock music and comic strip art. The greatest paradox of pop art is that it never became truly popular; it circulated within a circuit of well-endowed museums, galleries, and private collectors. The irony was symptomatic of the state of visual arts after World War II, as painting and sculptures could no longer compete for attention with television.

Sports: Winning and Losing

During the Era of Uncertainty, no aspect of sports became more politicized than the Olympic Games. The Cold War competition between nations virtually dwarfed the competition among athletes. The United States and the Soviet Union each strived to win the most medals to prove the superiority of their system. The United States usually finished first or second to the Soviets in medal count. Individuals also tried to make political statements. In the 1968 Summer Games American sprinters Tommie Smith and John Carlos raised their arms in a clenched fist Black Power salute and were stripped of their medals for their protest. Still, Americans took pride in outstanding performances. Bob Matthias became the youngest decathlon winner in 1948. Wilma Rudolph, once disabled, won three gold medals in track in 1960; and Bob Hayes tied the world record in the 100-meter dash in 1964. America fielded strong teams in swimming, track and field, and basketball.

Football replaced baseball as America's favorite spectator sport. College football, broadcast on television, became a major spectacle. Universities with the best teams became better known than elite academic universities. Every year, colleges pursued the national championship and players competed for the Heisman Trophy, given to the best player. Among professionals, the National Football League expanded to the South and West. Its stars included quarterback Johnny Unitas of the Baltimore Colts and Cleveland Browns fullback Jim Brown. Yet the real star of the Era of Uncertainty was not a player but a coach, Vince Lombardi of the Green Bay Packers. When Lombardi took over the floundering Packers had great players who were playing out of position or sitting on the bench. Lombardi excelled as a strategist, a disciplinarian, and a motivator. The Packers, running a simple, bone-crushing offense and fielding an unyielding defense, developed a mystique, playing in the league's smallest town. Lombardi, emphasizing the team concept, coached the Packers to five world championships in nine years. Salaries soared after Alabama quarterback Joe Namath signed with the New York Jets of the upstart American Football League for $427,000 in 1965. Desperate to end the salary wars that ensued, the NFL and the AFL merged in 1970. After Namath predicted that his underdog Jets would defeat Unitas's Colts in the 1969 Superbowl, he helped fulfill the prophecy.

Baseball gave sports some of its most memorable moments. Don Larsen of the New York Yankees pitched a perfect game in the 1956 World Series. Yankees outfielder Roger Maris hit a record sixty-one home runs in 1961. A plethora of hard-hitting outfielders, including Ted Williams, Joe DiMaggio, Stan Musial, Willie Mays, Hank Aaron, and Mickey Mantle, thrilled spectators. The Yankees garnered a collection of championships that nearly equaled their dynasty of the 1920s. After Jackie Robinson broke the color barrier in 1947, teams rushed to recruit African American players. Baseball, more than football, planted teams in the West and the South, aided by jet travel. Curt Flood sued to invalidate the contract clause binding players to teams. He lost, but took a step toward free agency.

Basketball flourished. The Minneapolis Lakers, with the first great big man, George Mikan, dominated the late 1940s and early 1950s. The greatest dynasty of the Era of Uncertainty, perhaps in any sport, was the Boston Celtics, coached by Arnold "Red" Auerbach and featuring center Bill

Russell and guard Bob Cousy. Russell's chief competitor at center was the seven-foot Wilt Chamberlain, who scored a record one hundred points in one game while averaging over fifty points per game in a season. In college basketball, dynasties shined at the University of Kentucky in the late 1940s and 1950s and the University of California–Los Angeles in the 1960s. College basketball suffered point-shaving scandals in 1951 and 1961. Players on top teams accepted bribes to lose games or shave points to ensure gamblers won by the point spread.

Boxing existed in the shadows of brutality, organized crime, and fixed fights. Out of the shadows emerged Cassius Clay, an Olympic gold medal winner. He restored luster to boxing by defeating Sonny Liston for the world heavyweight championship in 1964. Clay converted to Islam, changed his name to Muhammad Ali, and denounced racism and the Vietnam War. Ali refused induction to the army in 1967, claiming he, and all Muslims, were ministers. Stripped of his title and imprisoned, he was later released and regained his title in 1971. At one point in time, Ali had the highest name recognition of any American in the world.

The Rise of the Counterculture

Asked to define the counterculture, one student in the 1960s, responded: "Look at what the mainstream culture is not. That's us." In clothing, music, lifestyle, and sexual standards, the counterculture was the counterpoint of their parents' culture. Like many cultural rebels against the mainstream, the students of the 1960s ultimately merged with it. Their fashions, philosophies, and practices, such as free love, likewise influenced the "straight" culture. The counterculture was about style, not politics. Its counterpart on the left, the New Left, was about politics.

The fashions included miniskirts for women and wide-lapeled coats and broad ties for men. Men sprouted beards, mustaches, and sideburns as well as long locks. Women often wore their hair straight. Both sexes went barefoot or wore sandals. Recreational drugs and profanity were part of the lifestyle. Hippies accused mainstream Americans of racism and narrow-mindedness, yet there were few black hippies and little tolerance of conventional lifestyles. Violence, and rough sports were scorned. There was tolerance for gays and lesbians. Having a variety of sexual partners was not considered disloyal, and partners frequently lived together before marriage. Love and peace were praised, but materialism and hard work were rejected. Like other protesters against capitalism, war, and poverty in the Era of Uncertainty, most hippies were not poor, or were poor by choice. They contributed an element of freedom and free thinking diversity to America, yet discouraged respect for standards.

A smaller number of students, constituting the New Left, were political activists, critical of the Right, the Center, and the Old Left. The best known organization was the Students for a Democratic Society (SDS), which was heavily influenced by anarchism and Marxism. SDS was critical of American democracy, capitalism, religion, technology, and bureaucracy. "We would replace power rooted in possession, privilege or circumstances, with power in love, reflectiveness, reason and creativity," SDS announced in its 1962 manifesto, the Port Huron Statement. The students found the large university bureaucracy repulsive. Mario Savio, a leader of the Free Speech movement at the University of California, Berkeley in 1964–1965, in a metaphor incorporating the students' ambivalence toward technology, told his followers: "You've got to put your bodies upon the gears, and upon the wheels, upon the apparatus, and you've got to make it stop."

The majority of students who demonstrated against the Vietnam War, for free speech, and for more individualized treatment by administrators were members of neither SDS nor the counterculture but a cross-section of the college community, vocal, though never a majority.

The lack of direction of the New Left—its indecisive, divided leadership and its vague goals—undermined its role in practical political change, though it contributed an element of idealism and self-sacrifice. However, its activities too often degenerated into senseless violence, attempts to provoke police, and rowdy demonstrations, sometimes directed at the wrong people. Perhaps its worst strategic mistake was the violent demonstration at the Democratic National Convention in Chicago in 1968, which helped defeat Democratic nominee Hubert Humphrey, generate a conservative backlash, and elect Republican Richard Nixon. Whatever the bravery and idealism of the New Left, what was most sadly lacking was good judgment and the temptation to demonize even potential allies, such as Humphrey.

Some of the New Left's criticism of materialism, militarism, hypocrisy, and the excessive influence of big business were justified. Yet the students' violent rhetoric and sometimes violent behavior belied their language of love, and their dogmatism was no more flexible than that of their adversaries. Communism and anarchism were no solutions to the shortcomings off capitalism and democracy. For most people, expressions of love were more appropriately expressed to other people or to deities than to ideologies or doctrines. On all sides as well, hate parading as love is the ultimate hypocrisy; it is the stuff of tyrants.

The Rainbow of Power

The Black Power movement inspired demands for power among groups such as Indians and Chicanos. In the mid- to late 1960s the civil rights movement shifted from the moderate desegregation objectives of Martin Luther King Jr. to the aggressive tactics and economic, cultural, and esteem issues promulgated by "Black Power." Malcolm X, an opponent of integration and nonviolence and an advocate of black pride and self-sufficiency, laid the groundwork for the doctrine. He was assassinated by rival Black Muslims in early 1965. Stokely Carmichael used the term "Black Power" at a march of the Student Nonviolent Coordinating Committee" (SNCC) in Mississippi and it caught on. H. "Rap" Brown, who succeeded Carmichael as SNCC head, translated "Black Power" into more threatening terms. Brown insisted that instead of trying to "love that honky [white man] to death," African Americans should shoot "shoot him to death." The Black Panthers, established in 1966, armed its members to guard black neighborhoods and clashed violently with police. The Panthers embraced black pride, wearing traditional African hairstyles and clothing and demanding black studies programs. They also sponsored community centers and school breakfast programs. Yet the "Black Power" slogan was incendiary. Few politicians asked openly, yet they knew that middle-class whites wondered how black people would feel if white people marched through their neighbors with upraised clenched fists chanting "White Power." Worse, the slogan was divisive among blacks and whites alike. It marked a turning away from integration just as it was making progress, and a return to a philosophy similar to the doctrine of white supremacy.

Young Hispanics challenged the social and economic status quo, led by Cesar Chavez of the United Farm Workers. Chavez struggled to obtain union recognition and better working conditions for migrant farm workers. Like Martin Luther King Jr., a believer in nonviolence, he organized a grape picker strike in 1965 and grape consumer boycott in 1968. In addition, the young, militant Hispanic activists who swelled the "Brown Power" movement sought bilingual education and Hispanic studies programs in schools and Hispanic-only organizations.

For Native Americans, who suffered acutely from poverty and substandard education and housing, there was "Red Power." They worked to get Indian studies in classrooms and secured more federal assistance from Lyndon Johnson's administration. Yet they remained at odds with the federal government over old treaties that ensured them rights to land that whites had taken.

The American Indian Movement (AIM) imitated the Black Panthers in starting armed patrols to protect Indians; it sometimes employed violent tactics.

Black, brown, or red, the militant power groups diminished after the 1960s. The Black Power idea did not die, yet won few new converts because most African Americans were integrationists. Certainly the issue of racial and youth groups contesting for power, battling at the end to near exhaustion, and ending with a resurrection of conservativism, added turmoil, tension, and uncertainty to the times. A few capitalized on ideas whose time had come. Others grew disillusioned supporting causes that could not prevail. There were partial victories and scapegoating. But most important in the long term were the dreams of the young, which is their prerogative.

CHAPTER FIVE

New Frontiers, New Anxieties at Home, 1961–1968

DURING THE Era of Uncertainty, no decade was more uncertain than the 1960s. At home, it was a turbulent time of social experimentation and youthful rebellion, led by two presidents who were mirror images: John Kennedy, an idea man whose strong suit was inspiration, and his action-oriented successor, Lyndon Johnson. Following a decade of relative stability under Dwight D. Eisenhower, the hallmark of the 1960s was change. Americans, unusually optimistic under the youngest elected president, mourned when he died. When the decade ended they were a different people—spent, confused, and disappointed. Their initial optimism had sown discord, their expectations, accomplishments, and disappointments a potpourri of paradox.

The Frontier of the 1960s

John F. Kennedy thrived on inspiring rhetoric. His inaugural address on January 21, 1961, evinced a sense of history and a call to sacrifice: "Let the word go forth from this time and place, to friend and foe alike, that the torch has been passed to a new generation of Americans—born in this century, tempered by war, disciplined by a hard and bitter peace, proud of our ancient heritage." Kennedy summoned Americans to a crusade to bring justice to the nation and the world: "And so, my fellow Americans: ask not what your country can do for you—ask what you can do for your country. . . ."

John Fitzgerald Kennedy was born to a large Boston-area Irish Catholic family whose wealth, privilege, and political influence resembled American royalty. Patriarch Joseph Kennedy, a millionaire from investments in shipping, liquor, and real estate, had been a New Deal official. His isolationism before World War II and his ethnic and religious background denied him his political and social aspirations. Thus he drove his sons to achieve, hoping one would become the first Irish Catholic president. He laid the groundwork for John's career by using his influence to generate favorable publicity and by engineering the publication of John's senior thesis at Harvard as *Why England Slept (1940)*, a book about why Britain was unprepared for World War II. In 1946, young Kennedy was elected to the House of Representatives from Massachusetts. Taking his legislative responsibilities lightly, he nonetheless kept winning reelection and, in 1952, upset Republican incumbent Henry Cabot Lodge in a Senate race. While serving in the upper chamber, he published a Pulitzer Prize–winning collective biography, *Profiles in Courage* (1956), researched mostly by his staff and ghostwritten by his speechwriter, Theodore Sorensen. He unsuccessfully sought the 1956 Democratic nomination for vice president. Kennedy's 1958 Senate reelection made him the front-runner for the top spot on the ticket two years later, however.

Promoted as a vigorous chief executive who sailed, swam, golfed, and played touch football, the fit and manly image was at odds with the truth. Kennedy, known as JFK, was in pain virtually every day. On four occasions, he received the last rites of his church. JFK suffered from a degenerative back problem that required a cloth brace, hot baths, and four operations—one almost killed him in 1954. Sometimes he used crutches to get around the White House, although never in public. JFK also suffered from Addison's disease, a once-fatal withering of the adrenal glands treatable by cortisone, injected or in the form of pills. Nor was he as energetic as he liked to pretend. To fight fatigue and depression, he and his wife, Jacqueline, took injections of amphetamines, now known as illegal "speed," from Max Jacobson, known as "Dr. Feel Good."

Jacqueline Kennedy was a political asset. Beautiful, sophisticated, and glamorous, she proved a popular first lady. An elitist who found politics boring, she preferred the company of artists and intellectuals to that of officeholders. Americans were proud of her fluency in foreign languages, her social grace, and her jet-set fashions. Again, though, reality belied the Kennedys' public image. Although an attractive couple with charming children, both were remote, private, and introverted, partners in a union of convenience with little love. Kennedy was too competitive for the first lady's tastes and did not regard women with the seriousness he reserved for men. JFK was emotionally blocked, which kept him from bonding, and was manipulative.

Of the dark halves of these paradoxes, the public knew nothing. Americans read, heard, and saw only that Kennedy and his men proposed

THE PHOTOGENIC PRESIDENCY
John F. Kennedy stands in his car waving to a crowd at the
conclusion of a speech in downtown Detroit in October 1962.
(AP/Wide World Photos)

to lead the United States to a "New Frontier." Highly educated advisers
displaying an unusually assertive esprit de corps were summoned to
Washington. Robert Francis Kennedy, known as RFK, a younger brother
of the president, became attorney general and a key confidant. Robert
McNamara, a Republican and efficiency expert, was recruited from the
presidency of General Motors to serve as defense secretary. Historian
Arthur M. Schlesinger Jr. was named a special assistant and became one of
the chroniclers of the administration, writing the best-selling *A Thousand
Days: John F. Kennedy in the White House* (1965), a Pulitzer Prize winner.
Sorensen, who wrote for Kennedy the memorable speeches of cadenced
rhythms and balanced phrases, was chief counsel with responsibilities for
domestic policy.

The New Frontier celebrated power, toughness, and decisiveness. John
Kennedy, whom many intellectuals regarded as one of them, did not enjoy
serious culture, but he was probably the best-read president since Woodrow

Wilson, articulate, witty, respectful of artistic accomplishment, and eager to honor poets and philosophers. JFK appreciated the subtle ironies of life, including the fear of dying young, and believed that he had to live in a hurry. He enjoyed *Camelot*, a Broadway musical, and his friends referred to the New Frontier as the second incarnation of Camelot, the legendary kingdom of Arthur. Young Americans, energized by the glamour of the administration, rallied around their Arthur, a thought that was heartening, if not nearly enough to convince a self-described "idealist without illusions" that his quest would be easy in the Era of Uncertainty.

The Economic Frontier

In his relations with Congress, Kennedy faced obstacles. One was his lack-luster legislative skills. Despite fourteen years in Washington, he had few friends in Congress and lacked patience with the legislative process. Kennedy made little use of Johnson's legislative wizardry. The most critical hurdle, though, was that the president, elected by a razor-thin margin, lacked votes sufficient to overcome the conservative bloc of southern Democrats and Republicans. JFK was largely frustrated, getting just about one-third of his legislative proposals through Congress. The legislators defeated or deferred his bills to combat poverty, provide health insurance for the aged, and furnish federal aid for education.

There were some notable accomplishments. The 1962 Drug Industry Act tightened restrictions on the manufacture and sale of drugs after the births of deformed babies whose mothers had taken thalidomide, a sleeping aid. The 1963 Clean Air Act was a step to control pollution, a sign of an ecological awakening. Kennedy, who had a mentally ill sister, did more for mental patients than any previous president, and Congress appropriated $500 million to aid them. Turning from compassion to confrontation, the administration waged war on organized crime, led by RFK, whose pursuit of Teamsters Union boss James R. Hoffa led to Hoffa's conviction for jury tampering and pension fund fraud in August 1964.

Kennedy was successful in promoting economic growth. His first priority was to deal with a recession, and the administration secured adjustments. A small increase in the minimum wage was passed; the Area Redevelopment Act made grants and loans to communities and regions with persistent hardship; and $4.9 million was appropriated for housing. The economy rebounded in the spring of 1961, largely on its own.

The next year proved eventful. Kennedy gratified and angered big business. He achieved the former with a law that reduced business taxes by accelerating depreciation allowances and granting tax breaks for investment in new equipment. The latter was a product of Kennedy's showdown with United States Steel. Fearing inflation might blunt economic growth, he resorted to jawboning or implied threats to industry and labor to hold down wages and prices. Labor Secretary Arthur Goldberg persuaded the steel unions to accept a modest, noninflationary 2.5 percent wage increase, and because the steel industry had thus benefited from the federal intercession, it was expected to avoid an inflationary price rise. Yet on April 10, 1962, United States Steel President Roger Blough announced an increase of $6 per ton, or 3.5 percent. Kennedy felt betrayed and dismissed Blough's arguments, which had some validity, that profits were at a record low and that there had been no price raises since 1958. In a contest of wills the press likened to Theodore Roosevelt's dispute with J. P. Morgan, JFK criticized United States Steel and threatened it with antitrust lawsuits, the withdrawal of government contracts, and federal price-fixing investigations. Within seventy-two hours, the steel giant backed down, chastened because of meager demand for steel and Kennedy's actions. The press heralded Kennedy as a Robin Hood, but the affair shook business confidence, and the stock market plunged.

Reversing course after the stock slide, Kennedy spent the remainder of his administration attempting to reassure the business community, registering no complaints about two steel price increases in a year and making a tax cut the centerpiece of his program for 1963. His decision to seek reductions in personal and corporate taxes and to keep federal spending constant, while the government was running a deficit, a tool for stimulating growth, was paradoxical, for the recession had ended. Designed to promote long-term economic growth, the tax cut was languishing in Congress at Kennedy's death in November 1963. Still, the economy performed well on his watch. JFK's record on the agricultural economy was not as successful, as most farmers rejected mandatory acreage controls. The administration attacked the problems of overproduction and low farm income to limited effect, not surprising when one appreciates that Kennedy lacked empathy for rural America.

In the biggest New Frontier of all, space, a Soviet cosmonaut, Yuri Gagarin, was the first human to orbit the earth on April 12, 1961. Other Soviets followed. Almost a month and a half after Gagarin's feat, Kennedy said the United States should commit itself to landing the first man on the Moon and returning him safely to Earth during the 1960s. Over protests that these goals were too expensive or technologically impossible, scientists from the National Aeronautics and Space Administration (NASA) planned such a mission in the Apollo program. Meanwhile, the American manned space program, Project Mercury, began with Alan Shepard's suborbital flight in May 1961. A fellow astronaut, John Glenn, became the first American to circle the globe in 1962.

Civil Rights: Progress and Unmet Expectations

The frontier of human understanding on Earth might have seemed more distant than the frontier of the Moon. Kennedy's ascent to the White House held out hope to African Americans, but for much of his presidency, he took tiny, cautious steps. The chief executive feared large strides would alienate southern Democrats whose support he needed for legislation. His campaign promise to outlaw discrimination in federally funded housing by executive order went unredeemed for two years, until he issued a weak order that made barely a dent in segregation. Kennedy appointed a record number of African Americans to government posts, yet also picked white segregationists as federal judges.

The wave of agitation for civil rights in the South forced Kennedy's hand. Setting the stage, the Supreme Court in 1960 banned segregation in bus and train stations used for interstate travel, an edict that was ignored in the South. To expose this flouting of the law, the Congress of Racial Equality (CORE) sent "freedom riders" into the region, where violence awaited, in the spring of 1961. White mobs and Ku Klux Klansmen in Alabama assaulted the freedom riders in Anniston, Birmingham, and Montgomery before Kennedy deployed federal marshals to restore peace. Additional freedom rides and arrests of the riders led him to prod the Interstate Commerce Commission to enforce the law. JFK acted again in 1962. A federal court directed the University of Mississippi to enroll an African American student, James Meredith. Federal marshals escorted Meredith to the university, only to come under attack from mobs. Two were killed and scores were hurt before thousands of federal soldiers quelled the violence.

In 1963, Birmingham again became a focal point for civil rights. Rev. Martin Luther King Jr. launched nonviolent marches, sit-ins, and prayer demonstrations on Good Friday, April 12. Police Commissioner Eugene "Bull" Connor unleashed dogs, officers using electric cattle prods, and high-pressure fire hoses against the demonstrators. Some responded with stones and firebombs. King, jailed for instigating the march, penned the "Letter from Birmingham Jail," justifying civil disobedience to protest segregation. A federal Justice Department official helped negotiate an agreement whereby major city department stores agreed to desegregate and hire African Americans, and black leaders agreed to halt the demonstrations and cease boycotting of segregated businesses. On May 11, though, bombs exploded at King's brother's home and a motel that African American leaders used, triggering more rioting and violence in the Birmingham ghetto.

Newspaper and television scenes of the police brutality outraged Americans. Now Kennedy was convinced the government had to direct the pace of civil rights to improve the image of the United States abroad. Alabama Governor George Wallace, pledging "Segregation now! Segregation tomorrow! Segregation forever!" tried to keep two black students out of the University of Alabama in June 1963. Kennedy federalized the state National Guard to enforce a court desegregation order and forced Wallace to back down. Kennedy also delivered a televised speech, prodding the enactment of civil rights. Days later he introduced a civil rights bill that bogged down in Congress.

The movement responded with a March on Washington on August 28, attracting about 250,000 people, black and white, to the Lincoln Memorial.

MARCHING ON WASHINGTON Martin Luther King Jr. and supporters, 1963. (National Archives)

Kennedy opposed plans for the gathering, meant to show support for his bill, until he was assured the march would be peaceful. In fact, the event marked the apogee of the nonviolent, racially mixed phase of the crusade. The crowd heard speeches that King capped with a rousing address describing his vision of a just society. Promising that he and his allies would not rest until African Americans were free of discrimination, King said, "I have a dream" that the descendants of slaves and of slaveholders could unite in brotherhood. He envisioned his children judged "not on the color of their skin, but on the content of their character." Finally, he foresaw "that all of God's children, black men and white men, Jews and Gentiles, Protestants and Catholics, will be able to join hands and sing in the words of that old Negro spiritual: 'Free at last! Free at last! Thank God almighty we are free at last!'" The crowd, too, sang of freedom, including the hymn that became the anthem of the civil rights movement, "We Shall Overcome."

There was, regrettably, much to overcome. On the night of Kennedy's televised speech in June, a sniper killed NAACP field secretary Medgar Evers just outside his home in Jackson, Mississippi. The civil rights bill remained bottled up on Capitol Hill, notwithstanding the resolve of King and his marchers. And in September 1963, a bomb took the lives of four black girls in a Birmingham church. Murder took three civil rights workers in 1964 and six in 1965—four of them white—in the South, compounding the outrage. Blacks took notice of the promise of progress under Kennedy—and of the gap between promise and progress.

The Assassination of JFK

Even after Kennedy's early missteps, his star never shined as brightly as it did in the fall of 1963. Recent triumphs with the economy and diplomacy and signals of more victories helped give him high approval ratings. He was looking forward to reelection in 1964 over the likely Republican presidential nominee, Arizona Senator Barry Goldwater. But there was a feud between the liberal and conservative factions of the Texas Democratic Party. On November 22, Kennedy was in Dallas to close that breach and to make speeches.

Large, friendly crowds, bright skies and warm temperatures welcomed Kennedy's motorcade. Because the weather was pleasant, the president ordered the Secret Service to remove the bulletproof bubble top from his limousine. Shattering the scene, shots rang out, two of them striking the president in his neck and head. Jackie Kennedy, her pink suit splattered by her husband's blood and brain, climbed on the back of the car, only to be pushed back by bodyguards. The car pulled from the motorcade and sped to Parkland Memorial Hospital, where Kennedy was pronounced dead. Vice President Johnson was sworn in as chief executive aboard the presidential plane hours later at the Dallas airport.

Lee Harvey Oswald, twenty-four, an unstable former Marine and a communist sympathizer, probably fired the lethal shots from the Texas School Book Depository. His motives remain lost to history, for a few days later, nightclub owner Jack Ruby shot and killed Oswald, saying he wanted to punish the president's assassin. Johnson appointed a panel under Chief Justice Earl Warren to investigate the assassination, and in 1964 the Warren Commission concluded that Oswald, acting alone, killed Kennedy. Many of the commission's methods were flawed, making millions doubt the panel's conclusions and generating a minor industry of attempts to ferret out conspiracies behind the assassination. One theory had Cuba seeking vengeance on Kennedy for CIA attempts to kill Fidel Castro. Another said the underworld was retaliating for RFK's crusade against organized crime. Yet another implicated white southerners who considered JFK a threat to the racial status quo. No one, however, has convincingly refuted the commission's basic findings. A House committee later investigated the case and, in 1978, essentially agreed with the commission, but noted that acoustic evidence and witness testimony indicated the possibility of a second gunman on a grassy knoll ahead of the motorcade.

In the twenty-first century, many Americans could remember what they had been doing when they learned of Kennedy's assassination, just as many people could remember everything about the day Pearl Harbor was bombed. Millions watched television for the next three days, as all three networks halted programming to cover the funeral. The nation seemed to shift—instantaneously—from the sunshine of optimism to the darkness of despair. By the end of the decade uncertainty was ingrained as Americans had come to expect shock and trauma, despite notable domestic accomplishments by Kennedy's successor, including racial progress and an economy hitched to a locomotive. Still, the purpose and vision JFK had provided the nation vaporized, leaving the nation empty inside, like a flat balloon.

The Kennedy brothers often said that life is unfair, a notion that JFK's (and, later, RFK's) life made poignant. John Kennedy was the beneficiary of unearned wealth, was elected to the most powerful office in the world while young, was elevated to heroic status—and was borne to his grave at age forty-six. His slaying touched off a wave of adulation, myth-making, and nostalgia. The Treasury soon began minting 50 million Kennedy half-dollars and could not keep them in circulation because they were hoarded as souvenirs.

As for the verdict of history, it is mixed. Kennedy was regarded highly for his charisma, his power to inspire, his ability to master ideas and words, and his articulation of goals, but his administration was not effective at translating its ideals into deeds. JFK's intellect was not as great as his vice president's; his rugged, macho persona concealed physical weakness; his charm belied a calculating, ruthless mind and—for all his calls for sacrifice—a streak of selfishness. Kennedy made the early 1960s seem simple and heroic, an extension of the stable 1950s with the excitement of Camelot, even though his White House was no Camelot. His reign merely represented the calm before the storm.

Lyndon Baines Johnson

Lyndon Baines Johnson (LBJ) ranks as one of the most important political figures in American history, and as one of the most paradoxical. LBJ was intelligent but not book-smart, crude but crafty, serious but a teller of tall tales, naive but a wheeler-dealer supreme, idealistic but cruel—a man waging a battle to the death against himself. He spent most of his life running scared, superhuman energy yielding occasionally to crushing depression and self-doubt. Extremely ingratiating, Johnson insisted on being the center of attention, a quality that left him greatly loved and greatly hated.

Born in the Texas hill country, raised on a ranch and in small towns, Johnson loved his home yet felt a sense of inferiority because of it. He learned politics from his father, Sam, a tough, folksy man and state lawmaker, and identified with his mother's cultural pretensions. Trying to earn the love of two very different parents made Johnson insecure, taught him that compromise was a means to political achievements, and helped him treat politics as a means to earn love. His Disciples of Christ religion and his year of teaching poor Mexican American schoolchildren reinforced LBJ's desire to do good, compassion that clashed with the Texan's callous treatment of his wife Claudia, known as "Lady Bird." She laid the foundation of the Johnson fortune, owning radio and television stations, and stayed with her husband despite his temper and insistence on total domination.

Entering politics as a congressional aide, Johnson excelled and was ambitious. He became Texas director of the National Youth Administration (NYA), a New Deal post that led to his adoption of FDR as a political role model. He won election to the U.S. House of Representatives in 1937 and was narrowly elected to the Senate in 1948, on his second try. The

TAKING THE OATH OF OFFICE
Lyndon B. Johnson being sworn in as president aboard
Air Force One after Kennedy's assassination, November 22, 1963.
(Lyndon B. Johnson Presidential Library)

Senate was his habitat, in which he rocketed to power as Democratic whip in 1951, minority leader in 1953, and majority leader in 1955. A master legislator, persuasive in personal encounters, Johnson cooperated with the Eisenhower administration to pass the 1957 Civil Rights Act, and sponsored the 1958 measure that created NASA.

Unhappy as vice president, Johnson thought that Kennedy was overrated, more style than substance. LBJ knew he was better prepared for the Oval Office than Kennedy, who respected Johnson; but JFK's subordinates disdained LBJ as a crude deal-maker and gave him almost no role in shaping policy. There was talk of replacing Johnson on the 1964 Democratic ticket. When Kennedy's assassination tested LBJ's ability to soothe in a moment of national anguish, he was superb, sensitive, and poised. Five days after Kennedy died, Johnson addressed a joint session of Congress, reminding his audience that in JFK's inaugural speech, Kennedy proclaimed, "Let us begin." Now, Johnson said, "Let us continue." Actually, LBJ wished not only to continue Kennedy's priorities but to expand them. Johnson wanted to exploit his predecessor's martyrdom and employ his own persuasive talents to enact a far-reaching program of civil rights and antipoverty measures that would mark him as a great and beloved president like FDR. Securing passage of Kennedy's civil rights and economic measures, especially the tax cut and the antipoverty legislation, Johnson reasoned, would give him a solid record on which to run in 1964. Thus he demanded that Congress pass them quickly, and lawmakers did, in 1964.

The tax cut ushered in the most prosperous period of the postwar era to that time. The gross national product increased 7, 8, and 9 percent in 1964, 1965, and 1966, respectively. Unemployment fell below 5 percent, amounting to "full employment," according to economists. By 1968, average family income would be twice that of ten years earlier. The 1964 Economic Opportunity Act, the most far-reaching federal effort to help the poor, followed his declaration of an "unconditional" War on Poverty and his vow to eliminate poverty in a decade. The law created the Office of Economic Opportunity, with a budget of $800 million, to oversee Project Head Start, which offered education for preschoolers from poor families; a Job Corps to train the young in employment skills; and the Volunteers in Service to America (VISTA) program that put youths to work in poor areas, a domestic version of the Peace Corps. Most daring was the Community Action Program, including local job training, legal aid, community health, welfare reform, and educational measures. The poor were to have the "maximum feasible participation" in deciding how local antipoverty funds were administered.

Another 1964 law, the Civil Rights Act, stands as one of the two greatest achievements of the liberal decade, the other being the Voting Rights Act of 1965. If Kennedy fired the hearts of African Americans, Johnson went further, cementing their claims to a stake in American life by pushing the two bills through Congress. He acted because of his political aspirations, because his passion for civil rights had grown during his vice presidency, and because of his need to feel loved. To pass the 1964 law, LBJ pried the stalled JFK bill from a House committee and, with the aid of Republicans, broke a fifty-seven-day Senate filibuster. The measure banned racial discrimination in public accommodations, prohibited discrimination on the basis of race, national origin, religion, and sex in employment, and denied federal funds to programs and institutions that practiced discrimination. "We can understand without rancor or hatred how this all happened," Johnson said. "But it cannot continue. Our Constitution, the foundation of our republic, forbids it. The principles of our freedom forbid it. Morality forbids it."

Then Johnson set out to personalize his program, which he called the "Great Society." There must be "an order of plenty for all our people" and "an end to poverty and racial injustice," he said. Nor was that all: LBJ's quest was "to advance the quality of our American civilization," to "create a place where the city of man serves not only the needs of the body and the demands of commerce but the desire for beauty and the hunger for community." First, however, he had to be president in his own right.

1964: Lyndon's Landslide

Within the Democratic Party, Johnson's chief challenger was George Wallace, who advocated small government, law and order, and segregation. Entering some 1964 presidential primaries without much money or organization, he stunned liberals by winning 34 percent of the vote in Wisconsin, 30 percent in Indiana, and 43 percent in Maryland. In June, Wallace announced that he would run for president on a third-party ticket, but withdrew before the November election, fearing that his candidacy would divide conservatives. Johnson also faced trouble from blacks at the Democratic convention in August in Atlantic City, New Jersey, where the Mississippi Freedom Democratic Party (MFDP) challenged the all-white delegation from the state and demanded to be seated. LBJ sympathized yet worried that southern whites would bolt the convention if the MFDP demands were met. With his backing, the convention seated the regulars and disappointed the African Americans by giving them only two at-large seats and a pledge to ban future discrimination by state delegations. The other significant development at the convention was Johnson's selection of Minnesota Senator Hubert Humphrey as his running mate. (Johnson initially served as president without a vice president. The Twenty-Fifth Amendment, which Congress passed and the states ratified in 1967, closed a gap in law by assuring continuity in the executive branch. It provided that the vice president could become acting president if the chief executive were incapacitated but not dead. Also, it provided for the appointment of a vice president upon the president's death, so the office would not have to remain vacant.)

After Wallace's withdrawal, right-leaning voters united behind the Republican nominee, Barry Goldwater, who distanced himself from moderates, announcing at the GOP convention in San Francisco that "extremism in the defense of liberty is no vice. . . moderation in the pursuit of justice is no virtue." His campaign slogan was "In your heart, you know

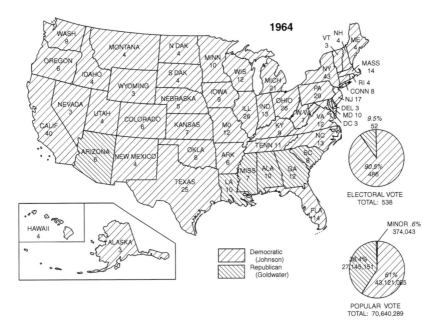

Election of 1964

he's right," and he vowed to offer "a choice, not an echo." Goldwater preached a sermon of personal responsibility, a stronger national defense, and limited government that would cease meddling in civil rights and social problems. Democrats exploited fears that he would eviscerate Social Security by making it voluntary and depicted him as a warmonger.

Johnson craved for a vote that would eclipse even FDR's margins. LBJ did not accept Goldwater's desire for a real debate on the issues or address directly the senator's attacks on his administration. He did not have to worry, as any Republican would have been unlikely to overcome the martyrdom of Kennedy and Johnson's legislative feats. LBJ won more than 43 million popular votes, 61 percent of the total—the greatest percentage that a presidential candidate ever received—and 486 electoral votes. Goldwater won 27 million popular votes and 52 electoral votes, carrying only his home state and five Deep South states. Democrats gained big majorities in Congress, giving liberals the margins they needed to pass Johnson's program.

In less than a year, Johnson seemed to have forged a magnificent coalition. Yet many people voted for him out of reverence for JFK and fear of Goldwater's ideas and personality rather than support for the incumbent. Johnson's base was broad but shallow, leaving him vulnerable to the backlash against liberalism in 1968 that helped drive him from the White House. Goldwater's candidacy was not the last gasp of an exhausted conservatism; it was the herald of a grassroots revival that would enable conservatives, mainly from the South and the West, to wrest control of the GOP from eastern moderates and realize future presidential triumphs. Goldwater was the ideological John the Baptist who presaged the coming of Ronald Reagan sixteen years later.

The Great Society

Moving swiftly to capitalize upon his election, Johnson directed a legislative assault for the Great Society, marching more than two hundred bills through Congress in 1964 and 1965, the pace rivaling that of 1933. His rhetoric gave an urgency to his commitments and raised hopes, contributing to one of the paradoxes of the postwar United States: no matter how great the nation's successes, expectations ran higher. Poverty was no worse than it had been earlier. Yet LBJ envisioned a government that could be kind and competent. Never seeking a major redistribution of income, he wanted a harmonious society that met the needs of all classes. To avoid conflict and decisions that defined winners and losers, Johnson, unlike FDR, refused to wage class war. By targeting specific groups for help, the Great Society made them conscious of their identities.

Congress built on the 1964 Great Society programs by approving a variety of measures. The Elementary and Secondary Education Act made more than $1 billion available for school textbooks, library materials, and special education programs; the Higher Education Act earmarked $650 million for scholarships and loans to college students and funds for libraries and research facilities. The Medical Care Act created Medicare, a federally financed program of health insurance for older Americans, and the Medicaid program provided money for states to give free health care to the poor. Other laws funded research on heart disease, cancer, and strokes and required cigarette packages to carry warnings that smoking is hazardous to health. The Omnibus Housing Act set aside $8 billion for housing for low- and middle-income families and rent aid for qualifying families. The Model Cities Act, the centerpiece of the new Department of Housing and Urban Development under Robert Weaver, the first black cabinet secretary, provided grants for redevelopment in slums. Environmental protection was the object of laws setting standards for auto emissions and air and water quality. Consumer safety motivated standards for cars and stricter rules for the labeling and packaging of food, drugs, and cosmetics. Cultural improvements included aid to museums, establishment of the Public Broadcasting System, and creation of

National Endowment for the Arts and Humanities. Other laws furnished $1 billion for development of depressed regions of Appalachia; and funds to enable cities to improve mass transportation, build sewers, and train police. Johnson's sweeping reforms created the Transportation Department; ended the national origins quota system for immigration; and promoted highway beautification, a project of the first lady's.

An Activist Supreme Court

Augmenting the liberal program, the Supreme Court under Earl Warren continued its activist agenda. Bolstered by two appointments each from Kennedy and Johnson—among them Solicitor General Thurgood Marshall, the first African American on the Court—the justices handed down major constitutional rulings. They ordered states to apportion legislatures on the principle of "one man, one vote," increasing the representation of urban minorities. They held that poor defendants in felony cases had a right to publicly financed legal counsel and struck down prayers and Bible readings in public schools. Melding the sexual revolution and technology, the court invalidated a law banning the sale of contraceptives. It also rejected prohibitions on interracial marriage and limited the impact of antipornography laws. Highly important, *Miranda v. Arizona* (1966) stated that police must advise suspects of their right to remain silent and to have counsel during questioning.

Liberals were disappointed when Warren announced his intention to retire near the end of Johnson's term. LBJ hoped to promote Justice Abe Fortas to replace Warren, but Fortas was forced to resign when it was disclosed that he had advised Johnson on political matters while a justice, a conflict of interest. When Johnson left the presidency and no successor to Warren had been designated, the next chief executive, Richard Nixon, appointed a conservative, Warren Burger.

Racial Rights and Wrongs

After 1964, the civil rights movement focused on voting rights. CORE and SNCC emphasized this goal through the Mississippi Freedom Summer Project of 1964, in which young volunteers went to that state to register blacks to vote, set up "Freedom Schools" that offered instruction in black pride, and established the MFDP. The volunteers found themselves harassed by law enforcement officers and Klan members, who firebombed churches and meeting places and threatened, beat, and even killed civil rights workers.

But shortly after King won the 1964 Nobel Peace Prize for his civil rights crusade, his Southern Christian Leadership Conference staged protests in Selma, Alabama, to dramatize the barriers that kept African Americans from voting. Sheriff Jim Clark had his men savagely attack the protesters, scenes that were shown on television and inflamed demands for federal action. Johnson spoke to Congress on March 15, 1965, pledging to end prejudice, urging lawmakers to pass a strong voting rights measure, and vowing, "We shall overcome." Nearly five months later, on August 6, he signed the Voting Rights Act. It allowed federal examiners to register qualified voters and to erase obstacles that were used to bar blacks, such as literacy tests. The law complemented the Twenty-Fourth Amendment (1964), which abolished the poll tax in federal elections. Across the South, the number of black voters skyrocketed, giving them clout to elect their candidates. During the 1960s African Americans won election to key offices, including seats in Congress.

Yet, paradoxically, the voting law and the 1964 civil rights law, however impressive, could not compete with rising expectations. Many African Americans remained members of an economic underclass and were losing patience with Johnson's leadership and with King's pace. Some became more militant, questioning the nonviolent tactics of the NAACP and the SCLC, espousing the slogan "Black Power." Only five days after Johnson signed the Voting Rights Act hostility erupted in the streets of Watts, a black ghetto in Los Angeles. White police and black youths clashed, triggering the largest race riot in twenty years. Fifty thousand blacks looted stores, bombed businesses, and fired at firefighters and law enforcement officers for six days and nights, a rampage that left thirty-four dead, almost four thousand arrested, and around $30 million in damages. African Americans in Chicago and Springfield, Massachusetts, soon rioted as well, a pattern that would intensify over the next three years. In 1966, more than twenty riots ripped northern cities. In 1967, more than forty riots tore at the nation, the worst in Detroit, set ablaze in a conflagration that claimed forty-three lives, injured more than one thousand people, and caused more than $50 million in property damage.

King denounced the violence, yet he understood blacks' frustration. He met with hostility when he and his followers tried to end housing segregation in inner-city Chicago. They rallied northern white support when targeting de jure legal segregation in the South, but failed to rally it by aiming at de facto segregation dictated by neighborhood patterns in the North. Once their movement headed north, public support waned. Another blow came when King announced opposition to the Vietnam War, angering

Johnson and turning some people away from the civil rights cause. Whatever the rifts, though, he was vital to the movement, which never truly recovered after a sniper, James Earl Ray, a white supremacist, killed him on April 4, 1968, in Memphis. King had flaws, but he was an example to millions. Like Gandhi, he turned to nonviolence to conquer a rage within himself and inspired the world with his patience, courage, and tolerance. "I may not get there with you, but I want you to know that we as a people will get to the promised land," King told supporters on the final night of his life.

Barely two months later, the unthinkable again occurred, and another young leader was cut down in his prime. Hours after winning the June 5 California Democratic presidential primary election on an antiwar platform, Robert Kennedy, forty-two, was shot in a Los Angeles ballroom, the victim of Sirhan Sirhan, a Palestinian who hated RFK's pro-Israel policies. A man of paradox, Kennedy was an investigator for Joseph McCarthy and an admirer of the communist-hunter, and a driven, ruthless campaign manager for his brother in 1960. A zealous attorney general, critics said he abused the law and suspects' rights in his pursuit of labor corruption and organized crime. A foreign policy hawk in the Kennedy administration, he was determined to have Fidel Castro removed. And since JFK's assassination, Robert Kennedy had become a senator from New York and an important advocate for the poor and minorities. Ironically, no longer a hawk during LBJ's presidency, he became the front-runner for the Democratic presidential nomination in 1968. When he became the third major leader to be slain in the 1960s, after John Kennedy and King, liberalism did not recover. As he said many times, in many parts of this nation, to those he touched and those who sought to touch him: "Some men see things as they are and say, 'Why?' I dream things that never were and say, 'Why not?'" eulogized his brother, Massachusetts Senator Edward Kennedy, the last Kennedy brother.

Contemplating the urban tumult that undermined RFK's, King's, and his own efforts, Johnson led the country in asking why rioting broke out despite so much social accomplishment. His National Advisory Commission on Civil Disorder blamed racism, saying that the United States was "moving toward two societies, one black, one white—separate and unequal," and calling for millions of new jobs and public housing units, a campaign against northern segregation, and money for national "income supplementation." Johnson knew such a prescription would not be accepted by white taxpayers, and personally, he complained of ingratitude. He passed one more important civil rights bill, the 1968 Open Housing Act. Yet, reflecting the dissonance of the times, it included amendments providing tough penalties for those who incited riots. The paradox of progress and pessimism ended Johnson's tenure on a note of uncertainty.

Assessment of the Great Society

The Great Society and the War on Poverty did much to ease suffering, and many of their programs outlasted 1960s liberalism. Besides the civil rights laws and Medicare, Head Start, for instance, proved so popular that it defied attempts to eviscerate it. But many of Johnson's measures, such as the local-level programs under Community Action, were poorly conceived and co-opted by local politicians. The War on Poverty did lift some people out of destitution, thanks in part to government programs. Johnson's backers cited statistics that apparently showed 8 million escaped poverty during his administration—but partly because domestic spending and Vietnam War outlays overheated the economy and elevated the poor with everyone else. Millions of poor Americans could not surmount poverty, though in five years, the federal government had doubled its regulatory role and the extent of its payments to poor people.

Significant wealth redistribution would have made a bigger impact upon poverty, yet Johnson believed that teaching job skills and education were preferable to direct distribution of money. Vietnam turned many liberals against Johnson, ending the momentum for domestic programs and contributing to the repudiation of liberalism by conservatives and the poor. At the end Johnson felt betrayed by the constituency he sought to help— the poor—because he could not keep up with their demands. Perhaps Johnson should not have tied the War on Poverty to a utopian pledge to eradicate poverty in one decade; a vow to mitigate poverty might have saved him from backlash. Further, poverty is a relative, not an absolute measurement, and in a free society some will always be poorer than others. In a period of emergency, such as the Great Depression, it might be possible to sustain the political and economic sacrifice necessary for such a program. But the decade of the 1960s was rich, not poor. People were inclined to ask, "Why now?"

Still, with the need for the Great Society and the opportunity to realize one, it would have been wrong not to pursue the vision. Individual programs were notable successes. In another context, without the Vietnam War (see chapter 18), for example, the Great Society might have done a great deal to uplift the nation. Conceived by Kennedy in a time of optimism, its fate was decided in a period of cynicism and uncertainty. Having the vision and the opportunity to uplift the poor, it seemed right to do so. Only by trying would we learn the possibilities, or whether it was an idea whose time had come.

The War on Poverty and the war in Vietnam taught Americans painful lessons in humility and paradox. They could lose wars like anyone else. Laws alone could not erase poverty. The optimism of the early 1960s was shattered by assassinations and violence. Yet the period was one of awakening as well as uncertainty. It was a time of fertility in politics, in the arts, and in technology. It was, doubtless, confusing. "We thought we knew society's rules," said a teacher who lived through the 1960s. "And every time we learned the rules, they changed them on us."

CHAPTER SIX

Foreign Anxieties, 1961–1968

THE PARADOX of John F. Kennedy's New Frontier in foreign affairs lay in the president's charisma and glitter on one hand, and his inexperience and poor judgment on the other. In the Era of Uncertainty, his brief administration is both the most dazzling and the most uncertain.

His cabinet and advisers, like the president, were considered macho intellectuals, ironically termed "the best and the brightest" because their judgment on Vietnam proved unsound. The brightest star, Defense Secretary Robert McNamara, became disillusioned with his own Vietnam policies and issued a mea culpa near the end of the century. Kennedy died before the ramifications of his policies, and what he might have done, became apparent, adding to the uncertainties of the era.

Kennedy and Castro

Next to Ronald Reagan, Kennedy was the most ardent Cold Warrior of the Time of Paradox. His inaugural address concentrated solely on foreign policy; he did not intend to be a domestic president. Kennedy inspired the nation with purpose as few presidents have done. His objectives were to win the Cold War, extinguish communism, and beat the Soviets to the Moon before the end of the decade. Rejecting Dwight Eisenhower's dangerous doctrine of massive retaliation, he substituted flexible response, which would enable the nation to fight brushfire wars. To combat guerrillas, he created the Special Forces, or Green Berets, trained in counterinsurgency. As in most presidencies, the most important events in foreign policy were the unexpected ones.

Kennedy's first challenge came from the south. JFK feared Fidel Castro's communist Cuba might attempt to spread communism through-

THE ROAD TO VIETNAM
Vice President Lyndon B. Johnson inspecting a textile mill in Saigon.
(Library of Congress)

out the hemisphere. Attempts to kill him by use of a poisoned cigar, injection of poison through a hypodermic needle concealed in a ballpoint pen, and shooting him were devised. To implement the plots the CIA employed experts—the Mafia. Castro survived.

Next, the CIA planned an invasion of Cuba to topple the dictator, led by anti-Castro refugees, fleeing Cuba daily by the thousands bound for Florida. On April 15, 1961, the operation began. Disguised American planes tried, but failed, to destroy the six-plane Cuban air force on the ground, which doomed the invasion. Kennedy canceled two subsequent bombing missions, fearing American involvement might become known. He hoped to win a minor war without acknowledging American involvement; in fact, the *New York Times* had already published rumors of the plan. On April 17, fifteen hundred anti-Castro Cubans landed at the Bay of Pigs. They were strafed by Castro's planes, which sank a ship carrying supplies and communications equipment. Castro's much larger army enveloped the refugee army. Surrounded by swamps, they were trapped. Five hundred died and one thousand were captured, later ransomed by American food and medicine. Castro preempted an uprising by imprisoning thousands of political opponents. Ironically, the American people applauded the attempt, despite its failure, and Kennedy's approval rating in the Gallup poll rose to 83 percent, the highest of his presidency. Americans shared the president's anticommunism and his loathing of Castro and gave the president credit for trying, however ineptly.

Hotspots in Berlin and Indochina

In the 1960s, nuclear war appeared most likely to occur over Berlin. The divided city was the centerpiece of the war in Europe, a place where a war of wills and prestige was aggravated by the flight of thousands of refugees daily fleeing the East to West Berlin and freedom. The dingy, bleak Eastern sector, rebuilt by the Soviets, contrasted to the thriving, bustling capitalist city to the West. In military strength, however, the advantage lay with the East, whose huge army faced just fifteen thousand Western troops. At the Vienna summit in 1961, Soviet boss Nikita Khrushchev threatened to turn the city over to the East German government, committed to ejecting the West by force. Kennedy called for additional money for defense, doubled draft quotas, called up two hundred thousand reservists, and launched an accelerated fallout shelter program.

Khrushchev did not follow through with his threat to have a proxy expel the West. Rather, he constructed a wall around West Berlin, which halted the hemorrhage of refugees. With the refugee issue settled, the Soviets no longer had a reason to drive out the West. Kennedy was criticized for letting the wall stand, but this might have been deliberate, as it stabilized the crisis. Khrushchev was condemned roundly in the West. Democracies, Western leaders proclaimed, do not build walls to keep their own people in.

The Cold War began in Europe but migrated to Asia. Initially, the chief trouble spot appeared to be Laos, which was neutralized at a major power conference in Geneva in 1962. The problem in Vietnam was more serious. In the context of the Cold War, a communist takeover in the former French colony would be a setback. The South thrived economically under capitalism, yet it was also riddled with corruption and religious divisions. In the North, the communist economy struggled, yet the population was more disciplined and determined, and the North boasted of its leader the charismatic Ho Chi Minh. As in some other cases in Third World wars, the communists seemed tougher than their capitalist foes. Further, some South Vietnamese sided with communism and rebelled, becoming known as the Vietcong.

The war did not explode out of control on Kennedy's watch, yet it was about to. Although about 80 percent of South Vietnam's population was

SEEKING THE ENEMY
Marines patrol the Rice Fields, 1965.
(National Archives)

Buddhist, an elite of Catholics, led by Ngo Dien Diem, governed the country. Buddhists demonstrated against the autocratic Diem, and some even burned themselves to death in protest. By August 1963, the Americans had lost faith in Diem and implied they would not interfere if a military coup toppled him. The coup succeeded and Diem and his brother, the corrupt Ngo Dinh Nhu, were murdered in the process. Kennedy approved the overthrow yet felt remorse for the assassinations, which came just three weeks before his own. By Kennedy's death, there were 16,500 American advisers and Green Berets in South Vietnam to train the South Vietnamese Army in counterinsurgency.

Luckily for Kennedy, the war did not become an albatross on his watch. Had he lived, he probably would have followed about the same policies as his successor, Lyndon Johnson. Kennedy was a more militant Cold Warrior than Johnson, unwilling to lose. Both presidents were highly competitive and found it inconceivable that a primitive guerrilla army could defeat American technology. Yet they did not enter, and remain, simply for pride; they believed in their cause. Kennedy left the situation worse than he found it. Initially, Lyndon Johnson believed continuity required the fulfillment of Kennedy's policies. Neither believed that America could play a great power on the cheap. Yet even with great effort, the outcome was uncertain, a bitter irony in the Era of Uncertainty.

The Cuban Missile Crisis

If Vietnam posed uncertainties to Kennedy, the lands to the south in the Western Hemisphere were yet more uncertain. Here Kennedy enjoyed successes and failures, and in his biggest trial gambled and won. To assist Latin America, he created the Alliance for Progress, which he outlined in his inaugural address. The United States would invest $20 billion and Latin American nations $80 billion to revitalize their economies over the next decade. Raising hopes extravagantly, the alliance produced only marginal improvements and failed to transform the economies or democratize the governments of the countries involved. Several military coups took place during Kennedy's presidency, producing oligarchic governments that had little interest in uplifting their people.

More successful was a small-scale, people-to-people enterprise, the Peace Corps, created by Kennedy in 1961 to tap the idealism of Americans, young and old, and to utilize their talents. Peace Corps volunteers, working for meager pay, lived among the common people and taught them skills such as reading, agriculture, home building, sanitation, and disease control. Though the program's bottom-up approach did not solve large problems, the Peace Corps volunteers were goodwill ambassadors for America. Launched with a high profile, the Peace Corps received less prominence from later presidents and became marginal.

The emerging nations of Africa, freed from European colonialism, languished in turmoil during the 1960s, although Africa was less a Cold War battleground than Asia. Kennedy paid more attention to Africa than previous presidents. The Peace Corps was popular there, and he treated Africa with dignity, sending highly qualified ambassadors to represent America. Africa seethed in turmoil as new nations emerged from the ashes of colonialism. Power struggles broke out, including Marxist factions, yet the superpowers rarely confronted each other directly. However, covert operatives were active, including the CIA. The stakes were highest in the largest of new nations, the Congo, once a Belgian colony. In 1960 a civil war broke out. Moise Tshombe led mineral-rich Katanga and several other provinces in seceding from the central government under President Joseph Kasavubu and Prime Minister Patrice Lumumba. The Moscow-trained prime minister requested Soviet military aid, and the pro-Western Kasavubu repudiated him. Lumumba retired to plan a comeback with Soviet assistance, but Kasavubu's men captured him and turned him over to Tshombe's forces, who murdered him. Earlier, the CIA had plotted to kill Lumumba. In the end, United Nations peacekeepers crushed the secessionists and restored order, allowing the government to remain in pro-Western hands. Kennedy backed the UN and avoided sending troops.

In October 1962, Khrushchev took the biggest gamble of the Cold War by installing intermediate range ballistic missiles in Cuba. From Cuba, the missiles could strike targets in the southern and eastern United States in eight minutes, compared to twenty-five minutes for missiles based in the USSR. They could also strike targets in Central and South America with deadly speed, intimidating these nations from aligning with the United States in a crisis. They might even make Berlin a pawn in a game of nuclear blackmail.

The installations were photographed by high-flying American U-2 reconnaissance planes on October 15. Kennedy convened a committee of his major advisers, called Ex-Comm, largely influenced by Attorney General Robert Kennedy, to expeditiously consider alternatives. They considered an invasion, air strikes, or a blockade of Cuba, deciding on the latter. If the blockades failed, the riskier options could be reconsidered. Provocatively, Kennedy announced the blockade on national television on October 22, placing the prestige of the superpowers on the line. With the world watching, the side that backed down, if either, would suffer humiliation. Khrushchev conceded rather than start a nuclear war. When the Soviet missile-bearing ships approached the picket line of American war vessels, they stopped or turned back. The usually diffident Secretary of State Dean Rusk gloated, "We were eyeball to eyeball, and the other fellow just blinked."

There was still the question of the missiles already in Cuba. In fact, Khrushchev claimed all the missiles had landed and work on the installations continued. On October 26 Kennedy received a letter from Khrushchev offering to remove the missiles in exchange for an American pledge not to invade Cuba. The administration was ready to accept when a second, tougher letter arrived, perhaps inspired by Khrushchev's hard-line colleagues in the Kremlin. It added a condition: America must remove its missiles from Turkey. Superficially, the condition was not unreasonable. The American missiles in Turkey were about as close to the Soviet heartland as the Cuban missiles were to America. Kennedy, though, termed the condition "nuclear blackmail" and said he could not remove them without Turkey's consent. Trading missile withdrawals would set a bad precedent, leaving some allies undefended. Privately, however, he authorized his brother to tell the Soviet ambassador that the missiles in Turkey would be removed in a few months. The president was not willing to sacrifice his prestige to make a deal, yet had placed Soviet prestige in jeopardy by appearing on television to announce the missile installations and the American blockade. As usual, superpower diplomacy resembled a game of blind-man's bluff. Meanwhile, Robert Kennedy suggested a solution to the problem of the two letters: accept the first and avoid comment on the second. This solution worked.

The Cuban Missile Crisis was the greatest American propaganda victory in the Cold War, one of Kennedy's most notable accomplishments, and the closest the superpowers came to a nuclear holocaust. Kennedy's popularity soared, yet was lower in the polls than after the failed Bay of Pigs invasion. Khrushchev later was removed from office by Kremlin leaders who believed he lacked the toughness to win the Cold War. Few then, or even now, noted that by backing down, the Soviet leader took the more prudent, even statesmanlike, course. On the other hand, he had been responsible for placing the missiles in Cuba in the first place. Some believed Kennedy had grown in office since his indecisive behavior in the Bay of Pigs. Others remarked that sometimes it was better to be lucky than to be good.

After the crisis, there was a temporary lull in saber rattling. The leaders established a teletype linking them for instantaneous communication and translation. It was not, literally, a "red telephone." At American University in Washington in June 1963, Kennedy made the most conciliatory speech of his presidency directed at his Soviet adversaries. We share a common planet, a stake in our children's future, and all of us are mortal, he proclaimed. Later that year the superpowers consummated a treaty banning tests above the ground or under water. Yet Kennedy could not resist piling up propaganda points against the Soviets, with a presidential election looming in 1964. In one of his last major Cold War addresses, at the Berlin Wall, he compared Berlin, the most contested spot of the Cold War, to Rome, capital of the ancient world. Just as people had once been proud to call themselves Romans, all free men were, in a sense, Berliners. He concluded, "All free men, wherever they may live, are citizens of Berlin, and, therefore, as a free man, I take pride in the words, "Ich bin ein Berliner!" (I am a Berliner). Thus, near the end of his life, Kennedy remained a Cold Warrior, though a more vacillating one. He had sheathed the sword at American University only to draw it at the Berlin Wall. In the Free World, Kennedy was almost universally praised for his tough and eloquent speech, and the magic of the place and the timing. Later, President Ronald Reagan would travel to Berlin, stand before the brick and mortar that fenced in a city, and challenge the Soviets to tear down the wall. Ultimately East Berliners would tear it down themselves.

LBJ: The Benefactor and the Gunslinger

John Kennedy turned over to Lyndon Baines Johnson a more troubled world than the one he inherited from Eisenhower. This was not entirely Kennedy's doing. In fact, science was the chief culprit. The superpowers could now destroy not only each other, but the world. It would have taken cemeteries stacked like high-rise parking lots to accommodate the dead, assuming there was someone left to bury them.

LBJ was a man of peace who yearned to become a great president by building a Great Society and eliminating poverty. Like Woodrow Wilson before, fate, not the president, set the agenda. With little experience in foreign policy, and hoping to ride in the wake of Kennedy's martyrdom to win election in 1964, Johnson tried to follow Kennedy's policies, and to guess what Kennedy would have done. He embraced the Alliance for Progress and the Peace Corps. He kept Robert McNamara and Dean Rusk, both hawks in the Cold War, and other Kennedy advisers. He was impressed by their polish and academic credentials, though his own breadth and imagination equaled theirs, if shrouded by insecurity and inarticulateness. Publicly cruder than Kennedy, LBJ was better at dealing with people in small groups, at least Americans. Yet he had never been curious or well read about the wider world, and now he found himself leader of it. Troubles for Johnson began in 1964, in the Panama Canal Zone. Panamanian students wanted to fly the Panamanian flag next to the American banner at schools in the zone. American students wanted only the Stars and Stripes to fly. In a compromise, Washington ordered that no flags be flown. Defiant Americans raised their flag, and their Panamanian classmates rioted. Twenty people were killed, and buildings and cars were burned. Panama broke diplomatic relations with the United States and demanded a renegotiation of the 1903 Panama Canal Treaty. Johnson at first took a militant stand, then agreed to talks to gradually integrate the Canal Zone into Panama. Diplomatic ties were restored.

In the Dominican Republic, politics resembled a maze with factions of all stripes scurrying through the hedges. There was a military faction, a leftist faction, and a moderate faction. What Johnson wanted was what America wanted throughout the Cold War, not the most democratic faction but the most stable pro-Western one. Like other American presidents, if the country seemed unstable, he was willing to impose pro-American stability. America did not necessarily favor dictators, however. For example, in 1961 the CIA connived in the assassination of longtime dictator Rafael Trujillo. A civil war followed and a coup brought leftist Juan Bosch to power, but only briefly. Bosch was toppled by an army-led coup. Later, Bosch won an election as president, but violence continued. Fearing Bosch was tilting toward communism, in April 1965 Johnson dispatched fourteen thousand Marines to quell the turmoil. Troops from the Organization of American States (OAS) began to replace Americans in the middle of the year, and the moderate Joaquin Balaguer came to power. LBJ restored stability, yet liberals complained that Bosch was a reformer, not a communist, and the intervention piqued the nationalism of some Latin American nations.

Direct superpower confrontation took a sabbatical under Johnson and he held only one summit with a Soviet leader. While he was president the Soviets attained nuclear parity with America after lagging badly at the time of the Cuban Missile Crisis. When the Soviets crushed a democratization movement in Czechoslovakia, termed the "Prague Spring," in 1968, LBJ did not take a strong stand. Johnson made some progress on arms limitations. In 1967 the adversaries signed a treaty guaranteeing peaceful uses of outer space and in 1968 agreed to a nuclear nonproliferation accord. The same year negotiations opened on arms limitations that culminated in the Strategic Arms Limitations Treaty, or SALT I, four years later.

The Middle East brought a threat of a superpower confrontation that never materialized.

In 1967, Israel, America's closest ally in the region launched a preemptive attack on three of its Arab enemies—Egypt, Jordan, and Syria—that Israeli intelligence showed were plotting war. The Israelis destroyed the Egyptian Air Force on the ground, punished the armies of all three rivals, captured the West Bank of the Jordan River and eastern Jerusalem from Jordan, and seized the Golan Heights from Syria. Like his predecessors and most of his successors, Johnson had few solutions to the intractable hostility in the Middle East.

Further east, diplomacy proved frustrating. China, especially in rhetoric, was militantly anti-American. North Korea seized an American spy ship, the *Pueblo*, in 1968 and held the crew hostage almost a year before releasing them. Despite the provocation, Johnson did not act because he was facing more serious problems in Vietnam, where the Vietcong had launched the Tet offensive. If China and Korea frustrated Johnson, Vietnam destroyed him.

The Little War That Wouldn't Go Away

When Johnson inherited the Vietnam War, there were just two feasible options: withdraw or escalate. Both entailed risks, and Johnson was not a seer. He wanted to win the conflict, avoiding personal and national humiliation, yet not risk a nuclear war in the process. He escalated incrementally, without a grand design, because each decision depended on how the last one worked. Unfortunately, the decisions did not go well and more force was applied, requiring additional troops. Finally, the president and the American military found themselves trapped in a swirling river, in which it was as far to swim to one bank as it was to swim to the other bank. The imbroglio not only ruined Johnson politically; it worried him to death.

Johnson ran for president in 1964 against Barry Goldwater as the peace candidate, telling Americans that if they voted for Goldwater, the Republican, a dangerous warmonger, would escalate the Vietnam War. One voter later reminisced, "They told me if I voted for Goldwater the war would be escalated, so I voted for Goldwater and, sure enough, the war was escalated." The escalation began even before the election, with the Gulf of Tonkin incident in August 1964. Johnson had been hoping that an event would provide him the rationale for crushing the North. On a stormy night in the Gulf of Tonkin, the destroyer *C. Turner Joy* radioed it was under attack from enemy torpedo boats. No visual sighting was made, and there was no conclusive evidence that the destroyer was attacked. Still Johnson described the affair as an unprovoked assault by the North and used it to obtain the Gulf of Tonkin Resolution from Congress, passed by lopsided votes. It authorized him to use force to protect American armed forces in Southeast Asia and to preemptively thwart aggression. It was as close to a declaration of war as ever passed. The act was repealed in 1970.

Johnson launched a retaliatory air strike, then other air strikes in retaliation to specific enemy provocations. These evolved into Operation Rolling Thunder, the systematic bombing of the North. Air bases were constructed to accommodate the bombers. The first ground troops were landed in 1965 to protect the airstrips. Then their duties were expanded to "search and destroy" missions designed to wear down the enemy in a contest of attrition. Progress was slow, so more troops were sent, rising from 23,000 soldiers in Vietnam at the start of 1965; 184,000 a year later; 485,000 by 1967; and 536,000 at the start of 1968. Americans attempted to impose technological advantages in air strikes, artillery barrages, and helicopter attacks. When the enemy melted into the jungle, the United States used defoliants, such as Agent Orange, destructive to plants, animals, and people. Frustrating the

Americans, the communists refused to meet them head-to-head in a major set battle. As the battles shifted territory through the swamps and forests, there were no static lines and no easy ways of measuring gains. The army resorted to counting the number of enemy dead and reporting them, in often inaccurate "body counts," because the mathematically minded McNamara demanded statistical measurements of victories.

Statistically speaking, bombing the North was probably the least effective means of defeating the communists. The United States spent $9.60 for every $1 of damage inflicted and used an average of several tons of explosives for each soldier killed. America dropped eight hundred tons of bombs each day from 1965 to 1968, three times the daily amount dropped on Europe, Africa, and Asia during World War II. The best means of ending the war would have been a negotiated peace, but neither side was willing to negotiate on terms the other would accept. The North wanted a bombing halt as a precondition to talks, but every time Johnson agreed to a temporary stoppage, the communists exploited the opportunity to infiltrate troops and supplies into the South. The communists also insisted on the removal of President Nguyen Van Thieu, president after 1968, and the removal of all American troops, while northern troops remained in the South. To Johnson, this constituted not a compromise but a surrender. He wanted peace, particularly for political reasons, but was not willing to forsake the years of sacrifice and Americans carried home in body bags.

Johnson's dilemma was partly an inescapable by-product of the Cold War and partly of his own making. Ultimately the war he could not win was not in Vietnam but in the streets and on the campuses of America. The war polarized Americans as no event since the Civil War. As in 1861, Americans turned to fighting each other. The antiwar movement, which began small, on college campuses, never constituted a majority. Even after antiwar sentiment spread off campus via television into the living rooms of Americans, and a consensus emerged that it was necessary to end the war, there was no consensus over how to do so. Almost equally, Americans were divided over whether to stop the physical and psychological hemorrhaging by risking massive escalation to win a victory, or by simply giving up and pulling out.

Johnson lost his confidence and his public credibility. He lost Robert McNamara, consumed with guilt, who resigned to become president of the World Bank, a less stressful job. Walter Cronkite, the highly respected CBS news anchor, concluded that the war was unwinnable. In fact, that was precisely the problem for many moderates, not that the war was immoral or that South Vietnam would flourish under communism, or even that the war was unusually bloody. After all, almost as many Americans died on the highways every year in the decade as died in combat during the ten-year involvement in Southeast Asia. Surrender would of course stop the deaths, but that is true in any war.

The real war of attrition took place in America. The public's patience and Johnson's nerves were wearing thin. The military draft disrupted the lives of American men even when it did not kill them. The cause was not clearly defined. Many Americans believed that because Vietnam was far away it was irrelevant. Others thought that there was a plot on the part of America to plunder the resources of Vietnam. If so, the plot backfired for America, which lost far more economically than it gained. Some groups believed Marxism was a superior system, a belief most prominent among leftist students and intellectuals. But if America had been winning, and winning quickly, none of this would have mattered.

If morale was low on the home front, it was also low among American troops in Vietnam. There are atrocities on both sides in all wars, but no previous war had been scrutinized so intensely by television and journalism. Because most of the journalists in the field traveled with American troops, most of the atrocities they reported were committed by Americans. They were nothing to be proud of, and the actions could not be justified by the pressure of warfare. As they sat in their living rooms, Americans watched soldiers casually setting Vietnamese peasants' huts afire with cigarette lighters. Soldiers abused drugs and participated in "fragging," or killing, their commanding officers, often with grenades.

Vietnam and the Election of 1968

By late 1967 and early 1968 some American generals, including General William Westmoreland, the commander in Vietnam, believed an American victory was in sight. This was dashed by the Vietcong's Tet Offensive of January 30, 1968. Tet was the Lunar New Year, a time when both sides traditionally observed a truce. Communists attacked cities, towns, and provinces in the South, as well as American military bases and the U.S. Embassy in Saigon. Rallying after initial setbacks, American and South Vietnamese troops inflicted forty-seven thousand casualties on the Vietcong. The Americans lost 1,100 killed and wounded, the South Vietnamese Army 2,300. It would have been an ideal time to launch a counterattack, because the Vietcong were spent, no longer a major force in the war. Yet if Tet was a tactical victory for America, it was a Pyrrhic one. What Americans remembered was not the follow-up fighting in which the Vietcong were decimated, but the initial shock from their simultaneous attacks, temporarily successful, at cities and bases believed secure. If they could penetrate the walls of the U.S. Embassy, they could strike anywhere. The first, daring

FIGHTING IN THE STREETS
Violent protests outside the Democratic National Convention, 1968.
(Chicago Historical Society)

victories of the Vietcong were broadcast on television and radio, and drove a nail in the coffin of LBJ's war. The light at the end of the tunnel Westmoreland had claimed to see before Tet "was a locomotive headed in his direction," an observer quipped.

The importance of Tet lay as much in its timing as in its psychological wound.

It occurred at about the time of the nation's first presidential primary in New Hampshire. Johnson was not on the ballot, though his understudy won, albeit barely. Minnesota Senator Eugene McCarthy won 42 percent of the vote, running as an antiwar candidate. This outcome was considered to be a referendum against the war, yet, paradoxically, a poll taken later showed that many of the McCarthy voters believed they were voting for Senator Joseph McCarthy, the infamous communist hunter. The anti-Johnson vote convinced Robert Kennedy, now a senator from New York, that Johnson was vulnerable, and he entered the campaign. On March 31, Johnson announced on television that he was dropping out of the race and devoting his total attention to ending the war. Peace talks would begin in Paris.

McCarthy and Kennedy waged a primary war, Kennedy leading, which culminated in Kennedy's victory in California, sealing his nomination. Yet that evening he was assassinated by an Arab nationalist. Stepping into the vacuum left by Kennedy's death, Hubert Humphrey won the nomination without waging a major primary campaign.

Richard Nixon, the Republican nominee started with an initial lead in the polls. Slowly, Humphrey began to catch up as he distanced himself from Johnson's war policies. The campaign lacked precision. It was difficult to determine who was the peace candidate: Humphrey promised a negotiated peace; Nixon implied he would end the war. Although the war was a major issue, it was not the only one. Many Americans considered the Democrats lenient on drug use, overly tolerant of the counterculture, and unable to rein in crime in the streets. Nixon talked tougher than Humphrey on these issues, yet George Wallace, the Alabama governor, talked even tougher. Wallace campaigned as the candidate of his own third party, the American Independent Party, to the right of both major parties. His tart message of toughness on crime, vigorous prosecution of the war, and veiled racism drew support from middle working-class Americans who disliked antiwar and civil rights agitators and longed for simpler times. To Wallace, the bigger the liberal, the bigger the target. Ironically, he probably took more votes from Nixon than from Humphrey because their regional and ideological constituencies overlapped. Paradoxically, the radical Left hurt Humphrey more and the radical Right hurt Nixon more.

In one of the closest elections of the century, Nixon won. He took 31.8 million popular votes (43.4 percent) and 301 electoral votes to Humphrey's 31.3 million (42.7 percent) and 191 to Wallace's 9.9 million and 46 electoral votes. Few had expected Nixon to arise from his defeats in the 1960s, yet timing means as much in politics as in hitting a baseball. Nixon's elevator ride through American history included one of the closest losses for president, in 1960, a victory that was almost as close, in 1968, and one of the most lopsided victories, in 1972, culminating, in his becoming the first president to resign, in 1974.

If Nixon's political career seemed like a script written for a tragic hero, Johnson's career fit the script even better. Johnson was everything Nixon was not; he was more popular, less shy, and early in his presidency seemed destined to become a great president. Like Nixon, timing was important to Johnson's resting place in history. He came to office almost totally in sync with his times and left it virtually an anachronism. He wanted to do good and he wanted credit for it.

Johnson returned to his ranch, resumed smoking despite doctors' warnings, let his hair grow long, ruminated, and waited for death, never

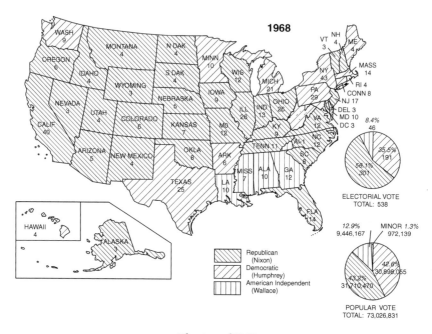

Election of 1968

to bask in the role of elder statesman. It must have seemed to Johnson that the harder he tried, the harder things got. Every group he had reached out to—blacks, students, the poor—seemed to have turned against him. American cities smoldered in riot-ravaged ruins that served as a metaphor for LBJ's reputation. Wanting to do the right thing, yet not knowing what the right thing was, he did not know whether he had come on too strongly or too weakly, whether the fault lay with him or with his critics. There is no monument in the nation's capital to the man who wanted to update and surpass Franklin Roosevelt's New Deal. Yet, to many, his memorial is a stone wall carved with the names of American servicemen who died in the war he did not start and could not end. The tall Texan's reputation had crested with the wave of public adulation in 1964 until it crashed upon the beach of Vietnam and rolled back in the other direction.

Lyndon Johnson, like Woodrow Wilson, wanted a world safe for democratic ideals as well as one that banished destitution. Like Wilson, Johnson was right in principle but wrong in degree. The aims of a Great Society and a world free for democracy were laudable, but as unachievable in 1968 as they had been in 1919.

Bibliographic Essay

Truman And Eisenhower

For general studies of the Era of Uncertainty, see James T. Patterson, *Grand Expectations: The United States, 1945–1974* (1997); Alonzo Hamby, *Liberalism and Its Challengers: FDR to Reagan* (1985); Eric Goldman, *The Crucial Decade—and After: America, 1945–1960* (1961); William L. O'Neill, *American High: The Years of Confidence, 1945–1960* (1986); and John Patrick Diggins, *The Proud Decades: America in War and Peace, 1941–1960* (1988).

Among the leading books on Harry S Truman are Alonzo Hamby, *Man of the People: A Life of Harry S Truman* (1995); William E. Pemberton, *Harry S Truman* (1989); David McCullough, *Truman* (1992), massively detailed and favorable to Truman; and Robert H. Ferrell, *Harry S Truman and the Modern American Presidency* (1983). On the Dixiecrats, see Kari Frederickson, *The Dixiecrat Revolt and the End of the Solid South, 1932–1968* (2001), practically definitive.

On domestic anticommunism, consult Richard Fried, *Nightmare in Red: The McCarthy Era in Perspective* (1990); Richard Gid Powers, *Not without Honor: The History of American Anticommunism* (1995); Ellen Schrecker, *Many Are the Crimes: McCarthyism in America* (1998); David Caute, *The Great Fear* (1978); and Harvey Klehr, John Earl Haynes, and Kyrill M. Anderson, *The Secret World of American Communism* (1998). The best biography of Joseph McCarthy is Thomas C. Reeves, *The Life and Times of Joe McCarthy* (1982), especially strong on McCarthy's rise to power. David M. Oshinsky, *A Conspiracy So Immense: The World of Joe McCarthy* (1983), does an excellent job of describing McCarthy's intellectual milieu. For the spy trials, see Allen Weinstein, *Perjury: The Hiss-Chambers Case* (1978). Ronald Radosh and Joyce Milton explore another famous trial in *The Rosenberg*

File (1983). For the Cold War, culture and politics, see Stephen J. Whitfield, *The Culture of the Cold War* (1991); Lary May, ed., *Recasting America: Culture and Politics in the Age of the Cold War* (1989); and Ellen Schrecker, *No Ivory Tower: McCarthyism and the Universities* (1986).

For diplomacy, see Wesley M. Bagby, *America's International Relations since World War I* (1999); Robert D. Schulzinger, *American Diplomacy in the Twentieth Century* (3rd ed., 1994); the succinct Ralph B. Levering, *The Cold War: A Post-Cold War History* (1994); Ronald E. Powaski, *The Cold War: The United States and the Soviet Union, 1917–1991* (1998); John Lewis Gaddis, *The United States and the Origins of the Cold War, 1941–1947* (1972), *Strategies of Containment* (1982), and *We Now Know: Rethinking Cold War History* (1997); Walter LaFeber, *America, Russia, and the Cold War, 1945–1988* (1990); Melvyn Leffler, *A Preponderance of Power: National Security, the Truman Administration, and the Cold War* (1992); Lloyd Gardner, *Architects of Illusion* (1970), *On Every Front: The Making of the Cold War* (1979), and *Meeting the Communist Threat* (1988); and Michael Hogan, *The Marshall Plan* (1987). On China, see June M. Grasso, *Truman's Two-China Policy: 1948–1950* (1987), and Warren I. Cohen, *America's Response to China* (rev. ed., 1980). For Vietnam in this era, see Gary R. Hess, *The United States' Emergence as a Southeast Asian Power, 1940–1950* (1988), and Lloyd Gardner, *Approaching Vietnam, 1950–1954* (1988). Among the histories of the Korean War are William Steck, *The Korean War: An International History* (1995); John Merrill, *Korea* (1989); and Paul M. Edwards, *The Korean War, 1950–1953* (1998).

On the 1950s, see David Halberstam, *The Fifties* (1993), a detailed popular history; J. Ronald Oakley, *God's Country: America in the Fifties* (1986), provocative, as is Paul A. Carter, *Another Part of the Fifties* (1983); also consult Tom Engelhardt, *The End of Victory Culture: Cold War America and the Disillusioning of a Generation* (1995), and Jeffrey Hart, *When the Going Was Good: American Life in the 1950s* (1982). The best biography of Dwight Eisenhower is Stephen E. Ambrose, *Eisenhower* (2 vols., 1983, 1984). Other valuable treatments are William B. Pickett, *Dwight D. Eisenhower and American Political Power* (1995); Alton Lee, *Dwight D. Eisenhower: Soldier and Statesman* (1981); Chester J. Pach Jr. and Elmo Richardson, *The Presidency of Dwight D. Eisenhower* (1979); John W. Sloan, *Eisenhower and the Management of Prosperity* (1991); Raymond Saulnier, *Constructive Years: The U.S. Economy under Eisenhower* (1991); and Jeff Broadwater, *Eisenhower and the Anti-Communist Crusade* (1992).

For an overview of Eisenhower's diplomacy, see Robert A. Divine, *Eisenhower and the Cold War* (1981); Richard A. Melanson and David Mayers, eds., *Reevaluating Eisenhower: American Foreign Policy in the*

1950s (1986); and H. W. Brands Jr., *Cold Warriors: Eisenhower's Generation and American Foreign Policy* (1988). Intervention abroad is chronicled in Richard W. Cottam, *Iran and the United States: A Cold War Case Study* (1988); Mark Gasiorowski, *U.S. Foreign Policy and the Shah: Building a Client State in Iran* (1991); and Piero Gleijeses, *The Guatemalan Revolution and the United States, 1944–1954* (1991). On covert operations, see Stephen E. Ambrose with Richard Immerman, *Ike's Spies: Eisenhower and the Espionage Establishment* (1981), and Blanche Wiesen Cook, *The Declassified Eisenhower* (1981).

Indochina is the subject of Melanie Billings Yun, *Decision against War: Eisenhower and Dien Bien Phu, 1954* (1988); Andrew Rotter, *The Path to Vietnam* (1987); David L. Anderson, *Trapped by Success: The Eisenhower Administration and Vietnam, 1953–1961* (1991); and James Arnold, *The First Domino: Eisenhower, the Military, and America's Intervention in Vietnam* (1991). For other aspects of policy, see Stephen G. Rabe, *Eisenhower and Latin America: The Foreign Policy of Anticommunism* (1988); Richard E. Welch Jr., *Response to Revolution: The United States and the Cuban Revolution, 1959–1961* (1985); H. W. Brands Jr., *The Specter of Neutralism: The United States and the Emergence of the Third World, 1947–1960* (1989); Isaac Alteras, *Eisenhower and Israel: U.S.-Israeli Relations, 1953–1960* (1993); Cole C. Kingseed, *Eisenhower and the Suez Crisis of 1956* (1995); Robert A. Divine, *Blowing in the Wind: The Nuclear Test Ban Debate, 1954–1960* (1978); and Michael R. Beschloss, *Mayday: Eisenhower, Khrushchev and the U-2 Affair* (1986).

Society and Culture

On civil rights, general studies include Steven F. Lawson, *Running for Freedom: Civil Rights and Black Politics in America since 1941* (1991); Harvard Sitkoff, *The Struggle for Black Equality, 1954–1992* (1993); Robert Weisbrot, *Freedom Bound: A History of America's Civil Rights Movement* (1990); Taylor Branch, *Parting the Waters: America in the King Years, 1954–1963* (1988); David J. Garrow, *Bearing the Cross: Martin Luther King Jr. and the Southern Christian Leadership Conference* (1986); and August Meier and Elliot Rudwick, *CORE: A Study in the Civil Rights Movement* (1975). White Southern opposition is discussed in Numan V. Bartley, *The Rise of Massive Resistance* (1966); Neil McMillen, *Citizens' Council* (1971), and Glen Jeansonne, *Leander Perez: Boss of the Delta* (2nd ed., 1995), the biography of a militant segregationist. The best book dealing with civil rights in the Eisenhower administration is Robert F. Burk, *The Eisenhower Administration and Black Civil Rights* (1984). Works on Martin Luther

King include Stephen B. Oates, *Let the Trumpet Sound: The Life of Martin Luther King Jr.* (1982), and David L. Lewis, *King: A Biography* (1978). Books on the civil rights movement in the 1960s include David J. Garrow, *Protest at Selma: Martin Luther King Jr. and the Voting Rights Act of 1965* (1978); Charles E. Fager, *Selma 1965* (1985); John Dittmer, *Local People: The Struggle for Civil Rights in Mississippi* (1994); Doug MacAdam, *Freedom Summer* (1988); Dennis C. Dickerson, *Militant Mediator: Whitney M. Young* (1998); David L. Chapell, *Inside Agitators: White Southerners in the Civil Rights Movement* (1996); Malcolm X (with Alex Haley), *The Autobiography of Malcolm X* (1965), a classic; William L. Van Deburg, *New Day in Babylon: The Black Power Movement and American Culture, 1965–1975* (1992); Mark Stern, *Calculating Visions: Kennedy, Johnson, and Civil Rights* (1992); and Hugh Davis Graham, *The Civil Rights Era: Origins and Development of National Policy, 1960–1972* (1990).

On the Earl Warren Supreme Court, see J. Harvie Wilkinson, *From Brown to Bakke: The Supreme Court and School Integration, 1954–1978* (1980); David J. Armor, *Forced Justice: School Desegregation and the Law* (1995); Richard Kluger, *Simple Justice: The History of Brown v. Board of Education and Black America's Struggle for Equality* (1975), the most complete account of the landmark decision; and James T. Patterson, *Brown v. Board of Education: A Civil Rights Milestone and Its Troubled Legacy* (2001).

Indians are discussed in Donald Fixico, *Termination and Relocation: Federal Indian Policy, 1945–1970* (1986); Ronald Dewing, *Wounded Knee: The Meaning and Significance of the Second Incident* (1985); and Charles F. Wilkinson, *American Indians, Time, and the Law* (1987). Among studies of other minorities, Ronald Takaki, *A Different Mirror: A History of Multicultural America* (1993), is a good general work. Also see David G. Guttierrez, *Walls and Mirrors: Mexican Americans, Mexican Immigrants, and the Politics of Ethnicity* (1995); David M. Reimers, *Still the Golden Door: The Third World Comes to America* (1985); and Ronald Takaki, *Strangers from a Distant Shore: A History of Asian Americans* (1989).

Women's history is covered in William Chafe, *The Paradox of Change: American Women in the Twentieth Century* (1991), especially strong on the 1960s; Sara Evans, *Personal Politics: The Roots of Women's Liberation in the Civil Rights Movements and the New Left* (1978); Cynthia Harrison, *On Account of Sex: The Politics of Women's Issues, 1945–1968* (1988); two classics by Gerda Lerner, *The Majority Finds Its Past: Placing Women in History* (1979), and *The Creation of Patriarchy* (1986); and Lillian Faderman, *Odd Girls and Twilight Lovers: A History of Lesbian Life in 20th Century America* (1991).

On television, see James L. Baughman, *The Republic of Mass Culture: Filmmaking and Broadcasting in America since 1941* (1992); Eric Barnouw, *Tube of Plenty: The Evolution of American Television* (1990); Lynn Spigel, *Make Room for TV: Television and the Family Ideal in Postwar America* (1992); and Mary Ann Watson, *Defining Visions: Television and the American Experience since 1945* (1998). On music, David Szatmary, *Rockin' in Time: A Social History of Rock and Roll* (1987, 1991), is informative; a recent account is Glenn C. Altschuler, *All Shook Up: How Rock 'n' Roll Changed America* (2003). Greil Marcus, *Mystery Train* (3rd rev. ed., 1990), is the best book on the place of folk, blues, country, and rock in culture. Works on motion pictures include Nora Sayre, *Running Time: Films of the Cold War* (1982), and Christopher Nicholas, *Somewhere in the Night: Film Noir and the American City* (1997), a penetrating study of social anxiety manifested in films. Robert Hughes, *Shock of the New* (1980), is a brilliant analysis of modernism and the arts. For literature, see Richard Ruland and Malcolm Bradbury, *From Puritanism to Postmodernism: A History of American Literature* (1991), and Ann Charters, *Beats and Company: Portrait of a Literary Generation* (1986), a fine introduction to the key Beats.

On religion, see Martin E. Marty, *Modern American Religion*, vol. 3, *Under God, Indivisible, 1941–1960* (1996), and Robert Wuthnow, *The Restructuring of American Religion: Society and Faith since World War II* (1988). On technology, see Alan I. Marcus and Howard P. Segal, *Technology in America: A Brief History* (2nd ed., 1999); Howard P. Segal, *Future Imperfect: The Mixed Blessings of Technology in America* (1994); Ruth Schwartz Cowan, *A Social History of American Technology* (1997); and Alfred D. Chandler Jr., and James W. Cortada, eds., *A Nation Transformed by Information* (2000).

The Sixties

William L. O'Neill, *Coming Apart: An Informal History of America in the 1960s* (3rd ed., 1975), is a lively account of politics and culture, especially strong on the counterculture. Other studies include W. J. Rorabaugh, *Kennedy and the Promise of the Sixties* (2002); Allen Matusow, *The Unraveling of America: A History of Liberalism in the 1960s* (1984), strong on the economic assumptions of the New Frontier architects; David Farber, *The Age of Great Dreams: America in the 1960s* (1994); John Morton Blum, *Years of Discord: American Politics and Society, 1961–1974* (1991); Dave Steigerwald, *The Sixties and the End of Modern America* (1995); Terry Anderson, *The Sixties* (1999); the balanced David Burner, *Making*

Peace with the '60s (1996); and Maurice Isserman and Michael Kazin, *America Divided: The Civil War of the 1960s* (1999). On the counterculture, see Terry Anderson, *The Movement and the Sixties: Protest in America from Greensboro to Wounded Knee* (1995); Timothy Miller, *The Hippies and American Values* (1991); Margaret Cruikshank, *The Gay and Lesbian Liberation Movement in America* (1992); and James Miller, *"Democracy Is in the Streets": From Port Huron to the Siege of Chicago* (1987). For the generation that entered college in the 1960s, see Landon Y. Jones, *Great Expectations: America and the Baby Boom Generation* (1980), and Helen Lefkowitz Horowitz, *Campus Life* (1987).

On John F. Kennedy, two massive accounts by insiders are still useful, although they conceal his flaws: Arthur M. Schlesinger Jr., *A Thousand Days: John F. Kennedy in the White House* (1965), and Theodore C. Sorensen, *Kennedy* (1965). Robert Dallek, *An Unfinished Life: John F. Kennedy, 1917–1963* (2003), is an excellent scholarly study. James N. Giglio, *The Presidency of John F. Kennedy* (1991), is a detailed administrative history. Herbert S. Parmet, *Jack: The Struggle of John F. Kennedy* (1980), and *JFK: The Presidency of John F. Kennedy* (1983), are balanced. Thomas C. Reeves, *A Question of Character: A Life of John F. Kennedy* (1991), is a devastating critique, as is Seymour Hersh, *The Dark Side of Camelot* (1997). For exhaustive books on JFK's assassination, see Sylvia Meagher, *Accessories after the Fact: The Warren Commission, the Authorities, and the Report* (1967), and Gerald Posner, *Case Closed: Lee Harvey Oswald and the Assassination of JFK* (1993). On Kennedy's domestic policy, consult Irving Bernstein, *Promises Kept: John F. Kennedy's New Frontier* (1990). For general works on JFK's foreign policy, see Michael R. Beschloss, *The Crisis Years: Kennedy and Khrushchev, 1960–1963* (1991). Crises regarding Cuba are chronicled in Peter Wyden, *The Bay of Pigs* (1979); Trumball Higgins, *The Perfect Failure: Kennedy, Eisenhower, and the CIA at the Bay of Pigs* (1987); William J. Medland, *The Cuban Missile Crisis of 1962: Needless or Necessary?* (1988); Raymond L. Garthoff, *Reflections on the Cuban Missile Crisis* (rev. ed., 1989); James G. Blight, *On the Brink: Americans and Soviets Reexamine the Cuban Missile Crisis* (2nd ed., 1990); Mark J. White, *The Cuban Missile Crisis* (1996); focusing on major participants, and the documentary history, Mark J. White, ed., *The Kennedys and Cuba* (2000). On other topics, see Norman Gelb, *The Berlin Wall: Kennedy, Khrushchev and a Showdown in the Heart of Europe* (1986); Bernard J. Firestone, *The Quest for Nuclear Stability: John F. Kennedy and the Soviet Union* (1982); Gerard T. Rice, *The Bold Experiment: JFK's Peace Corps* (1986); and Richard D. Mahoney, *JFK: Ordeal in Africa* (1983).

Among multivolume works on Lyndon Johnson, see Robert Dallek, *Lone Star Rising: Lyndon Johnson and His Times, 1908–1960* (1991), and

Flawed Giant: Lyndon B. Johnson, 1960–1973 (1998); Robert A. Divine, *The Johnson Years,* especially vol. 3, *LBJ at Home and Abroad* (1994); and Robert Caro, *The Years of Lyndon B. Johnson: The Path to Power (1982), Means of Ascent* (1990), detailed yet vastly overdrawn in their criticism, and *Master of the Senate* (2002). Paul K. Conkin, *Big Daddy from the Pedernales: Lyndon Baines Johnson* (1986), is balanced, with keen insights. Vaughn D. Bornet, *The Presidency of Lyndon Johnson* (1983), is a fine study. Michael R. Beschloss, ed., *Taking Charge: The Johnson White House Tapes* (1997), is gleaned from recordings LBJ made of his meetings. For efforts to combat poverty, see James T. Patterson, *America's Struggle against Poverty, 1900–1980* (1981), and Greg J. Duncan, *Years of Poverty, Years of Plenty* (1984). For the rise of conservatism, consult George H. Nash, *The Conservative Intellectual Movement in America since 1945* (1976); Michael W. Miles, *The Odyssey of the American Right* (1980); Paul Gottfried, *The Conservative Movement* (1993); John Ehrman, *The Rise of Neoconservatism: Intellectuals and Foreign Affairs, 1945–1994* (1995); and Kurt Schuparra, *Triumph of the Right: The Rise of the California Conservative Movement, 1945–1966* (1998).

On LBJ's foreign policy, start with H. W. Brands Jr., *The Wages of Globalism: Lyndon Johnson and the Limits of American Power* (1994). Of the voluminous Vietnam War literature, the best single-volume histories are George Herring, *America's Longest War* (2nd ed., 1986), and Robert D. Schulzinger, *A Time for War: The United States and Vietnam, 1941–1975* (1997). See also the government study of the war, *The Pentagon Papers, Senator Gravel Edition* (1975); David Kaiser, *American Tragedy: Kennedy, Johnson and the Origins of the Vietnam War* (2000); and David Halberstam, *The Best and the Brightest* (1972), a journalistic account of policy makers. General histories of the war include Stanley Karnow, *Vietnam: A History* (1991); Marilyn Young, *The Vietnam Wars, 1945–1990* (1991); George Donelson Moss, *Vietnam: An American Ordeal* (3rd ed., 1998); Gerard DeGroot, *A Noble Cause* (1999); and the brief but comprehensive Patrick J. Hearden, *The Tragedy of Vietnam* (1991). On the Johnson administration's role, see Brian VanDeMark, *Into the Quagmire* (1991); George Herring, *LBJ and Vietnam: A Different Kind of War* (1994); and Lloyd Gardner, *Pay Any Price: Lyndon Johnson and the Wars for Vietnam* (1995). On the antiwar movement, see Charles DeBenedetti with Charles Chatfield, *An American Ordeal: The American Antiwar Movement of the Vietnam War* (1990); Tom Wells, *The War within: America's Battle over Vietnam* (1994); and Melvin Small, *Johnson, Nixon, and the Doves* (1988). Milton J. Bates, *The Wars We Took to Vietnam* (1996), is an imaginative cultural study of the war and American stereotypes.

An Era of Diversity, since 1969

Prologue

DIVERSITY BY race, ethnicity, class, and gender was a major motif in the United States in the last third of the twentieth century. Yet the Age of Diversity also refers to the vast array of consumer products, new directions in science, religion, and philosophy, the end of the Cold War, and the challenges from international terrorism that followed. It involves regionalism, localism, revamped relations between the states and federal government, holistic health, and new priorities. The millennium and the century ended, old problems remained, past troubles were vanquished, new ones arose, and the world paused to give thought to what it all meant.

Group consciousness became a major factor in politics, consumerism, and labor organizing. Racial issues focused not on voting rights or public accommodations, but on busing to achieve school desegregation and affirmative action to give minorities a competitive edge. Blacks achieved political victories, electing mayors in many large cities, yet ordinary blacks struggled to enter the middle class.

Women entered the workforce in increasing numbers. They made political and legal gains as well, winning the right to abortion under the 1973 *Roe v. Wade* Supreme Court decision. Abortion opponents, many of them women, mounted a sustained attack on *Roe*, seeking to overturn the ruling or to restrict it. The Christian right, which became a cohesive political force, was instrumental in defeating ratification of the Equal Rights Amendment in state legislatures. Paradoxically, polls showed that men were slightly more supportive of "women's issues" such as abortion and the ERA than women.

The United States remained the most religious nation in the Western world, with a higher percentage of those attending a church, temple, or mosque than any developed country. By the 1980s Americans, especially conservatives, became more passionate and public about their religion, which they applied to politics. A fault line developed between conservatives and liberals, with each attempting to define the cultural standards in which families, sexuality, government programs, and education functioned. Conservatives stood for tradition and continuity, conventional moral standards, and discipline. Liberals advocated change, tolerance, and flexible standards. The vice of conservatives was self-righteousness; the vice of liberals was hypocrisy; and each side was vulnerable to the other's vices. Most Americans, whether right-center or left-center, remained centrists, rejecting candidates such as Barry Goldwater and George McGovern whom they deemed outside the centrist boundaries.

Some aspects of diversity might be more accurately called "variety," such as the broad range of products and services available to consumers. Americans had more choices than before, which might have been a mixed blessing. Cable television premiered in the 1970s and offered a virtual infinity of choices, but there were times the average person could scan a hundred channels only to complain, "Nothing's on!" Computers, especially personal computers, revolutionized communication, yet provided avenues for fraud and the irony of falling in love with a person one had "met" on the computer screen. There was computer dating, even "computer sex." Jeeps and cars could climb mountains and exceed the speed limit by forty miles per hour, but they polluted the environment, guzzled gasoline, and contributed to injuries and deaths in traffic accidents. By comparison with modern vans and sports utility vehicles, the chrome-plated, tailed-finned gas-guzzlers of the 1950s seemed minuscule—and safer.

The sexual revolution accelerated. Men and women lived in coed college dormitories, with condom machines in the restrooms. Viagra, a pill that could cure male impotence, removed obstacles to sexual intercourse. Viagra was followed by a variety of competitors and sexual stimulants, some prescription drugs, others sold over the counter, still others on sale at health food stores. Meanwhile sexual harassment complaints proliferated. Adultery, and lying under oath to cover it up, nearly brought the collapse of Bill Clinton's presidency in the 1990s. The nuclear family disintegrated. Most dangerous was AIDS, a fatal sexually transmitted disease that shut down the victims' immune systems.

Purveyors of variety, or diversity, did not necessarily represent progress. In the marketplace, huge stores such as Wal-Mart crushed smaller competitors by offering a vast amount of affordable goods, often of mediocre quality. Service was often substandard. The slogan "The customer is always right" became a relic. In politics and culture, some leaders of racial and ethnic groups asserted that their followers were entitled to privileged positions not by dint of work or ability but by virtue of group membership—ironically, a claim that minorities had long resisted by the majority. Big cities were a major focus of life, and towns were often dismissed as dying. Yet small town values lived on and continued to be the molders of presidents.

Richard Nixon, who had sought the presidency his entire career, finally won it in 1968. During the first summer of his presidency, American astronauts walked on the Moon in the greatest voyage of discovery since the 1400s. On Earth, Nixon opened avenues to détente with the Soviet Union, traveled to Moscow and China, helped slow the arms race, and withdrew America from Vietnam. But the Watergate scandal, a tangle of deceit and ineptness, drove Nixon from office. The economy, affluent in the 1950s and 1960s, stumbled because of foreign competition, slow growth, and a loss of high-paying manufacturing jobs. Gerald Ford, Nixon's successor, pardoned the former president, ensuring he would not have to stand trial for Watergate. The pardon and the slumping economy contributed to Ford's loss to Jimmy Carter, a Washington outsider, peanut broker, and former Georgia governor. "All the legislation in the world can't fix what's wrong with America," the Georgian said. Carter had passion; he seethed integrity, yet he lacked the ability to inspire even as he called upon Americans to make sacrifices, especially in conserving energy, that would change their lifestyles. Carter's failure to cajole Congress into enacting major programs, the national humiliation in the Iran hostage crisis, and a failed effort to rescue the hostages doomed his performance to the lowest poll ratings in history. Yet Carter ventured boldly into the morass of Middle East politics and made major breakthroughs at the Camp David Summit. The economic mess of the 1970s was, however, enough to sink a battleship. Carter lost to former California Governor Ronald Reagan in 1980. He completed his life as possibly the most useful, most respected former president in history, arbitrating international disputes and monitoring elections, speaking out for human rights, building houses for the poor, writing numerous books on subjects from fishing to philosophy, winning a Nobel Peace Prize, and remaining the modest, religious man he had always been.

While Carter was too involved in the details of governing, Reagan was detached. He came to office with a handful of major objectives and accomplished most of them. Others, he delegated. He was neither an outstanding intellect nor a dunce. As a Hollywood actor he was famed for his memory; by the time he became president it was failing. The Iran-Contra scandal tainted his administration. Some considered him rigid and overly ideological. Yet if Reagan was not a great president, neither was he a mediocre one. He pushed the Soviets into an arms race they could not win, using a weapon no previous president had employed: the dollar. He was blunt in his assessment of Soviet communism, calling it an "Evil Empire." Many ordinary Americans had long believed this, but few politicians had dared say it publicly.

Having pilloried the Soviets in his first term, he bonded with their president, Mikhail Gorbachev, in his second, meeting with a Soviet leader at more summits than any previous president. He reached a major arms agreement on his terms. He set up the Soviets for the kill and lived to see the tumbling of the Berlin Wall and the implosion of the Soviet Union.

In domestic policy, Reagan slashed taxes, rebuilt the military, slowed the rate of the government bureaucracy, and produced nearly a decade of prosperity. Yet his tax cuts and defense increases produced a yawning deficit that saddled the nation with an albatross of debt. Still, Reagan's most important accomplishment was not in policy. He shifted the mainstream of politics rightward, inspired Americans, and lifted the malaise that had shrouded Jimmy Carter's America like a fog. He was a magnificent orator when reading from a script, the best of the Era of Diversity. His patriotic sentences were poetic in their simplicity and might have seemed corny, except that he really meant them.

Reagan's successor, his vice president, George Bush, emphasized foreign policy. He invaded Panama and deposed dictator Manuel Noriega, a onetime ally who had become a drug-corrupted pariah. Bush led an American-dominated coalition to victory over Iraq in the Persian Gulf War, rekindling national unity, and presided over triumph in the Cold War. Communism cracked first in Eastern Europe, where the Berlin Wall was torn down by Berliners. Next the Soviet Union, crushed by an unworkable economy and fragmented by ethnic demands for independence, dissolved. In the United States the end of the Cold War was not greeted with the euphoria that might have been expected. Americans, suffering a recession, groaning under deficits, elected Democrat Bill Clinton in 1992.

Clinton stumbled early in his first term: his proposal for national health insurance fizzled, and in 1994 Republicans won control of the House of Representatives for the first time in forty years. But Clinton outflanked the GOP with spending policies that led to budget surpluses and helped make the 1990s the most prosperous decade in American history. Reelected in 1996, he became the first two-term Democratic president since FDR and weathered accusations of marital infidelity, illegal campaign contributions, a questionable real estate deal—and Republicans' vote to impeach him. In diplomacy, Clinton attempted to broker peace in the Mideast and Northern Ireland, aid Russia to build a capitalist economy, and end ethnic violence in Bosnia and Kosovo. Public approval of Clinton's job performance (as opposed to approval of him personally) was high. Despite the satisfaction with administration policies, though, his vice president, Al Gore, lost a close decision to Bush's son, Texas Governor George W. Bush, in the 2000 election. Gore won the popular vote but lost the Electoral College, where Bush's victory in Florida was decisive.

Diversity means many things. Since the assassination of the century's first president in 1901 to the horror of September 11, 2001, technology had abetted killing, leaving human problems unsolved. In technical terms America had traveled light years, had become part of a diverse global community, emerging from an insular, provincial one. Yet many things, good and evil, remained remarkably unchanged. As Americans turned the page on the millennium, the next page read not "The End," but "Chapter Two."

Time Line

An Era of Diversity, 1969–Present

July 20, 1969 Neil Armstrong and Edwin "Buzz" Aldrin Jr. become first humans to walk on moon.

July 1, 1971 Twenty-Sixth Amendment lowering voting age from twenty-one to eighteen ratified.

June 17, 1972 Police arrest five burglars in Watergate break-in.

January 22, 1973 Supreme Court legalizes abortion in *Roe v. Wade.*

January 27, 1973 United States and North Vietnam approve Paris Peace Agreement, under which American forces withdraw from Vietnam War.

October 10, 1973 Vice President Spiro Agnew, facing charges of corruption, resigns.

August 8, 1974 Nixon resigns, taking effect the following day, and Vice President Gerald R. Ford becomes president.

September 8, 1974 Ford pardons Nixon for any offenses committed as president.

April 29, 1975 South Vietnam falls to North Vietnamese.

November 4, 1979 Iranian students take members of U.S. Embassy staff hostage.

June 5, 1981 Acquired immune deficiency syndrome (AIDS) is reported by the Centers for Disease Control.

January 28, 1986 Space shuttle *Challenger* explodes.

November 25, 1986 Iran-Contra scandal breaks.

January 16, 1991 Persian Gulf War begins.

April 19, 1995 Bombing of Oklahoma City federal building kills 168.

December 19, 1998 House of Representatives votes to impeach President Bill Clinton.

February 18, 1999 Senate acquits Clinton of charges.

December 12, 2000 George W. Bush named President by the Supreme Court.

September 11, 2001 More than three thousand die in terrorist attacks on United States; World Trade Towers destroyed.

January 29, 2002 Bush says United States will fight preemptive wars against countries that develop weapons of mass destruction.

January 28, 2003 Space shuttle *Columbia* explodes.

March 19, 2003 U.S.–led coalition goes to war against Iraq.

December 13, 2003 Saddam Hussein captured.

November 2, 2004 George Bush defeats John Kerry for president.

November 11, 2004 Palestine Liberation (PLO) leader Yasir Arafat dies.

January 9, 2005 Mahmoud Abbas elected new PLO leader.

January 30, 2005 Large number of Iraqis turn out for free elections for Parliament.

February 10, 2005 North Korea announces it has nuclear weapons.

April 2005 Syria withdraws its troops from Lebanon.

May 31, 2005 W. Mark Felt revealed as "Deep Throat" in Watergate scandal.

CHAPTER SEVEN

The Nixon Years, 1969–1974

FEW PREDICTED that out of the ashes of the 1960s would arise Richard Nixon, whose political career included paradox in abundance. Admired and respected by millions, he had few personal friends and trusted barely a handful of people. Insecure and shy, he succeeded in a profession that rewards gregarious personalities. Detested by liberals, he was, relatively speaking, the most liberal Republican president of the twentieth century. An archetypal anticommunist, he became the architect of détente, a relaxation of tensions with the communist powers. He practiced the politics of division, but during his presidency, the race riots that had torn the nation ended and he accomplished much for civil rights—advances that were unintentional. He introduced humane and innovative domestic programs, yet is little remembered for them. Rather, Nixon is remembered for his bold opening to China and for his disgrace in Watergate, a tragedy that has the irony of a spider caught in his own web. Nixon's presidency bound together the strands of the age of diversity, metaphorically bundled in a time and man.

Richard Nixon

A native Californian, Nixon was born in Yorba Linda and grew up in Whittier, the son of Quaker parents who lived in near poverty and required him to work hard and be frugal. His mother, Hannah, was long-suffering yet rarely showed affection toward her children. Nixon's father, Frank, worked hard and had a violent temper. Losing two brothers to tuberculosis, Nixon grew up tough and determined, with a taste for the physical combat of football and the verbal sparring of debate in school, but deprived of love. After graduating from Whittier College, where he was a star student, he enrolled at Duke University Law School in Durham, North Carolina, impressed his peers by studying for long hours, and graduated third in his class. Briefly he searched for a Wall Street job, then returned to Whittier to practice law, met Thelma "Pat" Ryan, and married her.

In 1942, Nixon joined the Office of Price Administration, acquired a contempt for bureaucracy he never lost, resigned to enlist in the Navy, and served an uneventful tour of duty in the South Pacific. Then a group of Whittier businessmen asked him to run for the House of Representatives against the liberal incumbent, Jerry Voorhis. Nixon won a bitter 1946 campaign in which he accused Voorhis of being sympathetic to communism. He served two terms in the House, earning a reputation as an anticommunist by pursuing accused spy Alger Hiss, and on the strength of that renown, won an acrimonious campaign for the Senate in 1950. The Senate was a springboard to two terms as vice president under Eisenhower, from 1953 to 1961. But then came two successive difficult defeats, to John F. Kennedy for the presidency in 1960 and to Edmund G. "Pat" Brown for the California governorship in 1962. Nixon's heart was never truly in the latter campaign; he vowed he would not seek political office again. But he could not step away from politics for good, as he moved to New York, practiced law on Wall Street, and made his comeback in 1968.

In seniority, experience, and savvy, Nixon was the nation's senior politician, skilled at the craft he found unnatural and unenjoyable. From politics he had taken the bitter lessons that winning is all that matters and that he must destroy his enemies before they destroyed him. Since the 1952 campaign, when the alleged political slush fund that prompted his "Checkers speech" came to light, Nixon believed liberal newspapers were against him because he was a successful conservative. Consequently, he cultivated television, especially after his first 1960 debate with Kennedy, and ran slick TV campaigns in 1968 and 1972. Image matters more than substance in politics, Nixon and his aides sadly concluded.

In governance, too, Nixon's advisers reinforced the anger, paranoia, and the obsession with secrecy that marked the administration and helped defeat it. Chief of staff H. R. Haldeman ruthlessly limited access to Nixon and made enemies by insisting that the president's time could not be wasted. Vice President Spiro Agnew relished his public role of attacking young people, Democrats, and the press. Agnew's savage lyrics struck deep chords among the group that Nixon dubbed "the great silent majority," the white blue-collar workers and southerners who supported George Wallace in the 1968 election. They opposed affirmative action, school bus-

CULTURAL DIPLOMACY
Richard M. Nixon meets with Elvis Presley in December 1970.
(National Archives)

ing, abortion, recreational drug use, Vietnam War protesters, pornography, and "soft-on-crime" liberals.

Such inner workings of the administration belied an early theme of Nixon's presidency: his attempt to bring the country together after the tumult of the 1960s. "We cannot learn from each other until we stop shouting at one another," he told Americans in his first inaugural address. Aiding Nixon in his quest, astronauts walked on the Moon in the summer of 1969, fulfilling John Kennedy's wish that Americans reach Earth's satellite by the end of the decade. The lunar module *Eagle* from the *Apollo 11* rocket landed on the Sea of Tranquillity, and on July 20, Astronaut Neil Armstrong set foot on the lunar surface, informing an international television audience, "That's one small step for man, one giant leap for mankind." Armstrong and colleague Edwin E. Buzz Aldrin Jr. left an American flag and a plaque telling of their arrival "in peace for all mankind." Their feat foreshadowed other breakthroughs in space in the decades to come, among them longer Moon missions, rockets that brought back pictures from other planets, and space stations.

Fighting Inflation and Crime

Nixon served his tenure under the shadow of inflation, a holdover from the Johnson administration. The rate was 5 percent at the start of his presidency. At first he cut federal spending and prodded the Federal Reserve Board to raise interest rates. Unemployment rose and incubated a recession, yet inflation persisted. Now, wanting to end the recession more than curb inflation, Nixon reversed course on government expenditures in early 1971, proposing a Keynesian unbalanced budget. August brought more bad news, the first major trade deficit since 1890, which prompted another shift for Nixon. He imposed a 10 percent tariff on imports and said the value of the dollar would float, according to market conditions. In the most surprising change, Nixon imposed wage and price controls. These measures improved the economy, curtailing inflation and the trade deficit in time to help Nixon's 1972 reelection campaign. After he was inaugurated to a second term, Nixon changed directions. He ended the controls in favor of "voluntary" guidelines. Inflation rose to 9 percent.

Next, Nixon proposed a new approach to welfare reform. Aides drafted the most ambitious welfare proposal of the Era of Diversity, the Family Assistance Plan (FAP). Paradoxically devised by a conservative White House, it was more generous than anything offered by Lyndon Johnson. The Great Society's labyrinth of social programs would be replaced by direct cash payments. Whatever the causes of poverty, Nixon reasoned, the solution was to pay poor people a living. This was direct, simple, and actually less expensive. Each family of four would receive $1,600 plus $800 for food stamps. Able-bodied recipients except women with young children would be required to work or enroll in job training. The plan never passed Congress. Democrats, who controlled Congress, called it stingy and did not want credit to go to a Republican president. Many Republicans disliked the idea of paying people who did not work. Similarly, Nixon's plan for national health insurance faltered.

The Family Assistance Plan was part of a strategy Nixon called the "New Federalism." At its heart was "revenue sharing." Federal money was disbursed to the states and cities to use as they determined. Decision making would be decentralized. Nixon retained and even expanded some Great Society programs, including the Job Corps and housing subsidies. He supported a constitutional amendment lowering the voting age to eighteen. Nixon promoted the most progressive environmental program to that time. It included creation of the Environmental Protection Agency, the Clean Air Act of 1970, regulation of oil spill cleanups, and laws directed against pesticide contamination of water and noise pollution. The administration created the Occupational Safety and Health Administration (OSHA) to ensure job safety.

Nixon addressed middle-class concern about domestic crime and also targeted perceived domestic subversion. The FBI illegally wiretapped some leaders of the civil rights and antiwar movements. The CIA kept files on domestic radicals and infiltrated their organizations. Fearing leftist opposition to the government, Nixon established a group called "the Plumbers" to plug leaks. Among them were former FBI agent G. Gordon Liddy and former CIA operative E. Howard Hunt. An "enemies list" was compiled of persons to be harassed by federal agencies.

Nixon's ambition to impose "law and order" extended to his conservative nominees to the Supreme Court. His first two nominees, both southern conservatives, Clement Haynsworth and G. Harrold Carswell, were rejected. Northern liberals considered both men too far Right, and Carswell was said to have a second-rate mind. When he turned north for a conservative nominee, Nixon fared better, winning confirmation of federal Judge Harry Blackmun of Minnesota. In 1971 two more conservatives secured confirmation, Lewis F. Powell, of Virginia, a moderate, and William Rehnquist, a hard-liner who later became chief justice.

The Burger court proved moderate. It allowed the *New York Times* to publish the classified *Pentagon Papers*, accelerated school desegregation, and ordered Nixon to turn over Watergate-related presidential tapes to Special Prosecutor Leon Jaworski. Most important, in *Roe v. Wade* (1973) it legalized abortion in the months of pregnancy before a fetus could survive outside the womb.

Under Dwight Eisenhower, Vice President Nixon had been a leading advocate of civil rights. As the movement migrated leftward, he remained a supporter of civil rights, yet was less enthusiastic. Ironically, in a statistical sense, civil rights made great progress during his presidency. Nixon enforced court decisions and laws he personally opposed, such as school busing. At the beginning of his term, 68 percent of the African American children in the South attended segregated schools; by the end of his tenure only 8 percent did. To help blacks, Nixon created a program to lend money to start businesses. He became an early advocate of affirmative action, requiring contractors who worked for the government to design plans for hiring minorities. Neither did his Supreme Court roll back civil rights gains; in fact, it advanced them.

Emotionally, Nixon was most comfortable with white males, yet he adjusted to the changes that diversity brought to his times. He appointed more women to midlevel government positions than his predecessors. Yet there were none in the cabinet or the White House inner circle. Nixon

AMERICAN INDIAN
MILITANCY
The takeover of Wounded
Knee, a poster showing
Bobby Onco, a Kiowa,
and member of the
American Indian
Movement, holding
up a rifle.
(Library of Congress)

endorsed the proposed Equal Rights Amendment yet did not campaign for it. He opposed abortion as a means of birth control. The president enforced the law denying federal aid to schools and colleges practicing sex discrimination. Nixon insisted that the Civil Rights Commission enforce such requirements diligently and that child-care expenses become tax deductible when both parents worked.

The administration compiled a credible record in Indian affairs. Nixon broke with termination in favor of a program of enlightened self-determination and autonomy for tribes. The president appointed Louis R. Bruce, a Native American, as commissioner of Indian affairs and named Indians to the Bureau of Indian Affairs bureaucracy. The White House settled several claims against the government on terms that were generous to tribes, and the 1975 Indian Self-Determination and Educational Assistance Act was passed because of what the president had set in motion. Providing for direct negotiations between the tribes and the government to administer programs that the bureau formerly directed, the law was seen as the most important Indian-related law in more than forty years. Tribal fishing rights became contentious in the 1960s and 1970s. Sometimes whites staged violent protests, yet the courts usually favored the tribes. Native Americans grew assertive, emulating the militance of the Black Power movement. They occupied Alcatraz Island in San Francisco Bay, seized and trashed the offices of the Bureau of Indian Affairs and captured the village of Wounded Knee, site of the last major massacre of Native Americans. The White House responded calmly rather than punitively to the incidents.

Global Change: Détente and the Yom Kippur War

Nixon considered foreign affairs more important than domestic policy. The greatest presidents had drawn at least part of their reputation from international events. The president also had a freer hand in foreign policy; the security apparatus was less wieldly than Congress. Further, the minority party could initiate change, to some degree, without majority consensus, except for negotiating treaties. Nixon liked secrecy and surprises; he was skilled at intuiting what made foreign leaders tick; and he was a pragmatist. He wanted détente, especially with the Soviet Union and China, arms control, and an end to the Vietnam War. Henry Kissinger, his national security adviser, had a fine mind, a Harvard professorship, and like Nixon, an appreciation for intrigue. He exuded charm, talked tough, and got along with liberals. His colossal ego and desire for credit clashed with similar qualities in Nixon. The press debated whether Kissinger was the genius behind Nixon or Nixon the genius behind Kissinger. Although both men had fertile minds and were risk takers, Nixon devised the strategy, which Kissinger implemented.

Nixon was an anticommunist on principle, yet he believed in defeating the communists with finesse. Temporarily, he was content to lower tensions rather than overpower communism with force. Still, he prided himself on decisiveness, as did Kissinger. The president knew many communist rulers personally, they respected each other, and they had a common interest in survival. Nixon also believed he excelled at crisis management because of his experience under Eisenhower, his friendship with world leaders, and his extensive reading on foreign policy. For the most part, he did not intend to bully or be bullied. So long as he chained his temper and throttled the dark side of his personality, he might achieve this.

If creeping communism was anywhere apparent, it was in Cuba, the island ninety miles from American shores pointed like a dagger at Florida.

In 1962 John Kennedy had brought the world to the brink of nuclear war to keep missiles out of Cuba. In September 1970 American surveillance planes photographed a Soviet naval base being expanded to accommodate submarines carrying nuclear weapons. Nixon did not indulge in public brinkmanship, yet persuaded the Soviets to back down without losing face.

In Chile, the administration was more heavy-handed. In November 1970 Salvador Allende, a socialist allied with the Chilean Communist Party, came to power. Allende nationalized, with compensation, the property of major American companies such as Anaconda Copper and International Telephone and Telegraph. The United States suspended aid and loans to Chile and the CIA provided $10 million to forces opposing Allende. These actions helped the anti-Allende Chileans stage a coup that overthrew Allende in September 1973. Allende died in the coup, either by suicide or at the hand of revolutionaries. He was succeeded by General Augusto Pinochet, who established a repressive regime recognized by the United States.

Meanwhile, on the Asian subcontinent, Muslim Pakistan sparred with Hindu India over one-half of the nation of Pakistan. Pakistan was divided between eastern and western provinces, with India between. In 1972 East Pakistan seceded and proclaimed the nation of Bangladesh. Supported by India, it gained independence. The Nixon administration was divided, the State Department favoring India and the White House covertly tilting toward Pakistan, a Cold War ally. This split drove India into the arms of the Soviets, with whom India signed an alliance in 1972. The Soviet Union and India became major trade partners.

In the Era of Diversity, no nation was more diverse, and more mysterious to the West, than China, the world's most populous country. Nixon hoped the alliance between the communist superpowers might be pried apart by a determined finesse diplomat such as himself. China was an enormous potential trading partner, and Nixon saw trade and diplomatic avenues as the routes to cracking the cocoon that encased the communist giant. By normalizing relations with China while simultaneously practicing détente with the Soviet Union, the United States, as the uncommitted superpower, could wield the balance of power. This meant walking a diplomatic tightrope, which Nixon was willing to do. Détente would become a tripod, with the United States the base. Without the base, the other two sides would dangle.

Shortly after Nixon took office, the mating dance with China began. Nixon eased trade and travel restrictions. The Chinese invited, and thrashed, an American ping-pong team. Nixon erased the twenty-one year trade embargo. The UN expelled Taiwan and seated Mainland China on the Security Council. Then Nixon announced he would visit China in February 1972, an election year. He was the first president to go there since

DÉTENTE IN BEIJING
Nixon shakes hands with China's Mao Zedong in February 1972.
(National Archives)

Ulysses S. Grant in 1879. Nixon visited the Great Wall, talked with communist leader Mao Zedong and Prime Minister Zhou Enlai (Chou En-Lai), and conceded that the Chinese themselves must settle the fate of Taiwan. The two nations agreed to increase trade and normalize diplomatic relations. Formal diplomatic recognition did not come until 1979, under the administration of Jimmy Carter.

Détente with China enabled Nixon to negotiate from strength when he approached the Soviet Union. Like the Chinese, the Soviets were interested in trade and also in limitations of nuclear arms. For both sides, the weapons race had grown expensive and had reached the point of overkill. Nixon resumed talks on the Strategic Arms Limitation Treaty (SALT) that had begun under Lyndon Johnson and consummated the deal at a summit with Soviet President Leonid Brezhnev in Moscow in May 1972. The leaders also completed work on an Antiballistic Missile (ABM) Treaty. SALT set ceilings on the number of submarine-launched ballistic missiles and intercontinental ballistic missiles (ICBMs). The ABM pact limited each nation to protecting its capital. Nixon and Brezhnev also reached trade agreements: the Soviets committed to purchase $722 million of American grain for each of the next three years. Nixon hosted Brezhnev at Washington for a second summit in June 1973. At a third summit in Moscow during June 1974, the leaders discussed a SALT II treaty. By this time Nixon had been weakened by Watergate and lacked the credibility to make binding commitments.

At the first Moscow summit, Brezhnev warned of possible war in the Middle East, yet Nixon believed the Soviet leader overestimated the danger. Brezhnev said that Egypt and Syria were determined to retake territory seized by Israel in the Six-Day War of 1967. He suggested that the United States and the Soviet Union impose a settlement to preempt war. Brezhnev's intelligence reports were sound. On October 6, 1973, the Egyptians and Syrians struck. It was Yom Kippur, the Day of Atonement, the holiest day on the Jewish calendar. The Egyptians retook part of the Sinai Desert, and in the East, Syria drove Israel from the strategic Golan Heights. Well supplied with Soviet arms, the Arabs had never shown such military prowess nor such unity in their wars with Israel.

Israel had stockpiled weapons and ammunition for a three- or four-day war, yet this one seemed destined to last weeks. On October 13, the United States airlifted $2 billion worth of sophisticated weapons to Israel. Fortified, the Israelis counterattacked two days later, seizing all the territory they had lost and more. The Egyptian army was surrounded and in danger of annihilation when Washington and Moscow arranged a cease-fire. Meanwhile, on October 17, the Arab oil producers, united as the Organization of Petroleum Exporting Countries (OPEC), declared an embargo against the United States and its allies, leading to fuel shortages and inflated petroleum prices. Oil rose from $2.60 to $10 per barrel. To end the energy crisis and counter Soviet influence with Arabs, Nixon sent Kissinger on two years of "shuttle diplomacy," flying back and forth among Middle Eastern capitals, starting in November 1973. He helped arrange a cease-fire, Israeli withdrawal from lands captured in the recent war, and an end to the oil embargo, in May 1974. Nixon made a goodwill trip to Egypt, Saudi Arabia, and Syria in June 1974. A year earlier the Egyptians had ejected their Soviet military advisers and aligned with the Americans.

Withdrawal from Vietnam

North Vietnamese leader Ho Chi Minh died in 1969, yet the war in Vietnam went on. In America, the antiwar movement steamed ahead like a locomotive at full throttle. Nixon, having watched the war humiliate

Lyndon Johnson, realized he would be a one-term president unless he could defuse the issue. He decided to expand a policy begun late in LBJ's term: Vietnamization. American troops would be phased out and the fighting turned over to the South Vietnamese. The latter would be forged into an effective force with American training, weapons, and air and sea support. At home, Nixon dealt with the most divisive issue, the draft. First he devised a lottery, which provided some advance knowledge of the odds of being drafted. In 1972 he stopped sending draftees to Vietnam unless they volunteered. In 1973 the draft was abolished in favor of an all-volunteer army. These changes enabled Nixon to cut the number of American troops from more than five hundred thousand to less than thirty thousand.

To keep the pressure on, buying time for Vietnamization to work, American airpower pounded the North. The president secretly bombed supply routes in Cambodia and Laos. Early in 1970 North Vietnam infiltrated more soldiers into Cambodia to support the communist Khmer Rouge and make the country a staging ground for attacks on neighboring South Vietnam. Nixon reacted by ordering an American–South Vietnamese invasion of Cambodia in April, which killed two thousand North Vietnamese and destroyed several months' worth of enemy supplies but failed to locate North Vietnamese headquarters.

As American casualties declined, so did the antiwar movement. Yet each temporary escalation, such as the invasion of Cambodia, brought it roaring back to life, sometimes with tragic consequences. On May 2, 1970, Ohio National Guardsmen were sent to restore order at Kent State University after students burned down the Reserve Officer Training Corps building. On May 4, the troops panicked and shot into a crowd, killing four students and wounding nine. Ten days after the Ohio shootings, two died and twelve were hurt when state police fired into a dormitory at Jackson State College in Mississippi. Demonstrations erupted nationwide and seventy-five schools closed before the end of the academic year.

Escalations and protests continued in 1971. In January Congress repealed the Gulf of Tonkin Resolution. In February, American airpower supported South Vietnamese forces in an invasion of Laos to sever the Ho Chi Minh Trail, over which North Vietnam transported men and munitions. Initially the South Vietnamese fought well, yet when North Vietnam counterattacked, they fled in panic, some clinging to the skids of U.S. helicopters. Another blow struck the White House in June, when the *New York Times* began publishing the *Pentagon Papers*, a secret study of the Vietnam conflict that chronicled a record of government deception about American involvement. The papers, which former Pentagon analyst Daniel Ellsberg stole from the government and gave to the *Times*, revealed no information that discredited the Nixon administration; it ended before Nixon took office. Still, the president worried that other secrets might be published and that the papers' release weakened the security of government. The Justice Department obtained a court order against further publication. Appealing to the Supreme Court, the *Times* argued that the First Amendment prohibited prior restraints on the press, and the justices agreed, lifting the injunction. Infuriated, Nixon had the Justice Department indict Ellsberg for theft and spying and put "the Plumbers" on the case. Hunt and Liddy broke into the Los Angeles office of Ellsberg's psychiatrist in search of information that might prove him unstable. In 1973 a judge dismissed all charges against Ellsberg after it was disclosed that "the Plumbers" had burglarized the psychiatrist's office and had tried to bribe the trial judge by offering to name him FBI director.

By the election year of 1972 Nixon had achieved his objective of defusing Vietnam as an election issue. A settlement seemed possible because of his closer ties with the Soviet Union and China, which wanted American friendship and technical aid more than a communist South Vietnam. Best of all, while the two Vietnams battled, American casualties fell from three hundred weekly in 1968 to twenty-six weekly in 1971. In the last five months of 1972 casualties averaged only four per week. American troops in the field, aware that their efforts would soon be washed away, struggled merely to survive until their tour of duty ended. There were racial tensions, drug abuse, and "fragging"—the killing of officers by soldiers. Worse yet were massacres of civilians. As early as March 1968, army troops under the command of Lieutenant William Calley had murdered nearly three hundred and fifty women, children, and old men at the village of My Lai.

With the American presence in Vietnam declining and U.S. home front support weakening in 1972, the North Vietnamese launched their biggest offensive in Cambodia and South Vietnam, marshaling tanks and artillery. Nixon responded with bombing of the North and Cambodia and with the mining of North Vietnamese ports. Air and naval power stopped the advance and helped lead to a breakthrough in the Paris peace talks, which had been at a four-year impasse. Kissinger and North Vietnamese diplomat Le Duc Tho reached an agreement to withdraw all remaining U.S. troops, return American prisoners of war, and permit North Vietnamese soldiers to stay in the South. "Peace is at hand," Kissinger announced shortly before the 1972 election. But South Vietnamese President Nguyen Van Thieu balked over the communists' key demand, the provision letting North Vietnamese forces remain in the South. Concessions made to satisfy Thieu required offsetting concessions to satisfy the North. Kissinger broke off talks in hopes of bombing North Vietnam into agreement, and from

December 18 through 30, planes saturated the North in the most intense bombardment of the war. This "Christmas bombing" led the North Vietnamese to resume talks, and differences were worked out in a few days. Nixon promised Thieu that if he would sign the treaty, the United States would keep arming the South and employ airpower if the North violated the proposed cease-fire. If South Vietnam did not sign, Washington might terminate aid and sign the treaty alone. All parties signed the accord on January 27, 1973. Five days earlier Lyndon Johnson had died.

Some questioned whether a similar treaty could have been signed in 1969, averting four years of bloody war. The chief concession Nixon obtained during that time was North Vietnamese willingness to negotiate an agreement with Thieu still in power. Nixon believed he had given Thieu an opportunity to survive and had obtained an honorable peace. More realistic, Kissinger negotiated to provide a "decent interval" between the American withdrawal and a North Vietnamese conquest of the South. Nixon's promise to intervene if North Vietnam violated the terms proved worthless after his resignation. Congress curbed the power of future presidents by passing the 1973 War Powers Act. Presidents must notify Congress within forty-eight hours of troop deployment, and congressional approval is required to keep them in a war zone more than sixty days.

America's longest war ended in its most humiliating defeat. Although some believed the United States had no interest in the distant land, the war was fought in the context of the Cold War policy of containment. It was believed the Cold War was a zero sum game in which the superpower that accumulated and retained the most allies would triumph. Some 58,000 Americans died and 300,000 were wounded. In monetary terms it cost the nation $150 billion. Yet America's human losses paled in comparison to the other combatants. The South Vietnamese lost 184,000 killed and North Vietnam and the Vietcong a staggering 927,000. Ideologically driven, the North persevered despite these casualties. Yet the Vietnamese did not get the worker's paradise Ho Chi Minh had promised. What they got was "boat people"—desperate peasants and government officials fleeing communism, packed into flimsy boats which often sank, or were rejected by countries at which they sought asylum and reeducation camps in the south. Two dominos fell, Laos and Cambodia, the latter subject to massive genocide by the dictator Pol Pot. For the United States, the war was a lesson in humility. The military would be chained by the leash of public opinion for much of the remainder of the Cold War. Just as World War II had been the formative event of their fathers' coming of age, the baby boom generation was shaped by the failure in Vietnam. History, and historians, are more forgiving of winners than of losers.

Watergate

If ever there seemed a sure bet for reelection into a second term as president, it was Richard Nixon in 1972. He had neutralized the two most dangerous issues, Vietnam and the economy, although economic problems would return with a vengeance after the election. The Democrats nominated one of their weaker candidates, an antiwar senator from South Dakota, George McGovern. Liberal on economic and social issues, McGovern appeared indecisive after defending, then dismissing his choice for vice president, Senator Thomas Eagleton of Missouri. Learning that Eagleton had undergone electric shock therapy for stress, McGovern backed him to the hilt initially, then ordered him off the ticket. After several prominent Democrats refused second place, McGovern lined up former Peace Corps Director Sargent Shriver. George Wallace posed a threat on Nixon's right flank, yet was paralyzed in an assassination attempt and forced out of the race.

The only thing that could defeat Nixon was his own insecurity and in the long run it did. Long before polls revealed that Nixon had a lock on the White House, Nixon and his henchmen began a series of unethical and illegal acts that turned a magnificent victory at the polls into a devastating disgrace. Attorney General John Mitchell resigned to head the Committee to Re-Elect the President (CREEP): Democrats delighted in the acronym. The committee raised millions of dollars and poured some of the money into "dirty tricks" and domestic espionage on the Democrats. A bigger waste of money could hardly be imagined. Among various sordid ventures, the most historically significant one was an attempt to wiretap the Democratic National Committee headquarters at the Watergate office and apartment complex. Several attempts were made and bungled, especially the final one when the burglars were arrested. Some were traced to the White House, and they were paid hush money for their silence in court. Nixon professed ignorance, as did others at the White House. Nixon probably did not have prior knowledge of the break-in and was doubtless too savvy to authorize it. Yet almost from the beginning, he helped mastermind the cover-up and thereby broke the law. His main concern at the time was to contain the evidence of White House involvement until after the election.

The election was a Republican landslide. Nixon and Spiro Agnew were elected to a second term with almost 61 percent of the popular vote, second only to Johnson's percentage of the popular vote in 1964. They carried every state but Massachusetts and the District of Columbia. Nixon won 520 electoral votes to McGovern's 17, the greatest electoral rout since FDR's in 1936. Nixon was on top of the world; it was a long way down.

Nixon hoped Watergate would evaporate after the election, but his situation became grimmer. The Watergate scandal began to unravel when the five men who had broken into the Democrats' offices were caught, convicted after the election, and threatened with long prison terms. U.S. District Judge John J. Sirica said he would offer sentence reductions if the burglars informed on their superiors, and James McCord broke ranks to talk with prosecutors. Opening the floodgates on the administration, McCord admitted that top White House aides had known of plans for the break-in and said that the defendants, who claimed they had acted on their own, perjured themselves during the trial. McCord revealed the White House pressured him and other defendants to plead guilty and remain silent.

The Watergate investigation exploded onto the front pages of major dailies. *Washington Post* reporters Bob Woodward and Carl Bernstein published new revelations almost daily, relying on confidential informants. Their most important informant, known as "Deep Throat," remained secret until 2005, when he was revealed to be W. Mark Felt, second in charge at the FBI. In 1973 a Senate committee chaired by the folksy Sam Ervin of North Carolina opened hearings. Public pressure forced Nixon to allow Attorney General Elliott Richardson to appoint a special prosecutor. Richardson appointed his former law professor at Harvard, Archibald Cox, a Kennedy Democrat. Nixon hoped to head off the investigations by firing his chief counsel, John Dean, and accepting the resignations of his closest aides, Bob Haldeman and John Ehrlichman. Had anyone been willing to take the blame, the president might have been saved, but loyalty to Nixon proved thin. The Ervin committee, as it heard witnesses, uncovered skullduggery unrelated to Watergate, called the "White House Horrors," which cast doubt on the president's credibility. Still, there was no "smoking gun" pointing to the president. The committee's ranking minority member, Senator Howard Baker of Tennessee, summed up the issue they sought to resolve: "What did the president know and when did he know it?"

There was no direct eyewitness testimony, yet the committee stumbled across something better. White House aide Alexander Butterfield testified that the president had secretly taped almost every conversation in the Oval Office. Because the tapes were voice activated, the president soon forgot about them and talked normally, much to his later regret. When Cox subpoenaed the tapes Nixon refused to give them up on the grounds of executive privilege, and Nixon ordered Richardson to fire him. Richardson refused, as did his subordinate. Finally Solicitor General Robert Bork wielded the ax. The affair was called the "Saturday Night Massacre."

His credibility further strained, Nixon allowed the appointment of a new special prosecutor, Leon Jaworski, a distinguished Texas lawyer.

Jaworski proved as aggressive about getting the tapes as Cox. The House Judiciary Committee began hearings to impeach Nixon. Meanwhile, Vice President Agnew stepped from the shadows into the limelight. Agnew was indicted for accepting bribes and kickbacks while governor of Maryland and vice president. He pleaded "no contest," resigned the vice presidency and paid a $10,000 fine. For the first time, the provisions of the Twenty-Fifth Amendment, which allowed a president to appoint a vice president when the office was vacant, were invoked. Nixon, passing over controversial nominees, nominated the friendly, uncontroversial U.S. Representative Gerald R. Ford of Michigan, who was confirmed.

The issue of the presidential tapes continued to plague Nixon. Still refusing to turn over the originals, yet unwisely failing to destroy them, he issued edited transcripts. The transcripts were replete with omissions, typographical errors, and profanity described as "expletive deleted." The published transcripts became instant best sellers. Still, the Judiciary Committee and Jaworski appealed to the Supreme Court to order Nixon to provide the originals. In a 9-0 ruling in *United States v. Nixon*, the justices, many of them Nixon appointees, ruled that he must do so. Meanwhile, the Judiciary Committee voted three articles of impeachment: abuse of power by using the government to harass political enemies; contempt of Congress for refusing to honor a subpoena demanding the tapes; and obstruction of justice in trying to cover up the White House involvement in the Watergate break-in.

The tapes yielded the "smoking gun"—direct evidence of presidential involvement in the cover-up. Six days after the break-in, Nixon had ordered Haldeman to use the CIA to block the FBI's Watergate investigation on the grounds it might compromise national security. Even Nixon's own attorneys could not defend this breach of faith. On August 7, 1974, a group of respected Republican leaders informed Nixon that impeachment and conviction were certain unless he resigned. Nixon, who had prided himself on his perseverance, of never being a "quitter," now had to face the humiliation of resignation or the greater humiliation of conviction and removal from office. On August 8, the president announced his resignation, a one-sentence letter addressed to Secretary of State Henry Kissinger that became effective the next day. He became the first president to resign. "Our long national nightmare is over," declared Ford, who became the first unelected president.

Americans awakened from their nightmare to a world that was different than the one they had known. They were cynical about politics and politicians, about foreign adventures, and high-priced petroleum. For some time, the best qualifications for the White House were virtually no qualifications. Like Diogenes, Americans carried a lantern looking for an honest man.

Never before had a president soared to the pinnacle of success, then plunged into the abyss of repudiation as quickly as Nixon. The system worked, in a way: even the president was not above the law. But the price was high, the wound was deep, the ramifications were broad. Watergate and Vietnam were serious blows to presidential credibility. The media and the public imposed higher moral standards that proved difficult for some of Nixon's successors to meet. Congress gained power at the expense of the chief executive. The concept of a strong presidency was undermined.

History will probably be kinder to Nixon than his contemporaries, partly because he led a productive life as an ex-president. His legislative achievements were minor, yet he set an agenda that was ambitious, especially in foreign policy. Consistently overcoming adversity, except for his last political crisis, Nixon was the toughest man in politics in his generation, but toughness resulted in meanness; he was not generous in victory, a flaw that led to his downfall. Members of his White House staff wrote that Nixon's personality, deeply complex, had light and dark sides or, alternately, many layers, such as those of a cake. One biographer told the former president that he found Nixon too complex to get on paper. "Aha," Nixon replied, "now I know you are really getting somewhere."

CHAPTER EIGHT

Healing and Malaise: The Ford and Carter Administrations

I N THE Era of Diversity, politics demonstrated a striking range of diversity. There were elements of paradox as well, sometimes in parties and elections, sometimes wrapped up in individuals. Presidents are judged on their accomplishments and flaws. Richard Nixon had more of both than Gerald Ford. Nixon and Ford were both conservatives, yet they were better known for their differences, especially in temperament. Nixon was moody; Ford was even-tempered. Nixon was passionate; Ford lacked Nixon's win-at-all-costs mentality. Nixon was a loner; Ford liked people. Nixon was vindictive; Ford was forgiving. It was ironic that Nixon's landslide reelection was followed by the accession of the first unelected president.

The Tribulations of Gerald R. Ford

Both Nixon and Ford liked football, yet Ford was a better athlete, starring in high school and at the University of Michigan. He turned down professional offers in order to attend the Yale University law school, where he earned high grades. Ford worked his way through by coaching junior varsity football and boxing, learning boxing entirely from books. He returned to Grand Rapids, practiced law, and enlisted in the navy after Pearl Harbor. Ford served four years, two on an aircraft carrier, on which he saw combat. After the war, Ford starred in politics. He won a seat in the U.S. House of Representatives from Grand Rapids and remained there until he was confirmed as vice president in 1973. After eight months, he became president. Down-to-earth, humble, known for his integrity, Ford was a contrast to Nixon, and that was an asset.

Like her husband, First Lady Betty Ford was candid and forthcoming. She impressed the nation with her courage when she talked about her mastectomy for cancer in 1974. Even her flaws endeared her to the public because she shared them. Admitting to alcoholism after her White House years, she helped establish a clinic for alcohol and drug abusers. A feminist, she lobbied for ratification of the Equal Rights Amendment (ERA), supported *Roe v. Wade*, and pressed her husband, without much success, to appoint more women to office.

Ford was an instant president, barely briefed by Nixon. He mixed his own staff with Nixon's. The holdovers and newcomers clashed, and the White House, initially, was chaos. Trying to unite the liberal and conservative wings of his party, Ford nominated Nelson Rockefeller, a favorite of liberals, vice president. Ford promised Rockefeller he would coordinate domestic policy, yet the promise proved empty when Rockefeller was unable to overcome bureaucratic infighting.

The political bombshell of the administration, just thirty days after Ford took office, was his pardon of Richard Nixon for crimes he committed or might have committed. Ford's purpose was to end the bitterness over Watergate rather than prolonging it in a long trial of the former president. Nixon receded in the public mind, at least to a degree, as Ford hoped. Yet the pardon damaged Ford politically; some even said that he had agreed to the pardon when nominated for vice president, an agreement that is unlikely.

The nation did not forget Watergate sufficiently soon to avoid making the Republicans the underdogs in the 1974 congressional elections. To prevent disastrous losses, Ford embarked on a speaking tour to back Republican candidates. While on tour, there were two attempts to assassinate the president, both in California. First, Lynette "Squeaky" Fromme, a member of the "family" of young girls attracted to mass killer Charles Manson, aimed a handgun at Ford, but it did not discharge. Later, Sara Jane Moore, a former FBI informant, fired at Ford but missed, her aim deflected by a bystander. Neither brought much of a sympathy vote to Republicans, who lost the congressional races badly.

The economy brought equally bad news, spiraling downward. The condition was called stagflation, the rare occurrence of simultaneous recession and inflation. Interest rates were high, too high to buy or build homes. Many large cities, including New York, teetered on the brink of bankruptcy. New York begged for federal loan guarantees to survive the crisis. Initially, Ford refused, leading the New York *Daily News* to splash the headline: "FORD TO CITY: DROP DEAD." Ultimately, Ford changed his mind on the condition that New York begin operating on a balanced budget. Paradoxically, the federal budget remained sunk in red ink.

Ford's fiscal prudence induced him to call for tight money and tax increases, which were unpopular. His political prudence then led him to call for two tax cuts, which passed. The energy crisis was paradoxical. High prices were an incentive to conserve fuel, yet created inflation. Congress and the president worked out a bill that would temporarily roll back the price of domestically produced oil, yet would phase in price decontrol, a strategy that worked one way in the short run and just the opposite way in the long run. As for inflation, Ford said the solution was not to buy goods at stores that charged high prices. As encouragement he produced "WIN" buttons, standing for "Whip Inflation Now." Presumably most Americans had the common sense to buy cheaper goods anyway. Ford did not start inflation and did not end it; inflation soared into the stratosphere under his successor and beyond.

Another kind of strife surfaced in Boston, where a federal judge mandated a busing plan to mix students from an all-black high school with those from an all-white school. White parents boycotted the school system and violence broke out, in which a white student was stabbed and white adults threatened black students. Civil rights were not a priority for Ford, who believed that busing should be used to end deliberate segregation, not segregation that occurred as consequence of neighborhood patterns. He would not mobilize the National Guard, despite the tumult. Finally, in January 1975 Boston school officials produced a program for large-scale desegregation, and the plan was implemented with minimal violence that fall.

Less controversial was Ford's single nomination to the high court, federal Appeals Court Judge John Paul Stevens, unanimously confirmed in the Senate late in 1975. Modest, moderate, and scholarly, he replaced the longest-serving Justice William O. Douglas, who resigned after a debilitating stroke. Stevens frequently joined the liberal wing of the court in his opinions.

Overlapping domestic politics and foreign policy, the CIA was purged under Ford, and three investigations of the agency ensued, one internally, one under Vice President Rockefeller's Commission, and one under a Senate committee. The inquiries discovered serious abuses, including plots to assassinate foreign leaders. The Senate and the House established oversight panels.

The Fall of Saigon

If domestic affairs produced headaches for Ford, foreign policy brought migraines. Détente dissolved. Kissinger's star descended because of information implicating the Nixon administration in the fall and perhaps murder

FOREIGN POLICY HEADACHES
Henry Kissinger in decline.
(Gerald Ford Presidential Library)

of Salvador Allende in Chile. Ford was shackled by the War Powers Act and straitjacketed by public opinion and congressional suspicion. More than at most times during the Cold War, foreign policy became passionately partisan. Though Ford was a peacemaker by temperament, the only significant peacemaking on his watch came inadvertently in Vietnam, by surrender.

Crisis had erupted on Cyprus during the Nixon administration. Fifty miles off the coast of Turkey, the island was claimed by the Turks on the basis of proximity. Yet its population was four-fifths Greek, and on that basis Greece claimed the island. In 1974 the Cypriot National Guard, under Greek army officers, seized the government, prompting a Turkish invasion. After peace talks broke down, Ford sided with Turkey. His position was unpopular with Congress, which forced Ford to cut off military aid to Turkey. The Turks countered by closing American military bases on their territory. In 1975 Turkish Cypriots created a separate state in the area they controlled, on the northeast part of the island, and expelled Greeks.

The African nation of Angola ignited a further setback for Ford. When Portugal announced it would free its colony and withdraw in 1975, three factions competed for leadership of the new nation. Covertly, Washington aided factions opposed to the leading group, which had backing from the

Soviet Union and Cuba. When the pro-Soviet group gained the upper hand, Congress ended CIA aid to the other factions—the first time Congress had canceled a secret operation. Meanwhile, the United States and the Soviet Union continued to funnel money and weapons into other areas of Africa, intensifying civil wars and turning the continent into a bloody battleground of the Cold War.

Ford's record in dealing with Moscow and Beijing was mixed. He lacked Nixon's finesse and friendships with Soviet and Chinese leaders. The president talked with Mao about extending diplomatic recognition to China in Beijing, yet the discussions failed because Ford was unwilling to break relations with Taiwan. Ford was more successful with Leonard Brezhnev, signing a Strategic Arms Limitation Treaty negotiated by Nixon during a summit at the Soviet port of Vladivostok. In 1975 the Cold War adversaries met again at Helsinki, Finland, for a Conference on Security and Cooperation in Europe. The leaders agreed to peacefully settle conflicts over human rights, ratify the permanence of the boundaries of post–World War II Europe, and refrain from interfering in the affairs of other nations. The agreement was unpopular among many Americans, who claimed it legitimated the grip of communism on Eastern Europe.

In Southeast Asia, 1975 brought communist regimes to power in Vietnam and Cambodia. Saigon fell to a conventional invasion from the North, and the last Americans were evacuated by helicopter. Vietnamization had failed; the hard-fought American defense of South Vietnam had done no more than delay its conquest. Cambodia fell under the dictatorship of the communist zealot Pol Pot, who fanatically murdered his own people in order to impose his brutal version of communism. In terms of percentage of the population killed, he exceeded Hitler and Stalin. Pol Pot became a pariah even among other communist nations. Flexing their muscles, the Khmer Rouge seized an American freighter, the *Mayaguez*, headed from Hong Kong to Thailand. Wanting to prove the United States could be tough and decisive, Ford approved a rescue operation to free the crew of thirty-nine. It succeeded—although forty-one Americans died. To complaints that more men were lost than saved, Ford said his choice was a matter of principle. The nation rallied around him, raising his approval rating 11 percent in polls.

Patriotism, in need of replenishment, received a boost from the nation's bicentennial celebration on July 4, 1976. Tall sailing ships paraded in New York harbor, as millions watched and fireworks exploded. Hallowed public documents were displayed and exhibits of America's historic symbols toured the nation. It was a small step in restoring national unity in the wake of trauma, a mission of Ford's administration.

The Election of 1976

With the 1976 presidential primaries approaching, Ford faced difficult opposition from former California Governor Ronald Reagan. Ford won the early primaries, nearly eliminating the Californian. Then Reagan won a string of victories in the South and West that enabled him to pull nearly even. Taking a risk, hoping to attract the votes of liberal delegates before the convention, Reagan picked Pennsylvania Senator Richard Schweiker as his running mate. Ford edged Reagan for the nomination and chose Kansas Senator Robert Dole to complete the ticket. Reagan, once dismissed as an extremist, had come closer to taking the nomination from a sitting president of his own party than any candidate in the Time of Paradox.

Now Ford faced another outsider, ex-Georgia Governor Jimmy Carter, whose hard work and meticulous planning won the Democratic nomination. A complex mixture of virtue and ambition, an intense campaigner, Carter exploited Watergate by promising never to lie to the American people; however, he was also naive, inexperienced, and stubborn. Carter appeared at one of the rare moments in American history when a candidate lacking in Washington savvy and name recognition could lead a major party. (Carter's running mate, Minnesota Senator Walter Mondale, however, was a seasoned lawmaker with strong ties to liberals and organized labor.) The first campaign to be partly funded with public money, one of the Watergate-spawned election reforms, deprived the Republicans of their customary advantage of outspending Democrats. Ford chipped away nearly all of Carter's advantage in the polls, but the Democrat won narrowly, getting 50.1 percent of the popular vote and 297 electoral votes to Ford's 47.9 percent and 240. Among factors that contributed to Carter's victory were Ford's pardon of Nixon, a stagnant economy, and Reagan's divisive challenge to Ford. The president tripped in a debate with Carter by denying that the Soviet Union dominated Eastern Europe. Mondale outclassed Dole, who appeared shrill, in the vice presidential debate. Further, some wanted to punish the GOP for Watergate and elect a fresh face, someone with few connections to Washington.

Ford might have lost the presidency, but he helped restore respect for the institution and helped exorcize the demons of Vietnam and Watergate. He did not provide direction or vision. Then again, the switch from Nixon was so abrupt that few expected Ford to articulate goals; it was enough that he could pull the country from its morass of corruption. His transparent decency made Americans feel more confident. Ford gave the country an antidote of midwestern simplicity and humility, much needed after years of secrecy, arrogance, and self-destructiveness. "If I'm remembered," Ford said, "it will probably be for healing the land."

Jimmy Carter

The new president appeared a paragon of virtue and intelligence. A graduate of the Naval Academy, James Earl Carter Jr., who preferred to be called "Jimmy," had been a naval officer, a nuclear engineer, and a wealthy peanut warehouse broker from the hamlet of Plains, Georgia. A Southern Baptist evangelical, he expressed spirituality through service to humanity. He served two terms in the Georgia Senate and one term as governor, one of a new breed of southern chief executives who were conservative on fiscal issues and progressive on racial and social problems. Carter was nonetheless virtually unknown when he launched his race for the Oval Office. Even his mother, Lillian, had doubts. When he told her he was running for president, Lillian asked, "President of what?"

Striving to bring the presidency closer to the people not long after Nixon made it seem aloof, Carter walked instead of riding in a fancy car in his inaugural parade, dressed informally in a cardigan sweater for his first White House speech, and enrolled his daughter, Amy, in public school. He carried his own luggage, and discouraged the playing of "Hail to the Chief." Sleeping only six hours nightly, he was at the Oval Office by 6:00 A.M., ready to tackle part of a workweek that had grown to eighty hours, including thirty hours of paperwork. Initially there were no clearly defined organizational lines in the White House; cabinet secretaries had direct access to Carter, and no chief of staff limited the flow. Acting as his own staff chief, he read memos voraciously. Carter intended to run an open administration, in contrast to Nixon's. Overly conscientious, the president made himself a victim of a "tyranny of the trivial." He pushed his self-improvement to his limits—jogging until he collapsed, listening to classical music, reading a chapter of the Bible in Spanish each night, and still finding time to teach Sunday school. Some found him a humorless workaholic, and none of his assistants could keep pace.

First lady Rosalynn Carter was diligent and persevering as well. She had been eighteen when the couple married and they had four children. Rosalynn kept the books for the Carter Warehouse, handled family finances, made business decisions, and campaigned effectively in 1976. The Carters had a close, intimate marriage. Neither a social butterfly nor a policy wonk, Rosalynn concentrated her activities in a few areas: promoting ratification of the ERA and advocating equal pay for equal work, improving education, and improving care for the aged and the mentally ill.

At the outset of his administration, Carter stuffed the hoppers of Congress with an overload of bills. His proposals included tax reform and welfare reform, which were deferred and watered-down. He submitted a bill to create a federal Energy Department, which passed; an office of consumer affairs, which failed; and economic measures which languished. Straining his relations with Congress, lawmakers, Carter threatened to veto pork-barrel dam and irrigation projects, only to restore half of them under pressure. Impatient with interest-group politics, he appealed to national interests and angered traditional Democratic constituencies. Uncomfortable with the ego-stroking expected on Capitol Hill, the Georgian abstained from false flattery. Carter was neither capable of leading Congress in a collegial fashion nor inspiring the masses as a speaker. What he did was call for sacrifice, especially in conserving energy, which was necessary, yet unpopular.

The Economy and Malaise

Carter's campaign promise to hold down spending and balance the budget collided headlong with a recession. At first he attempted to combat the recession with corporate tax cuts, job programs, and a $50 rebate to each taxpayer. In April 1978, with the economy improving and inflation rising, Carter abandoned the rebate before it came to a vote. Worse, the specter of stagflation shadowed Carter's presidency. Seldom have the economic furies aligned against an administration been so powerful: trade deficits, a falling dollar, and a plummeting stock market. Carter's other measures—budgetary austerity, high interest rates to rein in expansion, and wage and price controls—proved ineffectual and unpopular. Democrats complained about his lack of spending on cities, education, and health care. Carter vacillated. However, even an experienced president might not have pushed through Congress a program that could address economic troubles without angering important groups. Inflation rose from 6.5 percent in 1977 to 7.6 percent in 1978, 11.3 percent in 1979, and 13.5 percent in 1980, when unemployment was 7.0 percent.

Energy was the chief culprit behind inflation. Since the Arab oil embargo of 1973, American dependence on imported energy had increased from $8.4 billion to nearly $40 billion in 1977. Referring to the crisis as "the moral equivalent of war," Carter presented comprehensive energy legislation. To encourage conservation and exploration, he sought measures such as punitive taxes on gas-guzzling cars, rebates for purchases of fuel-efficient vehicles, and taxes on crude oil and gasoline. The price of domestically produced oil would be allowed to rise to world levels, with rebates helping poor families pay the higher costs. Also, production of coal and nuclear power would increase. The House passed the complex bill nearly intact, yet the Senate Finance Committee dismembered the measure. Nearly a year and a half after

★ Barbara Jordan: A Voice That Commands Respect ★

Barbara Jordan was the first African-American elected
official to become an American hero.

—MARY BETH ROGERS

UNITY AND DIVERSITY
Barbara Jordan shares
her vision for America.
(Library of Congress)

IN THE Era of Diversity, Barbara Jordan was confident that unity could emerge from differences. Born to a lower-middle-class family in Houston, she excelled in school, graduating with honors from Texas Southern University and participating on the college debate team that defeated Yale and Brown and tied Harvard. In 1959 Jordan received a law degree from Boston University, passed the Texas bar examination, and entered politics by campaigning for John F. Kennedy for president. She then ran for the Texas Senate in 1962 and 1964, losing both times, but she then won a seat after redistricting in 1966. She became the first African American to serve in the body since 1883, and the first African American woman ever.

Six years later, once again aided by redistricting, Jordan was elected to the U.S. House of Representatives, the first black woman in Congress from a southern state. She became one of the stars of the House Judiciary Committee while it considered impeachment charges against President Richard Nixon for offenses during the Watergate scandal. "Now she had a message that matched her voice," biographer Mary Beth Rogers wrote.

Jordan worked even better outside the limelight. With a talent for getting along with people that rivaled her talent for public speaking, she became a consummate political insider, trading favors and dealing with the political structure on equal terms. "It is dangerous to enter the struggle to establish a civil society as a purist if, as a purist, you are unwilling to take in others and be flexible," Jordan wrote.

The breakdown in the nation's political order paralleled a decline in Jordan's health. In 1974 she was diagnosed with multiple sclerosis, a degenerative muscle disease. Jordan remained silent about her illness even after she began using a cane, then a walker, then a wheelchair. Still, she delivered keynote addresses at the Democratic National Conventions in 1976 and 1992, played a key role in renewing the Voting Rights Act of 1965, and led President Bill Clinton's commission on immigration reform.

In December 1977, Jordan announced her retirement from the House at forty-three. Her body was ravaged, and she wanted to pursue new interests: teaching, sitting on corporate boards, and speaking about national harmony. The policies of the Reagan and first Bush administrations, as well as new manifestations of black nationalism, disturbed Jordan, who warned, "A sense of harmony can only survive if each of us remembers that we share a common destiny."

In 1994 Clinton awarded Jordan the Presidential Medal of Freedom, the nation's highest civilian honor. Two years later, suffering from multiple sclerosis, diabetes, failed kidneys, heart problems, and leukemia, Jordan succumbed to blood cancer. A paradox of visible strength in a diseased body, she demonstrated the verities of the lyrics of the black spiritual "We Shall Overcome." She said, "The greatest motivation . . . has to come from inside you."

Sources: Studies on Barbara Jordan include Mary Beth Rogers, *American Hero* (1998); Barbara Jordan and Shelby Hearon, *Barbara Jordan: A Self-Portrait* (1979); Ira B. Bryant, *Barbara Charline Jordan: From the Ghetto to the Capitol* (1977); and James Haskins, *Barbara Jordan* (1977).

it was unveiled, in September 1978, the Senate approved a weaker version that removed most punitive taxes. By deregulating the price of natural gas and establishing a single price structure for intrastate and interstate gas, however, Congress and the administration had made an important contribution to ensuring consistent gas supplies nationwide.

Carter's energy proposals alienated environmentalists. Increased use of coal would cause pollution, and opening wilderness areas in Alaska to oil exploration would harm wildlife. Alarms over nuclear power multiplied after an accident in March 1979 at Three Mile Island near Harrisburg, Pennsylvania. A pump failure at the plant led to a breakdown in the reactor cooling system, the precursor to a possible meltdown of the reactor core. Fortunately, conditions stabilized and disaster was averted.

Carter's energy proposals, which included taxes on high energy uses, threatened to aggravate inflation and to anger taxpayers, just as the national mood had turned against high taxes. In California a tax revolt led by Howard Jarvis succeeded in placing limits on property taxes. So Carter decided to place his ideas about the energy crisis before the nation in a major televised speech and retreated to Camp David to write it. The Camp David plans expanded into a domestic summit at which Carter consulted national leaders. In his speech, Carter addressed problems beyond energy, a national crisis of spirit and morale. The press labeled it the "malaise" speech, although Carter never used the word. In the finale of the talk, Carter did address energy. Instead of calling for more sacrifice and higher taxes, he switched gears and emphasized new sources for fuels. His program included decontrol of oil prices to encourage exploration, complemented by a wind-fall profits tax to prevent price gouging. The government would subsidize the development of synthetic fuels for coal and oil shale. Also, an Energy Mobilization Board would cut red tape. The windfall profits tax and a scaled-down version of the synthetic fuel program passed Congress. The Energy Board was defeated because of concerns it would violate environmental regulations and states' rights. Following the speech, Carter asked cabinet members to resign and accepted five resignations. Early polls showed the speech was a success, but the cabinet shuffle backfired.

Interest Groups

Carter encountered political difficulties by alienating traditional Democratic interest groups. Black organizations, for example, believed he was penurious with appropriations for programs that helped their constituents. Race riots flared in Boston; Wichita, Kansas; and Tampa, Florida. Still, most African Americans supported Carter rather than his Republican opponents. Befitting the Era of Diversity, he appointed more blacks to high positions, including the cabinet, than any prior president. A black women, Patricia Harris, served successively in two cabinet positions. Two black men, Andrew Young, followed by Donald McHenry, served as ambassador to the United Nations.

One of the remedies to discrimination, affirmative action, faced a test from Allan Bakke, a white man twice denied admission to medical school at the University of California-Davis, which reserved slots for minority students whose grades and test scores might not qualify them. Bakke sued, claiming the school was guilty of reverse discrimination by rejecting him even though his grades and scores were better than those of the minority applicants accepted. He prevailed in lower courts, and the case went to the Supreme Court. In the most important civil rights ruling since *Brown v. Board of Education*, the justices held 5-4 in *Regents of the University of California v. Bakke* (1978) that Bakke should be admitted but that affirmative action was acceptable if it did not employ rigid quotas. Race could be considered among a variety of factors in deciding whether to admit a student, the court said.

Feminists criticized facets of the Carter administration, yet, in principle, the president tried to advance feminist aims. Besides his appointment of women to government posts, Carter joined his wife in supporting the ERA and favored an extension of the seven-year ratification deadline for the amendment. However, women criticized Carter on budgetary grounds, calling for more funding of projects such as day care. Although Carter, ideologically, was liberal, his fiscal austerity and strong belief in a balanced budget generated criticism among economic liberals, yet he won important objectives, including in 1980, a $1.6 billion "Superfund" to clean up areas contaminated with toxic waste, and a bill that more than doubled the size of the national parks and wildlife refuges. The amount of land designated wilderness almost tripled.

By 1980, with the domestic travails and the Iran hostage crisis (explained below), Carter's approval rating in the polls had fallen to 21 percent, lower than Nixon's 24 percent in the depths of Watergate, and Truman's low of 23 percent. Liberal Massachusetts Senator Edward M. "Ted" Kennedy was favored over Carter in a race for the Democratic presidential nomination, surveys indicated. Carter's identification of a deep-seated national crisis was unpopular, if well-founded. Americans did indeed lack faith—in Congress, in the business community, in the intellectual establishment, in the commitment of allies, and in the restraint of adversaries.

Cold Warrior and Peacemaker

Carter had even less experience in international affairs than in national politics. He failed to set a hierarchy of priorities and pitted a hawk national security adviser, Zbigniew Brezezinski, against a dovish secretary of state, Cyrus Vance. The arrangement muddied the administration's direction and made it unpredictable. Eventually, Vance resigned over a hostage rescue attempt in Iran. At the United Nations, Andrew Young also resigned after meeting secretly with Arab leader Yasir Arafat, who headed the Palestine Liberation Organization (PLO), which the United States did not recognize.

Just as Gerald Ford sought to banish the ghost of Watergate by pardoning Richard Nixon, Carter attempted to bury the memory of Vietnam by pardoning draft evaders. Both served their purpose in the long run, yet hurt each president politically. Idealistically, Carter sought to base his foreign policy on respect for human rights, applied not only to communist countries but also to nations that were our allies. Carter was critical of apartheid in South Africa and repression in Rhodesia and South America. He also publicized the plight of dissidents in the Soviet Union.

The Soviet Union considered Carter's policy meddling, and relations deteriorated. Still, the two nations had a common interest in arms control and negotiated SALT II in 1979. However, the treaty stalled in the Senate. To ameliorate misgivings, Carter authorized the development of the MX missile. Based on the principle of a shell game, these nuclear rockets would be placed on railroad tracks and shuffled among numerous shelters to mislead the Soviets about their location. Still, Carter rejected plans for other new weapons. He canceled the B-1 bomber as too expensive and the neutron bomb, which killed people with radiation yet left buildings intact.

With the communist superpowers, it was the best of times with China and the worst of times with the Soviet Union. After waiting since 1949, Mainland China received diplomatic recognition on December 15, 1978, requiring the United States to break relations with Taiwan. Yet when the Soviet Union invaded Afghanistan a year later to implant a communist dictator, Carter's vision of communism was transformed. The Soviets really did intend world conquest, he concluded, and now he would play hardball. The United States smuggled military aid to the Islamic rebels fighting the Soviets. Carter withdrew the SALT II treaty from Senate consideration and ceased high-technology exports to the Soviet Union. The president also declared an embargo on grain sales and ordered a boycott of the 1980 Moscow Summer Olympic games. According to the Carter Doctrine he proclaimed, the United States committed to defend the territorial integrity of the Persian Gulf region. Carter also abandoned fiscal austerity to begin a major arms buildup that continued through the Reagan years. Congress approved his request for a 5 percent increase in military spending, the largest arms program in thirty years. Young men were required to register for a potential draft. Promised military spending cuts were abandoned. Carter took credit for military technology developed during his administration—the cruise missile and the Stealth bomber that was virtually invisible to radar. The new password was "peace through strength."

In the late 1970s, after détente fell from favor, a new consensus began forming that America must take a tougher stand against communism. Ford had banned the word "détente" from his foreign policy vocabulary because of its unpopularity. More minds were changed by the invasion of Afghanistan, Soviet and Cuban soldiers in Africa, the leftist rebellion in Nicaragua, and the brutal regimes in Cambodia, Laos, and Vietnam.

Carter's attempt to forge a new relationship with Panama encountered pressure from the resurgence of nationalism in Central America. Carter believed the canal was a vestige of colonialism and could not be defended without Panamanian cooperation. Conservatives, most prominently Ronald Reagan, considered the canal a symbol of American achievement that should not be yielded. Nonetheless, Carter prevailed narrowly in winning Senate approval for his treaty with Panama that would incrementally turn over sovereignty in the Canal Zone to the people of Panama by 2000. The United States has priority passage and the right to defend the canal.

Carter's command performance came in the thicket of Middle Eastern politics. Since Egypt had broken with the Soviet Union, a window of opportunity had opened for peace with Israel. The initiative came from the leaders of the two nations. Egyptian President Anwar Sadat accepted an invitation from Israeli Prime Minister Menachem Begin to visit Jerusalem in 1977, followed by a Begin visit to Cairo. Never before had Arab and Israeli leaders talked face to face. Once the euphoria wore off, negotiations bogged down, and Carter invited Sadat and Begin to Camp David, where he acted as mediator. For Carter, the Camp David Summit was a huge risk, as failure would have been humiliating. The conference did not fail, however, partly because of Carter's persistence. After thirteen days of tough, sometimes acrimonious talks, he announced on September 17, 1978, that two accords had been reached. Israel and Egypt agreed to negotiate a peace treaty within three months, and Sadat and Begin decided that issues of Palestinian autonomy would be determined in long-range negotiations. When the postaccord discussions slowed and the rivals could not conclude a treaty by the deadline, Carter again intervened. After taxing negotiations

HANDING OVER THE WHITE HOUSE
President Jimmy Carter shaking hands with Egyptian President Anwar Sadat
and Israeli Prime Minister Menachem Begin at the signing
of the Egyptian-Israeli Peace Treaty, 1979.
(Library of Congress)

climaxing in a Middle East trip by Carter, an Israeli-Egyptian pact was signed on March 26, 1979, in Washington. Despite uncertainties and an evident inability to follow through on promises, the Camp David Accords laid a more pragmatic basis for future talks. Trying to settle long-held differences in a region that had resisted solutions, Carter enjoyed his finest hour as president.

In the Western Hemisphere, Marxist rebels, the Sandinistas, pressured the dictator, Anastasio Somoza, a longtime U.S. ally, to abdicate. The United States attempted to force Somoza to implement reforms, and when he did not, withdrew economic and military aid. Somoza fled Nicaragua, and the Sandinistas seized power. Carter courted the new Marxist regime, only to become disillusioned when it accepted Cuban military aid and encouraged Marxist revolutions elsewhere in Latin America. Moreover, the Sandinistas were no more willing to hold free elections than Somoza had been.

An ocean away in Africa, Carter and Young were sympathetic to black aspirations for majority rule. Like Kennedy, they believed the key battlegrounds of the Cold War were in the Third World. The administration helped ensure the transition from white minority rule to rule by the black majority in Rhodesia, employing sanctions against the repressive regime. Unfortunately, the new government, under Robert Mugabe, proved autocratic. In the horn of Africa, Somalia claimed Ethiopian land, and war ensued. The Soviets backed the Marxist Ethiopian government and Cuba sent troops. Ethiopia triumphed but the region remained unstable. The Cuban soldiers remained, a distraction for Washington.

Humiliation in Tehran

But the worst came in Iran. Shah Reza Pahlavi, an American ally who came to power in a CIA-backed coup in 1953, led a repressive regime that Islamic fundamentalists sought to overthrow. Agitation led by the Islamic religious leader, Ayatollah Ruhollah Khomeini, living in exile in Paris, climaxed in a general strike in 1979. The shah fled the country. Khomeini returned, and a new constitution was drafted, based on Islamic law, making Khomeini ruler for life. Such perceived Western vices as alcohol, rock music, and informal attire were banned. The new government labeled the United States "the Great Satan."

Carter admitted the exiled shah, dying of cancer, to America for medical treatment on humanitarian grounds. Outraged, Iranian fundamentalists vowed vengeance against the United States and demanded it return the shah to Iran to face "revolutionary justice." Finding a way to avenge themselves, Islamic students seized more than fifty hostages at the U.S. Embassy in Tehran. Chanting in the streets, flaunting the impotence of America to free the hostages, the crisis slowly eroded Carter's political status. Carter resisted military intervention for months, fearing it might result in the deaths of the hostages. In April 1980 he severed diplomatic relations with Iran and imposed a trade embargo. Finally, he dispatched a complicated rescue attempt that ended in tragedy. Mechanical problems on three helicopters forced cancellation of the mission at the desert rendezvous. In the withdrawal, a helicopter and a transport plane collided, killing eight servicemen. Carter's hopes for a second term lay smoldering in the Iranian desert. If the daring plan had succeeded it is possible that Carter would have been reelected in 1980. If so, the subsequent history of the 1980s might have been quite different.

The 1980 Election

Carter's chief opponent in the Democratic primaries was the youngest, and only remaining Kennedy son, Edward M., "Ted." Ted shared the liberalism of John and Robert; in fact, he had moved to the left of John. Yet he did not share their intellects or abilities. In a television interview, he was unable to define why he wanted to be president. Troubling memories were resurrected: he had left a young woman to drown on Chappaquiddick Island in 1969; earlier, he had cheated in college. Southern Baptist Carter quipped that if Kennedy ran in the primaries, he would "whip his ass" and he did, winning so many primaries it embarrassed Kennedy.

The Republicans nominated ex-California Governor Ronald Reagan after he brushed aside George Bush, a former House member, CIA director, ambassador to China and the United Nations and chairman of the Republican National Committee. Reagan picked Bush as his running mate. Reagan focused his campaign on a few big objectives: he promised to cut taxes, increase defense spending, and balance the budget. The tone of the campaign was upbeat and optimistic, conveyed by Reagan's mastery of public speaking and the mystique of television. A third candidate, John Anderson, a liberal Republican, offered voters a choice. The U.S. Representative from Illinois, however, threatened to deprive Carter of liberal votes.

Carter had Achilles' heels on both feet: on one the poor performance of the economy, on the other the humiliation of the hostages. Reagan, like Carter, was a Washington outsider, yet he made the election a referendum on Carter's failures. "Are you better off than you were four years ago?" he asked Americans. Clearly, they were not. Americans warmed to Reagan's folksy style and tough talk against communism. The Republican ticket overwhelmed the Democrats with 43.9 million votes (50.7 percent),

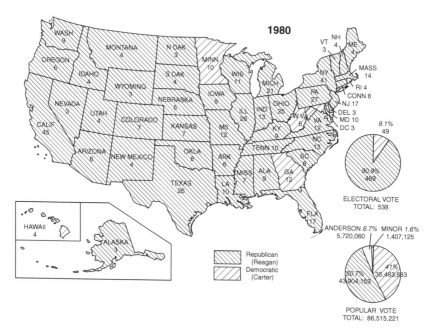

Election of 1980

to 35.5 million (41.0 percent) for Carter, and 5.7 million (8.3 percent) for Anderson. The totals were staggering in the Electoral College, Reagan receiving 489 votes, Carter 49, and Anderson none. Carter became the first president since Herbert Hoover to lose a bid for a second term. On January 20, 1981, just after Reagan completed his inaugural address, the Iranians released the hostages, having held them for 444 days.

In time Carter rebounded, answering the question, "Is there life after the presidency?" with "Absolutely!" He became a valuable elder statesman—the model of a successful former president, *Newsweek* magazine declared. He wrote major books, helped build homes for the needy through the Habitat for Humanity organization, and promoted social and political activism via the Carter Presidential Center in Atlanta. He advanced democracy by monitoring elections in Panama, Nicaragua, and Haiti, among a number of countries; traveled the globe speaking out for human rights, including Cuba, where in 2002 he became the highest-ranking American official to visit during Fidel Castro's regime; and won the 2002 Nobel Peace Prize for his efforts on behalf of international understanding.

Still, Carter's postpresidential activities did not redeem his performance in the White House; most historians rank Carter as a mediocre president. In both domestic and foreign affairs, his administration, like Ford's, was longer on good intentions and character than on accomplishments. Carter brought to government an engineer's intelligence, not a poet's vision, and the disturbing messages that sacrifice and restraint were necessary to meet national goals and that America did not have the resources to move simultaneously on all fronts at home and abroad. In fairness, it must be said that the country sought recovery and rest, not innovation and bold programs. Carter governed in the eye of the storm that still swirled around Watergate and Vietnam. Like Ford, he renewed respect in the presidency and gained grudging respect for his honesty, decency, adherence to principle, and peacemaking.

Carter knew his limitations. He enjoyed comparing himself to a man in a joke who was accused of getting drunk and setting his bed afire. "I admit that I was drunk," the man said. "But the bed was already on fire when I got in it."

★ CHAPTER NINE ★

The Reagan Rebellion

THE PARADOXES pile up for Ronald Reagan, a rebel of the right who vowed to change the status quo of conciliatory diplomacy, the welfare state, big government, and high taxes. He was, ironically, a greater advocate of change than any president since Franklin Roosevelt, and yet a conservative. In the Era of Diversity, purveyors of change came in all shades.

The liberalism that led to Barry Goldwater's burial under Lyndon Johnson's landslide in 1964 waned by 1968. Voters harkened to the conservative mantra that government had grown up too fast, was drunk on power, and needed to live within its means. With Richard Nixon, they elected a centrist who became the engine of his own destruction, followed by Gerald Ford, a right-center Republican, honest, but lacking charisma, and drowning in the muck of Watergate. Without Watergate there probably would not have been a Carter presidency, and perhaps not a Reagan one either.

Ronald Reagan

History is built on near misses. Republicans said they wanted a real conservative, like Goldwater, but without Goldwater's snap judgments. In Reagan they found one. Men who knew both said Dwight Eisenhower was calm on the surface, but Ronald Reagan was calm through and through. He took office wanting to accomplish a few big things and achieved most of them. He ended the country's drift and dispelled the fog of malaise that shrouded Jimmy Carter's America. Even people who were hurt by the former actor's economic or social policies sometimes voted for Reagan because he lifted their spirits. This paradox seems most perverse in the remark of a Milwaukee drug dealer who said he voted for the law-and-order Republican because Reagan made him feel good about himself.

Reagan, at sixty-nine, was the oldest man to assume the presidency. He delivered a polished performance when reading from a script, but faltered before extemporaneous questions. Once he nodded off at an audience with the pope. His spokesmen conceded that the president often forgot the names of those he worked with. He spoke to visitors to the Oval Office from note cards. Once, at a trade meeting with businessmen in the White House, he picked up the wrong note cards and delivered the wrong speech.

Reagan sympathized with poor people as individuals, yet he believed in personal responsibility. Ever since the New Deal, Americans had looked to the federal government to solve their problems. Once a New Dealer himself, Reagan warned that the federal government could not expand infinitely. Government was no longer the solution, he suggested; it was the problem. Reagan's detractors warned that the old man in the White House believed in a Hollywood version of reality where there were simple answers and a happy ending to every script. In the real world there were no simple answers. Reagan demurred: "There are simple answers," he said, "but there are not always easy ones."

Reagan remembered his hometown of Dixon, Illinois, as a place where neighbors and families cared for each other from a sense of Christian charity. "A Samaritan crossed over the road and helped the beaten pilgrim himself," he said. "He did not report the case to the nearest welfare agency." A lower middle-class boy known as "Dutch," Reagan was a churchgoer, a football star, and a lifeguard who saved seventy-seven people on the Rock River in seven summers. He starred in school and church plays and was class president, maintaining a low "B" average. His mother was a teetotaler and amateur playwright; his father was an alcoholic and a salesman.

Reagan continued to star in athletics and extracurricular activities at minuscule Eureka College, where he also earned a low "B" average. He was a mediocre football player but a fine swimmer and a star of the stage. He was also elected student body president. Reagan made the best of his assets: a pleasant, nonaggressive personality, a fit, athlete's body and handsome demeanor, a retentive memory, an eloquent voice, and a sense of humor. Many things came easy to him, but he rarely gave up when they did not.

Graduating in 1932, when the nation's cupboard was bare of jobs, Reagan visited Chicago radio stations, seeking work as an announcer. Advised to search in smaller towns, he was hired at WOC in Davenport, Iowa, to broadcast football games. In 1933 the station merged with the larger WHO in Des Moines, and Reagan gained fame as a sportscaster. In 1937, when Reagan covered the Chicago Cubs' training camp near Los Angeles, he took a screen test and signed a seven-year contract with Warner

Brothers. As an actor he made fifty-three films, including some hits, but never reached the pinnacle of the profession. *Knute Rockne: All American* (1940) and *Santa Fe Trail* (1940) established him as a promising star, and *King's Row* (1941) might have made him a top talent had not home front military service in World War II interrupted his career. Meanwhile, he met actress Jane Wyman on a film set, married her in 1940, and soon had two children. But the marriage and the movie career crashed about the same time: Wyman filed for divorce in 1948, when the postwar glut of younger talent made roles scarce for Reagan. Taking a different type of lead role, president of the Screen Actors Guild, he concluded that communists aspired to take over Hollywood, part of his conversion from liberal Democrat to conservative Republican. His ideological script was completed in 1952 when he wed another actress, Nancy Davis, who was from a solid GOP family.

Two years later, Reagan became host of the television's General *Electric Theater*, giving speeches for the company that extolled big business and small government. The talks made him a celebrity in the Republican Party. After the program left the air, Reagan became host of *Death Valley Days* in 1964 and devoted increasing time to politics. Effective speeches for Goldwater in 1964 led to an invitation from wealthy Californians to run for governor in 1966. Edmond G. "Pat" Brown, Reagan's Democrat opponent, attempted to label him an extremist yet could not make it stick because of Reagan's placid demeanor. Reagan defeated Brown, benefiting from a backlash against student antiwar demonstrators on California campuses. Turning the governor's responsibilities into a nine-to-five job, he reluctantly raised taxes. Despite this, the state deficit increased. After a lackluster second term, Reagan became a speaker, syndicated columnist, and radio commentator. He lost the Republican nomination for the second time in 1976, but in 1980 won the nomination and the election.

The Reagan Enigma

A politician, actor, and public speaker for much of his life, Reagan had many acquaintances, yet few close friends. The Republican Party championed family values, yet the chief executive's own family was dysfunctional. Reagan espoused religion yet rarely attended church and did not instill spiritual values in his children. Nearly all of Reagan's children, at one time or another, were estranged from their parents. Some felt the bond between the president and Nancy was so great it excluded them. Son Michael said his father "just finds it difficult to hug his own children." Nancy Reagan was criticized for extravagant spending on clothes, and, after an assassination attempt on her husband, for using an astrologer to help plan his trips. Registering the lowest public approval ratings of any modern first lady, she began to focus on her campaign against illegal drugs and her popularity improved. Yet, she influenced her husband, particularly in the hiring and firing of staff members and planning of the White House schedule. In that sense she was a powerful first lady. Nancy, for example, also persuaded her husband to take a softer line in the Cold War and use less threatening language.

In delegation of detail, Reagan was the opposite of Carter. He had little intellectual curiosity; rather, he waited for his staff to bring things to him. Despite his inclination to follow his staff's script, he did not inevitably do so. Reagan was an old-fashioned, people-oriented president who disliked cold, impersonal solutions to problems, and relied on intuition. The president was confused by computers and wrote everything longhand.

For his political confidants, Reagan relied mainly on Californians who were personal friends. They were not specialists but generalists who understood Reagan. They had common aims and were loyal. The first term was

MORNING IN AMERICA
Ronald Reagan minutes before being shot, 1981.
(Ronald Reagan Presidential Library)

managed by a triumvirate of Chief of Staff James A. Baker III, a friend of Vice President George Bush; Edwin Meese III, who handled policy issues; and Michael K. Deaver, who was close to Nancy Reagan. This trio controlled access to the president. Reagan's cabinet had only a few strong members, such as Donald T. Regan, who served as treasury secretary and later as White House chief of staff; Caspar Weinberger; and George Shultz, defense secretary and secretary of state, in turn.

The troika of Baker, Meese, and Deaver was more important than the cabinet because they understood Reagan and his priorities. Baker, a skilled operative, played a key role in shepherding legislation through Congress. He helped persuade Reagan at the outset of the administration to focus on cutting domestic spending and upgrading the military rather than on divisive social issues

The Battleground of the Budget

The heart of Reagan's domestic program pulsated to the economy. He planned to cut taxes 25 percent over 33 months, pare overall expenses, but boost defense spending. Reagan was a convert to "supply-side" economics, the theory that the existence of consumer goods would create customers for the products, in contrast to the conventional idea that demand generated supply. With lower taxes and fewer regulations, businesses would grow, create more products, and stimulate consumer demand for them. In turn, federal revenue from taxes would rise, even though tax rates were reduced. Most economists and political theorists were skeptical of what some labeled "Reaganomics." If the budget cuts were not deep enough, the loss of revenue from the tax cuts would lead to lopsided unbalanced budgets. Politically, it was easier to cut taxes than to prune programs. Lawmakers and interest groups rushed to defend their constituencies' funding.

Reagan made the package of tax and spending cuts his highest priority in his program to shrink government, devoting virtually all his energies to that objective. Then, as he was leaving a Washington hotel on March 30, 1981, he was wounded in an assassination attempt by a mentally disturbed gunman, John Hinckley. A bullet lodged less than three inches from the president's heart. Reagan's coolness and courage reaped respect. Wheeled into an operating room, near death, he told his doctors, "I hope you're all Republicans." The public rallied around Reagan and his programs. Congress, too, came around, thanks to "boll weevil" Democrats, southern conservatives who favored lighter taxes and fewer government programs. In August, Reagan signed into law measures slashing $40 million from the budget and cutting personal income taxes 25 percent over three years.

The economy slid into recession, largely because the Federal Reserve Board raised interest rates high to cool inflation. By 1983 the board's policy and lower world oil prices pushed inflation down to 4 percent. The recession, however, was worse than those in the 1970s. Factories operated below capacity, unemployment soared, and the underprivileged suffered because their income declined and because spending cuts reduced social programs. In January 1983 some twenty thousand people lined up in Milwaukee to apply for two hundred jobs at an auto frame factory. American products became more expensive overseas because the steep interest rates made the dollar more valuable than foreign currency. United States exports fell and imports increased, creating huge trade deficits. The slump in exports pinched farmers who depended on selling grain abroad, as well as businesses such as automakers, steel mills, and heavy equipment manufacturers in the Northeast and Midwest "Rustbelt."

Meanwhile, the highest budget deficits in history loomed. A harbinger of trouble would arise in the Social Security system as baby boomers retired and the number of workers paying into the system decreased. To address deficits, Reagan accepted a 1982 tax increase that restored one-third of the reductions he had sponsored the previous year. He also approved changes in Social Security that boosted payroll taxes, raised the retirement age to sixty-seven by 2027, and taxed benefits of high-income recipients. Finally, he scaled back the cuts in social spending and the increases in defense funding. Still the administration ultimately increased annual military spending by 7 percent above the 5 percent yearly boosts called for in Carter's last budget. Over Reagan's eight-year presidency, military spending rose 70 percent, and $1.5 trillion was spent by the Pentagon.

Congress tried to solve budget problems in 1985, enacting the Gramm-Rudman-Hollings Act to downscale the budget until it was balanced in 1991. Under the law, if federal forecasts predicted the budget would not meet its targets, they would trigger across-the-board cuts unless Congress acted to reduce the budget or raise taxes. In 1986 another tax reform act, which Ronald Reagan initiated, recouped more of the revenue the government lost as a result of the 1981 tax cuts. The last major domestic initiative of Reagan's second term, the law cut some rates and brackets and closed loopholes.

Despite deep deficits, 80 percent of Americans thought they were better off because of the measures enacted during Reagan's first term. In 1983, with inflation curbed, the Federal Reserve Board reduced interest rates and the money supply. By April, the economy began to recover and went on to record the longest period of sustained economic growth in modern twentieth-century America up to that time. People went on a buying binge. During the Reagan years, they purchased 105 million color television sets, 88 million cars and light trucks, 63 million videocassette recorders, 62 million microwave ovens, 57 million washers and dryers, 31 million cordless phones, and 30 million telephone answering machines. A bull market began in stocks, with the Dow Jones Industrial Average peaking at 2,722 in August 1987. Less than two months later, in October, the market plummeted 508 points, the largest one-day drop ever, yet because the economy was basically sound, the crash was not followed by a depression or even a recession.

Another component of Reagan's economic policy, deregulation, led to corporate destabilization. The program lifted regulations on business, relying on competition rather than rules. Billion-dollar business mergers and takeovers resulted. Sometimes floating high-risk, high-yield "junk bonds" to finance their ventures, a capitalist or a company would pay stockholders above market prices for their shares in a firm. If the takeover failed, it was costly to the company that prevented it. If the takeover was successful, the new owners were burdened by the huge debt they had just incurred. Often they found it necessary to gut their new companies by selling operations and cutting jobs to pay the debt.

Wall Street greed expanded on a staggering scale, as financiers began buying stock in companies that were takeover candidates. With corporate "raiders" and others trying to purchase control of the firms, the stock grew volatile, and many shareholders were glad to sell to avoid risk. Among this new breed of speculator, Ivan Boesky used his contacts to select companies that were susceptible to takeovers before that vulnerability became public information. He went to prison and paid the Securities and Exchange Commission $100 million, half as a fine for his insider trading and half as reimbursement of his illicit profits. He still had a fortune of $100 million when he left prison. To reduce the charges against him, Boesky told the SEC about his accomplices, including Michael Milken, a junk-bond specialist. Milken paid the commission $600 million in fines and served a prison term for securities fraud. Even after paying the fines, he was left with $1 billion.

The administration also relaxed restrictions on savings and loan associations, known as "thrifts." The government, which insured their deposits, allowed them to invest more aggressively. The tactic backfired when reckless investments and criminal activities forced many of the savings and loans into bankruptcy. By the time Reagan's successor, Bush, took action in 1989, the bankruptcy bailouts were costing the federal government $35 million a day. By 1996 the total cost had risen to $480.9 billion and was forecast to mount to seven times that amount before it was paid off, more than the cost of World War II.

The administration had tense relations with organized labor, especially after Reagan fired striking air traffic controllers in 1981. Subject to long hours and severe stress, the controllers felt they deserved better pay. But legally, they could not strike. When they walked out anyway, Reagan dismissed those who did not come back to work within forty-eight hours. Military controllers and returning employees directed landings and departures until new workers were hired. There were no major accidents, although controllers' conditions remained difficult. Also, Reagan's commitment to free trade angered some unions, who feared loss of jobs. Reagan signed a free trade agreement with Canada and worked for one with Mexico, to be concluded by his successors.

Reagan molded the federal judiciary to his conservative ideology, appointing more than four hundred judges, almost half the federal bench. The tactic of appointing young jurists assured they would still be shaping law long after his tenure expired. On the Supreme Court, some of his appointments were landmarks. His first Supreme Court appointee, in 1981, was federal Appeals Judge Sandra Day O'Connor, the first woman justice. When Chief Justice Warren Burger retired in 1986, Reagan elevated Associate Justice William Rehnquist, the most conservative justice. To replace him, the president appointed Antonin Scalia, another staunch conservative. Then Justice Lewis Powell retired in 1987, leaving Reagan the opportunity to nominate Robert Bork. Bork was controversial because of his conservative views expressed in a long paper trail of opinions and articles. Civil rights organizations and feminists helped liberal Senate Democrats defeat the nomination. Conservatives complained that Bork was rejected solely for his views, not for any blemish on his record. Moreover, Bork had a keen legal mind. In 1988 the Senate confirmed Reagan's choice of Anthony Kennedy, a more moderate conservative. Rehnquist and his colleagues shifted the Court to the right.

African Americans received little and contributed little to Reagan's political agenda. They voted for him in low percentages in 1980 and even lower in 1984. Not personally prejudiced, Reagan had little experience with blacks and was insensitive to their concerns. He never supported the use of federal power to advance civil rights, had opposed the 1965 Voting Rights Act, and inherited some of George Wallace's followers. His administration opposed affirmative action and busing to desegregate schools, and cut funds for legal services for the poor and minorities.

Reagan was unpopular among feminists because he opposed abortion and the ERA, because their concerns were not a priority, and because there were no feminist women in Reagan's inner circle. Women who dealt with

Reagan personally did not find him sexist, however, and he was popular with homemakers.

"Morning in America"

In the 1984 campaign, several Democrats sought their party's nomination to oppose Reagan, including former Vice President Walter Mondale and the Reverend Jesse Jackson, a civil rights activist. Mondale won and selected New York Representative Geraldine Ferraro as his running mate, the first woman nominated for vice president by a major party. Rejecting political expediency, Mondale said he would raise taxes. Reagan would raise them too, Mondale said, but would not admit it until after the election. Republicans depicted Mondale as a tax-and-spend liberal. Reagan ran a carefully scripted campaign that emphasized patriotic themes. The pall of the Carter years had receded, Reagan proclaimed, and it was "morning in America." Once more, one could be proud to be an American, enjoying prosperity and the protection of a strong military.

Because Reagan would be in his late seventies by the time he completed another term, his age and health became issues. In his second debate with Mondale, Reagan dismissed the question of his age with humor, saying: "I will not make age an issue of this campaign. I am not going to exploit, for political purposes, my opponent's youth and inexperience." Voters buried Mondale's aspirations. Reagan carried every state but his foe's home of Minnesota and the District of Columbia, polling 59 percent of the popular vote (54.4 million) and 525 electoral votes to 41 percent (37.5 million) and 13 for the Democrat. No gender gap materialized, for 56 percent of women voted for Reagan. He won just 9 percent of the African American vote and lost the Jewish vote, but took 63 percent of the white vote and 71 percent of the white Protestant vote. Polls showed people were more positive about Reagan than were negative about Mondale. The former vice president was frustrated by the outcome. "I tried to get specific and Reagan patted dogs," he complained.

In domestic policy, Reagan's second term was more difficult than his first. His major domestic goals had been achieved early. Most important, the triumvirate that planned his domestic agenda broke up. James Baker changed places with Donald Regan at Treasury, with Regan becoming chief of staff. Meese became attorney general, and Deaver became a political consultant. Regan, an egotistic, serious, austere personality, decided that the president should deemphasize public relations and focus more on substance. This was not playing to Reagan's strengths. Regan tried to push the president too fast. When Regan and his assistants spent weeks on a policy agenda for the second term, the president said simply, "OK" and did not read it. To the old actor, policy was not much different from "show business." It had worked during his first term when he was surrounded by nurturing aides. To make Reagan's administration succeed, one must understand him. For all his drive and wealth of administrative experience, Donald Regan did not know the president.

After the 1984 election, Reagan undertook few new initiatives except for tax reform and immigration reform. The Immigration Reform and Control Act of 1986 made it more difficult for illegal immigrants to enter America and obtain employment, yet offered an amnesty to those who had lived in America since January 1, 1982.

America's space program continued to soar, and, in one tragic accident, to crash. The Apollo program continued, yet near disaster struck *Apollo 13* in 1970, and the astronauts aborted their Moon mission and returned to Earth. In the 1980s, the reusable space shuttle became the major vehicle for manned space exploration. On January 28, 1986, the near tragedy of *Apollo 13* was eclipsed by the horror of the fourth space shuttle, *Challenger*, which exploded in the Florida sky seconds after liftoff. All seven astronauts were killed, and the shuttle program was grounded for thirty-two months.

On the ground, a new scourge surfaced, erecting roadblocks on the avenue to the sexual revolution. Acquired immune deficiency syndrome (AIDS), caused by a virus transmitted through unprotected sex with an infected person, the sharing of needles for drug injections, and transfusions of tainted blood, gave rise to a deadly pandemic. The human immunodeficiency virus destroyed the immune systems of patients, leaving them vulnerable to diseases. First diagnosed in 1981, the disease initially struck homosexuals and bisexuals who had unsafe sex, then moved into the population at large; 97,000 cases were reported by 1989, when 46,000 had died of AIDS. Medical experts, among them Reagan's surgeon general, C. Everett Koop, warned people to take precautions against AIDS, including the use of condoms during intercourse. New drugs were discovered to extend the lives of patients, but in the twenty-first century the stubborn virus defied efforts to find a cure, and emphasis continued on prevention.

Reagan and the "Evil Empire"

Whereas Nixon had ushered in détente and Carter focused on human rights, Reagan's initial foreign policies focused on combating communism. His objective was not continued stalemate or mere continuation of a fragile peace. His objective was to win the Cold War.

The scenario had surprises. The old warrior became a peacemaker, yet on his watch communism was set up for the kill. Few people, not even Reagan, foresaw the result, yet history proved again that surprise is its essence.

Early in the administration, prominent cabinet members such as Secretary of State Alexander Haig and Secretary of Defense Caspar Weinberger were bullish on America, skeptical of compromise with the Soviets. Reagan termed the Soviet bloc an "evil empire" destined for the "ash heap of history." His challenge invited ridicule, yet he was closer to the truth than anyone realized. Even Nancy Reagan cautioned her husband to temper his language.

Still, as Reagan entered the presidency, never had the Cold War seemed more wintry. As a series of Soviet leaders died in office, Reagan's first term lapsed without a single summit. Reagan complained that he could not meet Soviet leaders because they kept dying on him. Secretary Shultz, chastened for being a part of the first administration to go four years without a Soviet summit, retorted that he was not going to schedule a meeting merely to keep the record intact.

If Reagan was right about communism's destiny, he was wrong about the path it would travel to get there and about his role in the process. Yet he was determined to fight communism with all the tools available—military might, economic pressure, espionage, denial of technology, and withholding of credit and oil revenue, to squeeze the beleaguered economy. Whereas previous presidents had viewed trade as an avenue to understanding, Reagan viewed economic warfare as a weapon to add steam to the pressure cooker that was the Soviet economy. Meanwhile, the United States was armed to the teeth and extended aid to all nations resisting communism. Reagan rammed the MX missile program through Congress in 1987, and placed intermediate-range nuclear weapons in Europe to equal Soviet missiles there. The deployment inflamed the nuclear freeze movement in Europe and America.

As early as 1983 Reagan had added an untested new technology to the mix, proposing an intricate network of laser beams and missiles to destroy incoming missiles. Many American experts considered the Strategic Defense Initiative (SDI), nicknamed "Star Wars" after the popular science fiction movies, impractical. Star Wars was a dual threat to the Soviets: they could not match the technology and they could not afford the research. The new Soviet leader who came to power in 1985, Mikhail Gorbachev, realized that compromise and internal reform were essential for the communist system to survive, and he desired a more amicable relationship with the West. Gorbachev was ready to deal; Reagan, already holding the trump cards, was ready to play. In time, these two men bonded, and Reagan forged a closer relationship with Gorbachev than any president in history had established with a foreign foe.

Gorbachev embarked on policies of *perestroika*, or economic restructuring, and *glasnost*, or openness, and relaxed many of the restrictions on dissent in Soviet society. Fearful that the Cold War could consume his plans to build a viable consumer economy, he tried to reduce expenditures by relaxing tensions with the West at summits in Geneva, Reykjavik in Iceland, Washington, and Moscow. In 1986 at Reykjavik, the leaders struck the most sweeping arms agreement in history: to eliminate all nuclear weapons in ten years. But the accord never gelled because Gorbachev insisted that Reagan give up Star Wars. The Soviets took Reagan's missile defense plan seriously. Gorbachev believed Moscow would bankrupt itself trying to compete with SDI technology. For that reason, Reagan refused to give it up.

In 1987 Reagan traveled to Europe and, in a visit to West Berlin, stood at the Brandenburg Gate of the Berlin Wall, symbolic of the division of free

TAKING HIS MESSAGE TO THE HEART OF EUROPE
Ronald Reagan in Berlin, 1987.
(Ronald Reagan Presidential Library)

and captive worlds. "Mr. Gorbachev, open this gate! Mr. Gorbachev, tear down this wall!" Reagan said. Gorbachev did not then order the wall torn down, yet at a Washington summit later that year, the Soviets and the Americans signed the INF Treaty eliminating a whole class of weapons, intermediate-range nuclear weapons, and providing for on-site inspections to ensure compliance. Whereas previous treaties had limited growth of nuclear weapons, INF was the first to destroy weapons. Gorbachev and Reagan met once more, in 1988 in Moscow, cementing their relationship.

Meanwhile, Gorbachev was easing the Soviet grip on Europe. He cut the Soviet army by five hundred thousand soldiers and withdrew fifty thousand troops and five thousand tanks from Eastern Europe. Then he evacuated the last Soviet troops from Afghanistan, reduced aid to the Sandinistas, and asked Castro to remove Cuban troops from Africa. Gorbachev unleashed forces of liberation that he could not control, placing the Soviet Union on the brink of collapse. It needed only a nudge from nationalists in its republics, whom he would not crush with force. The denouement occurred under Bush, but Reagan was party to one of the greatest upheavals in world history. Historians differ over whether Reagan stage-managed the beginning of the end of the Soviet Union or whether he was mainly in the right place at the right time. They differ over whether he and Gorbachev rode the tides of history, beckoned them, or did a little of both. Regardless, they presided over momentous times and decreased the danger of nuclear war.

Other Foreign Challenges

Peace on a global scale, paradoxically, was easier to achieve than harmony in the Middle-East. Reagan, like his predecessors, found the region a place of problems with no solutions and crushed hopes. The Palestinians wanted a homeland, yet the Israelis considered that a threat to their security. Instead, Israeli leaders encouraged Jews to settle in the occupied territories to sustain their claim. Then in June 1982, the Israelis invaded Lebanon, a launching pad for terrorist raids by Yasir Arafat's Palestine Liberation Organization (PLO). The Palestinians evacuated Lebanon, leaving in their wake a civil war that pitted Christians against Muslims. Reagan sent two thousand Marines to Lebanon as part of an international peacekeeping force to supervise the PLO withdrawal, angering the Muslim militias. Violence struck the Americans on October 22, 1983, when a young Muslim detonated a truck-bomb that killed 239 Americans. Reagan tried to maintain the Lebanese mission, but in February 1984 the Lebanese government fell and the remaining Marines were withdrawn.

Jerusalem protested when Reagan sold tanks, missiles, and planes with sophisticated radar technology to Saudi Arabia, an American ally, yet an Israeli adversary. Washington opposed the Israeli bombing of Iraq's nuclear reactor in June 1981, yet benefited from the destruction later in its two wars against Iraq; otherwise, Iraq might have possessed nuclear weapons. Despite disagreements, Israel remained America's closest ally in the turbulent Middle East and the only democracy there. The administration promised not to have contact with Arafat and the PLO until it renounced terrorism and recognized Israel's right to exist. Not until Arafat satisfied the United States on these counts did Reagan's diplomats begin talking seriously to the Palestinians about a Middle-East accord. More intransigent, Libya became a target of a rare use of force by Reagan's administration. After U.S. naval maneuvers in the Gulf of Sidra, an area claimed by Dictator Muammar Qaddafi, Libyan jets harassed American forces, and U.S. planes shot down two of them. Washington later blamed Tripoli for the bombing of a German nightclub that claimed the life of an American serviceman. In retaliation, U.S. jets bombed Libyan military sites and Qaddafi's residence, killing one of his daughters.

Elsewhere, the administration had an easier time working its will. In 1982 the United States supported Britain against Argentina in the Falkland Islands War. Fighting broke out after Buenos Aires, backed by the Soviet Union and the Organization of American States, seized the islands off the South American coast, owned by Britain. A British naval expedition retook the islands, and Reagan won the gratitude of British Prime Minister Margaret Thatcher, his closest ally and ideological soul mate.

In 1983, shortly after the deaths of the Marines in Lebanon, the United States invaded the tiny Caribbean island of Grenada. Washington said it acted to rescue eight hundred American medical students. Also, it believed Soviet reconnaissance planes might use an airport under construction. In fact, the administration overthrew the Marxist government and installed leaders supportive of the United States. A force of American soldiers and small contingents from six Caribbean nations deposed the dictator, General Hudson Austin. The invasion was condemned internationally yet most Americans supported it.

Three years later, Washington helped oust two other dictators, Jean-Claude Duvalier of Haiti and Ferdinand Marcos of the Philippines. Duvalier had succeeded his father as ruler of his impoverished island and had continued the elder Duvalier's oppressive policies. Finally demonstrators drove him from power, after the United States warned Duvalier not to use force against them. Americans provided a plane to fly him to exile in France. Marcos, a longtime American ally, fell due to a declining economy and the

1983 murder of a popular opposition leader, which prompted a Marxist revolution. He surprised detractors by allowing elections in 1986 and won a rigged vote over Corazon Aquino, widow of the slain opposition leader. Popular demonstrations against Marcos followed, and part of the Philippine army defected to Aquino. Reagan withdrew his backing of Marcos and arranged for him to leave the country.

Central America drew much of Reagan's attention, and the United States became involved in two wars by proxy. It grew embroiled in battling Marxism, in one case supporting a government against guerrillas and in another case backing rebels against rulers. In El Salvador, leftists tried to overthrow the government, countered by death squads that assassinated leftists. Carter suspended aid to the Salvadoran government because of human rights violations, but Reagan restored it and sent CIA advisers. A reformer, Jose Napolean Duarte, elected president in 1984, implemented land reform, stopped the death squad killings, and opened negotiations with the rebels. Elections returned the right to power in 1988 after Duarte died. The war escalated, continuing after Reagan left the White House. In neighboring Nicaragua, the Sandinistas, who received aid from the Soviet Union and Cuba, tried to export revolution and vanquish the opposition Contras. Congress outlawed attempts to support the Contras or to overthrow the Sandinistas, yet Reagan continued aid.

The Iran-Contra Affair

Considering the Contras liberators, Reagan urged National Security Adviser Robert McFarlane to do whatever was needed to help them "keep body and soul together." A Marine officer on the National Security Council (NSC) staff, Lieutenant Colonel Oliver North, helped McFarlane secretly raise millions from third parties. North directed a covert operation that funneled supplies and information to the Contras. The actions defied the Reagan-approved Boland Amendments, which prohibited the government from furnishing support to the Contras. After journalists and members of Congress heard of the covert operations, McFarlane lied to House investigators in 1986, denying the NSC was involved.

Meanwhile, members of the Reagan administration hoped to establish links with Iranian moderates, selling them weapons and spare parts to use in their war against Iraq. In exchange, the Iranians were supposed to use their influence to free American hostages held by Islamic militants in Lebanon. The Iranians hoodwinked the Americans, led by North, stockpiling weapons but releasing few hostages. However, North also hoodwinked the Iranians by overcharging them for the arms he sold and giving the profits to the Nicaraguan

Contras. The transactions were illegal on both ends: law forbade trade with terrorist nations and Congress had cut off aid to the Contras. The subterfuge was exposed when the Sandinistas shot down a plane carrying weapons to Nicaragua in October 1986. The pilot, Eugene Hasenfus, confessed.

The United States denied knowing of Hasenfus's mission, but North, anticipating that Hasenfus would expose the operation, began to shred documents. Reagan admitted to the sales and to the aims of winning the freedom of American hostages and of courting Iranian moderates. Iranian-supported terrorism persisted despite the arms transfers, as groups took additional American hostages.

It was left to Attorney General Edwin Meese to scrutinize the affair and report to Reagan. North admitted to Meese that arms sales profits were diverted to finance the Contras, and when Meese informed the president of the discovery, Reagan seemed shocked. Someone in the administration had to take the blame, so North was removed from the NSC. Admiral John Poindexter, who replaced McFarlane as national security adviser—and who would reveal that he hid the fund diversion from Reagan to shield the president—resigned. Finally, a shaken Reagan and Meese revealed details about the Iran-Contra affair to the public and announced the creation of a board under former Texas Republican Senator John Tower to investigate. Reagan appeared before the country in a televised speech in March 1987, saying he accepted responsibility for what happened in his administration.

A House-Senate committee held televised hearings in the summer of 1987, in which North proclaimed that his actions, however illegal, were in the national interest, and appeared for a time as a heroic figure. The lawmakers did not conclude that Reagan personally knew of wrongdoing, yet assailed the administration for the flouting of the law and said that if Reagan did not know what his aides were doing, "he should have." Focusing on the illegalities, Lawrence Walsh, a court-appointed special prosecutor, indicted a number of Iran-Contra figures, including North and Poindexter, who were convicted. It took Walsh until 1994, five years after Reagan left office, to issue a final report in which he said that Reagan, although his actions fell short of criminal conduct, "created the conditions which made possible the crimes committed by others." Appeals courts overturned North's and Poindexter's convictions on technical grounds, though, and lesser figures received pardons from President George Bush.

Reagan's Legacy

Reagan was able to select his successor, Bush, who won the Republican nomination over a field that featured Kansas Senator Robert Dole, New

York Representative Jack Kemp, and televangelist Pat Robertson. Bush's running mate was the relatively obscure Indiana Senator Dan Quayle, who drew questions because he had used family connections to join the National Guard and avoid combat in the Vietnam War and because of doubts over his intelligence and experience. On the Democratic side, leading party members stayed out of the race, but there were plenty of contenders, among them Colorado Senator Gary Hart, who was the front-runner until it was learned that he apparently had extramarital affairs. The Reverend Jesse Jackson made the biggest impact of any African American candidate in American history. Massachusetts Governor Michael Dukakis won the nomination, largely because he revived his state's economy. He picked Texas Senator Lloyd Bentsen for the second place on the ticket.

WORKING FOR A BETTER FUTURE Reagan and Soviet leader Mikhail Gorbachev in Moscow, 1988. (Ronald Reagan Presidential Library)

Dukakis emerged from the Democratic convention with a substantial lead in the polls over Bush, yet lacked the passion to inspire voters. Bush exploited the public's fear of crime by running advertisements blaming Dukakis for the release of murderer and rapist Willie Horton, who committed more crimes while out of prison. The ads were labeled racist because Horton was black. Bush also boasted of his experience in foreign policy and cited the prosperity under Reagan. He won comfortably, with 48.8 million popular votes and 426 electoral votes to 41.8 million and 111 for Dukakis. The election was, in effect, another referendum on Reagan, a reaffirmation that he was one of the most popular presidents of the post–World War II era, although Democrats retained control of Congress.

If Reagan was not a great president, neither was he a mediocre one. He defined the 1980s as no president had defined a decade since Franklin Roosevelt in the 1930s. His greatest contribution was psychological, like FDR's. Reagan, like Roosevelt, was a gifted communicator with a sunny disposition who made decisions intuitively. With Reagan setting the pace, the national mood was upbeat. Reagan made patriotism fashionable and dispelled the sense of inferiority that had infested the military since Vietnam. But his flaws were real. Race relations suffered; greed proliferated; cities continued to decline; and the military-industrial complex operated at full blast. The Iran-Contra scandal violated the law. Though Reagan's defense expenditures bankrupted the Soviet Union, they also nearly bankrupted the United States. Still, the ending of the Cold War on his successor's watch was a landmark event in the Time of Paradox, comparable to winning World War II. If the danger of war did not disappear, at least it decreased, and if Reagan appeared Janus-faced, a likeable grandfather, and a hard-hearted militarist, he was in fact more complicated than he seemed. His story is fraught with paradoxes and contradictions, as is America's—and full of surprises.

Reagan hoped to spend his retirement largely at his ranch, riding horses, watching old movies, and being with Nancy. However, late in 1994, he told the public he had been diagnosed with Alzheimer's disease, a fatal ailment that destroys the brain and central nervous system, causing senility and dementia in patients whose bodies appear otherwise healthy. Because the disease acts slowly, and because of his mental lapses, some wondered whether he had suffered from the condition while president. In a handwritten public statement he announced: "I now begin the journey that will lead me into the sunset of my life. I know that for America there will always be a bright dawn ahead." On June 5, 2004, Reagan slipped from the twilight of Alzheimer's to the darkness of death. At ninety-three, he was the oldest ex-president in history.

CHAPTER TEN

A Culture of Diversity

B Y THE END of the twentieth century, popular culture was the oxygen of American life. Television shows and films gave more people a collective vision of themselves and reality than literature and painting. Even politics became a form of entertainment. American popular culture conquered the imagination of the world, integrating influences from other cultures and leaving its imprint. The arts addressed timeless human concerns, yet they lost their focus, as merchandising and marketing threatened to become the measure of success.

The Jaws of Hollywood

The 1970s were a golden age for Hollywood: artistry combined with box office success. But there was a descending spiral of violence, gratuitous sex, and graphic gore. Talented and untalented filmmakers felt free to extend the boundaries of decency. The 1970s brought a new generation of directors and landmark movies, among them Francis Ford Coppola with *The Godfather* (1972) and *Apocalypse Now* (1979), Martin Scorcese with *Taxi Driver* (1976), Steven Spielberg with *Jaws* (1975) and *Close Encounters of the Third Kind* (1977), and George Lucas with *American Graffiti* (1973) and *Star Wars* (1977). New actors became popular, notably Robert De Niro, Robert Duvall, and Harrison Ford. The best films of those years helped shape the culture of America and the world.

Millions of people imagined organized crime through *The Godfather*; *Apocalypse Now* helped Americans articulate their feelings about the Vietnam War; *Close Encounters* mirrored and magnified the growing belief that extraterrestrials were watching our world. *Star Wars* and its successors, the most popular science fiction ever, created a galactic mythology, embedded with moral and religious symbols.

Jaws, adapted from a novel about a killer shark that menaces a small resort town, had an enormous impact on Hollywood. It made so much money so rapidly that it invented the summer blockbuster and helped speed a reversal of the unprofitability of moviemaking (weekly admissions had reached an all-time low in 1971). *Jaws* inspired movies featuring bigger, louder, faster sensations rather than plot or character. The theme was spun off into toys, soundtrack albums, and, later, video games.

The blockbuster phenomenon rose to new levels with Spielberg's *Jurassic Park* (1993), a science fiction tale of dinosaurs resurrected. It grossed a record $50.2 million in its opening weekend, and, with video rentals, pay cable, and foreign markets, revenues surged to well over $1 billion. Spielberg made his mark as a serious filmmaker with *Schindler's List* (1993), a compelling exploration of good amid the evil of the Holocaust.

During the 1970s Hollywood discovered that films made for "niche" audiences, independently of the major studios could earn profits. Among the most successful "indie" producers were Spike Lee, *She's Gotta Have It* (1986) Quentin Tarantino, *Pulp Fiction* (1994), and Steven Soderbergh, *sex, lies, and videotape* (1989). These producers excelled at creativity rather than expensive special effects, often using handheld cameras. Lee gave a voice to the African American perspective and achieved a devoted following. Eventually, most of the successful "indies" were absorbed by the major studios. Another trend, often relying on special effects and thin plots, were movies based on comic book superheros of the 1950s and 1960s, such as Superman, Spiderman, and Batman.

When videocassette recorders became an appliance in most American homes in the early 1980s, doomsayers predicted the demise of movie cinemas. Instead, the 1990s marked a cinema building boom. Larger, multiscreen houses, often offering expensive customer amenities, rose at a furious pace. Video rentals and sales became a lucrative ancillary market, providing the studios with profits and even new outlets for distributing movies never shown on the big screen.

The Changing Sound of Music

Popular music continued its rapid development in the Era of Diversity, often in unexpected ways. Two of the biggest pop stars of the era, Michael Jackson and Madonna, represented the triumph of image and marketing made possible after 1980 by music videos, which revolutionized the way recordings and recording artists were sold to the public. Their fame was a facet of the cult of celebrity, raised to new levels because of the pervasiveness of television and the tabloid media. Neither Jackson nor Madonna was a musical innovator. By the 2000s Madonna's CD sales were in decline, though she seemed a fixture of tabloid journalism and celebrity television. Jackson's career plummeted as he was unable to stimulate public interest in his new recordings since 1990 and became embroiled in much-publicized charges of child molestation.

The sensibility of rock, grown mellow and theatrical in the 1970s, was shaken at the end of that decade by punk rock, an often abrasive but frequently ironic music born in New York. Punk rock inspired many younger musicians to follow less commercial paths, sometimes to great success, and spurred a number of developments, including the popularity of noncommercial college radio stations that promoted "alternative rock" (as much postpunk rock would be called).

POP ROYALTY
The Reagans and Michael Jackson at the White House Ceremony to launch the Campaign against Drunk Driving, 1984.
(Ronald Reagan Presidential Library)

Reggae, a Jamaican popular music drawing from American rhythm and blues, indigenous rhythms and postcolonial outrage, gained a following in America during the 1970s. It remained the most popular "non-American" music in the United States until a wave of Hispanic singers washed across the charts at the end of the century. Similarly, music called "rap" emerged to challenge rock as the idiom of youth culture. Originating among Jamaican immigrants in New York during the 1970s, rap began to displace rock from the music charts in the 1990s. Rap is essentially a rhythmic form of speaking in rhyme, rooted among Africans transported as slaves to the New World. Hip-hop, the music accompanying rap, created rhythm from turntables and by "sampling" a collage of excerpts from previous recordings. Although country music, long a staple of the working class, also enjoyed booming popularity during the years of rap's ascent, by 1998 rap for the first time outsold country. Like rock music before it, rap's lyrics became a source of concern among parents, politicians, and social activists. Many rappers described scenes of grotesque street violence; others appeared to glorify misogyny, violence, and unbridled materialism.

Sampling was the most radical development in music since the electric guitar. Electronic instruments called synthesizers became more accessible in the 1970s and turned up in everything from the most experimental rock to the biggest disco dance hits. Introduction of digital technology in the 1980s finally made the instrument widely affordable and easy to use. The dance music that young people enjoyed became an increasingly complex hybrid incorporating sampling, synthesized sounds, and the metronomic disco beat. But during the final decades of the twentieth century, upsurges of nostalgia accompanied innovation. In the 1990s younger audiences were fascinated with 1940s swing, 1950s rockabilly from the rural South, 1960s psychedelia, and 1970s disco. Jazz found a voice of neotraditionalism in trumpeter Wynton Marsalis, whose explorations of the music's prerock heritage led him to perform jazz in prestigious cultural centers, although the music's impact on record sales was meager.

Significant innovations in classical music occurred in the 1970s when modernist composers Philip Glass and Steve Reich responded to the hypnotic allure of Asian music and the forceful impact of rock. In the 1980s John Adams led postmodernists in a return to some of the tonality of an earlier age. Despite commissioning of new work, the core repertoire of American symphony orchestras was unchanged since the early twentieth century. The "early music movement," concerned with European compositions and instruments from pre-Mozart times, grew from a marginal subculture into an important influence on classical music in the 1990s.

★ MADONNA: MATERIAL GIRL IN A MATERIAL AGE ★

I know I'm not the best singer and I know I'm not the best dancer.
But I'm not interested in that. I'm interested in pushing people's
buttons . . . in being political and provocative.

—MADONNA

MATERIAL GIRL
1980s Pop Star Madonna poses at
the MTV Video Music Awards
in September 1984.
(AP/Wide World Photos)

THE AGE OF Diversity was epitomized by the political icon of the 1980s, President Ronald Reagan, and its cultural icon, the singer Madonna. Each represented one face of the decade, which featured political conservatism and cultural hedonism. Reagan was credited with bringing prosperity; Madonna flaunted her sexuality and touted herself as the "Material Girl." ("We are living in a material world, and I am a material girl," she sang.) Reagan made Americans feel good about themselves; he made patriotism and consumerism popular. Madonna freed Americans from their inhibitions and made them feel good about having fun. Although no Paul Revere of the sexual revolution, she plunged a dagger into the heart of conformity. Madonna dressed for shock value, championed her love of uninhibited sex, and became a celebrity superstar as much for her outrageous fashions and statements as for her modest talents as a singer and actress. "The arena I choose to express myself in is sexuality," she said.

Born Madonna Louise Ciccone in 1958 in Michigan, Madonna did not spend her formative years in the Hollywood entertainment industry in which she would make her career, but in the bohemian artistic and music culture of New York. There she absorbed the rhythms of contemporary dance music and was influenced by the gay subculture that spawned it. Her first big hit, "Lucky Star" (1983), was catapulted onto the charts because of MTV. The song launched a fashion fad, as millions of girls adopted the look Madonna had gleaned from New York street fashions.

Madonna continually reinvented her appearance, recycling the sexuality of such screen stars as Marilyn Monroe and surrounding herself with tuxedo-clad choruses of admiring men. Although First Lady Nancy Reagan urged young people to "just say no" to drugs and promiscuous sex, Madonna offered a countermessage. "Look, everybody has different needs and wants and preferences and desires and fantasies. And we should not damn somebody or judge somebody because it's different than yours," she said. Madonna attempted to portray just about every orientation imaginable in her music videos, stage performances, and her book *Sex* (1992).

Aside from her film debut, *Desperately Seeking Susan* (1985), Madonna's movies were usually greeted with critical hostility and public indifference. Although her high-profile marriage to actor Sean Penn ended in divorce, she continued to flirt with the cinema, picking up roles such as *Evita*, and marrying British director Guy Ritchie in 2000. Her recording career was not an unblemished record of success after 1990, but she remained almost ubiquitous in the media, which covered her interest in Jewish mysticism, her child-rearing, and her love of England.

Resolutely commercial and flaunting her ambitions, Madonna continued to update her image into the twenty-first century, assimilating new ideas in popular culture and reshaping them into commercial form. Her dominance in the spotlight prompts Americans to ponder whether she represents the light side or the dark side of their society.

Sources: Books containing useful sketches on Madonna include June Sochen, *From Mae to Madonna* (1999), and Tom McGrath, *MTV: The Making of a Revolution* (1996).

Enormous changes occurred within the recording industry in the 1990s and 2000s. Ownership was increasingly consolidated into the hands of a few corporate giants whose concerns had less to do with music than with short-term profitability. Classical music and jazz departments were gutted. Career development for rock and pop acts declined in an era when big, instant hits were expected. CD sales slumped because of widespread consumer dissatisfaction as well as the proliferation of file sharing technology, which allowed listeners to download music online. Being signed to a major record label was no longer the dream for many musicians, who began to manage their own careers by working through the internet or a network of small, independent labels whose owners were still concerned with quality.

Picturing and Wiring the World

By the 1990s the art business reached new heights of profitability, with powerful international auction houses setting records for sales of famous artists. Colleges conferred more master's degrees in visual and performing arts than in English, biology, and math. But the money that wealthy collectors spent at auction trickled into the pockets of relatively few contemporary artists, and the proliferation of art majors did not spur a new Renaissance. "All I see is art-school art," art historian Barbara Rose said.

"Basically it looks like homework, because what is homework but learning how to follow the teacher's rules?"

A gap remained between the general public and the visual arts, a problem since the birth of modernism. Public sculpture was seldom controversial until people no longer recognized the meaning of the abstractions being erected with their tax dollars. Even in New York, the art world's mecca, public complaints forced the federal government to remove Richard Serra's wall of curved steel, *Tilted Arc*, from the Federal Plaza in 1989. In the years that followed, cities and public agencies spent a larger amount of funds on public art, most of it decorative and whimsical rather than inspiring. An exception was Maya Lin's acclaimed Vietnam Veterans Memorial (1982) in Washington, a stark black wall bearing the name of every American killed in the Vietnam War.

In 1989 federal funding of the arts through the National Endowment for the Arts (NEA), established in 1965, became embroiled in a "culture war" between liberals and conservatives. The target was Andres Serrano's photograph *Piss Christ*, an image of a plastic crucifix submerged in amber-colored fluid. His work was a statement about the kitschy degradation of religious imagery. The Christian right and some members of Congress were outraged over a $15,000 grant Serrano received from a regional art center funded by the NEA. In 1990 similar fury erupted over an exhibition of Robert Mapplethorpe—photographs in Washington. Mapplethorpe's classically composed depictions of homosexuality and sado-masochism garnered accolades from the art world and denunciations from other quarters. Because federal money had funded the Corcoran Gallery, two prominent Republican senators—Jesse Helms of North Carolina and Alfonse D'Amato of New York—launched an attack that canceled the show.

Art of the 1990s often addressed sociopolitical topics such as AIDS, racism, and sexism. The most important political artworks—quilts memorializing AIDS victims—took their form from the oldest traditions of American folk art. By the end of the century, visual art had expanded to encompass video, performance art, and often room-size installations in addition to painting, printmaking, photography, and sculpture. Yet the ambitions of art seemed to have shrunk. Coherent ideologies engaged only a few artists, and there was neither a prevailing method nor a desire for one. Almost everything was acceptable, and nothing was particularly essential.

Postmodernism, the most popular catchall for cultural endeavors after the mid-1980s, found its most public and concrete expression in architecture. Philip Johnson moved architecture away from the rigid geometry of modernism to a style that honored, and often randomly appropriated, the past. The unadorned boxes of modernism became unfashionable, although the best postmodern architecture was witty, striking, and powerful. America nonetheless was soon covered with cheap, faceless buildings that aped postmodern styles.

Broadcasting underwent dramatic changes near the end of the twentieth century. Radio became an important national sounding board with the spread of call-in talk shows, many hosted by conservatives. The FM band, absent from many radio sets before 1970, was a growing industry. Programming became increasingly standardized, a dearth of variety that encouraged the popularity of noncommercial music stations. News-oriented National Public Radio, founded by the federal government in 1969, maintained high standards.

As radio evolved to satisfy the changing interests of its audience, television was transformed. A force for cultural uniformity in 1970, with millions of viewers glued to only three national networks (ABC, CBS, and NBC), TV became a vehicle for cultural diversity by 1999. New competitors brought the first changes. The corporation for Public Broadcasting established through federal law in 1969, won acclaim for its children's show *Sesame Street* and became an outlet for literate entertainment and documentaries. Other commercial networks, such as Fox and Warner Brothers, also gained reputations for creative programming in the 1990s.

Innovations sprang from technology. Hand-held remote controls allowed viewers to "surf" between programs. Cable TV, which became widely available in the 1980s, yielded hundreds of special interest channels. Viewers with satellite dishes could see still greater numbers of channels than cable provided. The global broadcasting market offered a variety of programming targeted at every conceivable audience, including sports, movies, fine arts, popular music, news, weather, comedy, and history. The introduction of videocassette recorders, a fixture in homes after the Supreme Court's 1984 ruling that home taping did not infringe on copyright laws, changed the way television was watched. It enabled viewers to record programs and watch them at their leisure.

The social changes and increased frankness stemming from the cultural upheavals of the 1960s had enormous impact on programs beginning in the 1970s. Among the groundbreaking series were *All in the Family*, which satirized middle-class prejudices; *M*A*S*H*, which satirized the military; *The Mary Tyler Moore Show*, which depicted an independent career woman; and *Saturday Night Live*, which pushed comedy to new levels of outrageousness. It introduced such stars as John Belushi, Eddie Murphy, Chevy Chase, Steve Martin, and Dan Aykroyd. Popular miniseries such as *Roots* influenced American perceptions of history. Sports, which had largely been

TV'S WORKING
WOMAN
Actress Mary Tyler
Moore holds two
Emmy Awards that she
won in 1974 for her
role on the *Mary Tyler
Moore Show*.
(AP/Wide World Photos)

confined to Saturday and Sunday afternoon telecasts, began to spread into the rest of the week.

A significant addition to programming during the 1980s was the debut of the cable channel MTV, whose fast-paced aesthetic left a mark not only on the music industry but also on television, advertising, and movies. Meanwhile, network shows developed new sophistication with *Hill Street Blues*, a police story whose flawed heroes, gritty realism, and open-ended narrative paved the way for such popular realistic dramas as *NYPD Blue* and *Law and Order*. Epitomizing the response of many Americans to media saturation, comedian David Letterman presented an ironic talk, comedy and variety show. Jay Leno succeeded Johnny Carson as host of the *Tonight* show, featuring monologues based on current events. *The Oprah Winfrey Show* was serious and emotional. American television's first nationally prominent black talk show host, Winfrey dispensed hugs, shed tears, and contributed diversity to the culture that pervaded the United States at the close of the century.

The signature shows of the 1990s were noteworthy for dysfunctional families and cynicism about national institutions. *The Simpsons*, a witty, sarcastic animated show, appealed to children for its visual gags and to adults for its lampooning of middle-class life. *Seinfeld* saw humor in life's petty annoyances. Cable News Network (CNN) brought news into homes twenty-four hours a day. The Persian Gulf War received saturation coverage. Reporting of the murder trial of ex-football star O. J. Simpson also blurred the line between news and entertainment. Once the most reticent medium, television was sexualized in content to a degree difficult to imagine only a few years earlier. New social attitudes, competition from pay-per-view channels, and the no-holds-barred Internet brought sexuality to the small screen. Early in the 2000s, "reality shows" proliferated. Beautiful women and rugged men competed for dates, mates, and money, by surmounting a series of physical and mental challenges. These shows, too, were infused with sexuality. More changes loomed from the enhanced visual quality of high-definition television and hybrid digital technology that promised to diminish the distinction between TV and Internet, ultimately fusing electronic communication into one mega-medium.

The Internet, a global computer network that transcended geography, political barriers, and time zones, accelerated communications. At the start of the 1990s the Internet was an open frontier, yet by the end of the decade, civilization had begun to cultivate and control the medium. By 1999, 80 million Americans were online, sending e-mail, shopping, making investments, applying for mortgages, viewing pornography, and even consulting physicians.

Churning news and rumor with unsettling speed, the Internet gave traditional news media a run for their audiences. Some worried the Internet would supplant the older media. Ratings plummeted for nightly network news programs, and newspaper readership declined. Other problems accompanied the growth of the Internet. There were legal questions: how to protect intellectual property rights online, how to resolve competing claims to names for Web addresses. Shoppers' credit card numbers could be stolen if the online connection was not secure. Sex abusers employed the Internet to lure victims. "Hackers" introduced computer "viruses" into the network illegally to sabotage victims' machines. Researchers cautioned that habitual Internet users were susceptible to depression and loneliness. The Internet was no substitute for human contact.

Attempting to coexist with the Internet and broadcast news, print journalism was less of a presence than it had been earlier. Competition from television, changing demographics, and expenses reduced the number of daily newspapers. Meaningful newspaper competition vanished in most cities.

Local ownership waned, swallowed in a wave of mergers and acquisitions by larger companies such as Gannett and Knight-Ridder. Gannett hastened the process with *USA Today*, a national paper introduced in the 1980s that stressed byte-sized news stories and use of color photos and graphics.

Writing and Performing in an Electronic Age

Battles over books raged in academia during the 1980s and 1990s. One of the fiercest skirmishes concerned the study of "great books," the classics of literature and philosophy. By the end of the 1990s, only a few universities still maintained a core curriculum of great books, which usually began with Homer and ended in the early twentieth century. But given the fractious state of the humanities and the withering of consensus over Western civilization, it became harder for educators to agree on what to include in a core curriculum. Now it was expected to reflect diverse perspectives, including non-Western cultures and such previously marginalized groups as women and racial minorities.

Some of the most important nonfiction books related to the feminist movement. Kate Millett's *Sexual Politics* (1970) found a political dimension in even the most intimate aspects of male-female relations. Germaine Greer's *The Female Eunuch* (1970) argues that women have been robbed of productive energy by being confined to passive sexual roles. Jean Bethke Elshtain's *Women and War* (1987) urges more nuanced understandings of gender roles. Camille Paglia's *Sexual Personae* (1990) asserts that female sexuality is humanity's most powerful force. She criticized feminism as single-minded, saying it was preoccupied with victimhood.

The velocity of change was the subject of Alvin Toffler's best seller *Future Shock* (1970), whose title became shorthand for the anxiety caused by rapid technological growth. Other influential nonfiction works were ambitious attempts at reporting recent events. Published during the author's exile from the Soviet Union, Aleksandr Solzhenitsyn's *The Gulag Archipelago*, 3 vols. (1973–1975) alerted the world to the Soviet Union's systematic abuse of human rights. *Washington Post* reporters Bob Woodward and Carl Bernstein published *All the President's Men* (1974), an indictment of the Watergate scandal that stimulated investigative reporting. Radio interviewer Studs Terkel compiled such acclaimed volumes of twentieth-century oral history as *Working* (1974) and *The Good War* (1984). Introduction of novelists' tools into nonfiction writing reached a controversial height with Edmund Morris's *Dutch* (1999), in which the biographer inserted a fictionalized version of himself into a biography of Ronald Reagan.

The American scientist of the late twentieth century with the greatest public recognition, astronomer Carl Sagan, authored several best sellers, including *Dragons of Eden* (1977), but reached his greatest audience by arguments in favor of extraterrestrial life in his television series *Cosmos* and appearances on the *Tonight Show*. Other science writers found nonspecialist readers, notably British astronomer Stephen Hawking, who popularized theories about the nature of the cosmos in his best seller *A Brief History of Time: From the Big Bang to Black Holes* (1988). In 2004 Hawking conceded that his theory of black holes was flawed and it might be possible for energy to escape from a black hole. James Gleick's *Chaos* (1987) stimulated the pondering of "chaos theory." Paradoxically, if the universe is sheer chaos, then chaos becomes its organizational principle. The popularity of those books is evidence that questions about the meaning of life, and the search for ultimate answers, has not gone out of style.

Many American historians were troubled over a lack of dialogue between historians and the public, blaming the national amnesia in part on academics more concerned with impressing peers than informing average readers. Despite some historians' tendency to retreat to ivory towers, others were determined to engage the public in the meaning of their country's history. Notable among them was Howard Zinn, whose *People's History of the United States* (1980) placed such previously ignored groups as women, African Americans, American Indians, and the poor into mainstream American history. History started being taught in a broader context, shifting the emphasis from Western civilization to world civilization. John Hope Franklin pioneered in the writing and teaching of African American history. Some historians lamented that politics and diplomacy were neglected, but important books about major leaders rolled off the nation's printing presses, including Robert Dallek's *Flawed Giant: Lyndon Johnson and His Times* (1998), and James MacGregor Burns's influential study of FDR, *Roosevelt: Soldier of Freedom* (1970). Historians used newly opened archives, especially Soviet sources on the Cold War, and such domestic sources as the private conversations taped by presidents John F. Kennedy, Lyndon Johnson, and Richard Nixon. Yet it was television, not books, that provided history with its greatest audience, especially Judy Crichton's compelling PBS series *The American Experience* and Ken Burns's epic PBS production *The Civil War*.

The most influential new philosopher was a Frenchman, Michel Foucault, who was interested in the mechanisms of power that underlie societies and the ways by which knowledge is translated into power. Pop psychology became one of the most profitable genres of publishing, beginning with Thomas Anthony Harris's bestseller *I'm OK, You're OK* (1969) and continuing through uncounted self-help manuals. Writers and speakers, including Deepak Chopra and Wayne Dyer, merged Eastern and Western religious beliefs, asserted that the human purpose was to become one with the universe, and taught their readers to manifest their desires through meditation. Practices such as meditation, yoga, Chinese and Japanese martial arts, and alternative medicine, part of the 1960s counterculture and dismissed as narcissistic in the "Me Decade" of the 1970s, were in the mainstream by the 1990s. Mysticism and non-Western philosophies and religions found a new open-mindedness, and people increasingly tended to trust their intuition, as artists long had done. Far more Americans visited health clubs than saw doctors. Herbal remedies often were preferred over prescription drugs; they were preventive, cheaper, and had fewer side effects. Jogging, bicycling, and weight lifting were increasingly popular for health and recreation. Psychology itself underwent a revolution during the final decades of the century. Clinical experiments with drugs led to pharmaceutical treatments that virtually supplanted Freudian analysis.

With films and popular music replacing literature for many younger people, and with most middle-class Americans wired to television and the Internet, book lovers had reason for pessimism. But Americans gathered in growing numbers to read and discuss books in clubs, which often were used to preserve time for reading in a society pressed for it. National bookstore chains displaced local stores and offered such amenities as coffee bars and musical entertainment. One of the most discussed Internet businesses, Amazon.com, started by selling books.

Literature wrestled with doubt, as some writers worried that fiction could no longer grapple with the truth of life and that society was changing too rapidly to be captured in a realistic "great American novel." Tom Wolfe defied the trend against realism with best-selling novels that depicted the lifestyles of America. In the 1960s Wolfe had been among the originators of "New Journalism"; later, he wrote novels and reached a large readership with *Bonfire of the Vanities* (1987), a social chronicle. Joyce Carol Oates, among America's most versatile authors, wrote scholarly and critical essays, poetry, and novels that explored social and economic history through personal narratives. Joan Didion used popular culture to ironic effect in her novels *Play It as It Lays* (1970) and *A Book of Common Prayer* (1977). Maya Angelou's best-selling autobiography, *I Know Why the Caged Bird Sings* (1970), was a raw account of a black woman growing up in the pre-civil rights South.

Science fiction continued to examine the implications of technology and social change. By the time of his death in 1986, Frank Herbert had completed six novels in his *Dune* series, a sprawling saga of galactic empire, and ecological devastation. William Gibson's groundbreaking novel about a computerized future, *Necromancer* (1984), was credited with coining the term "cyberspace" and envisioning the ramifications of the Internet and virtual reality. Anne Rice and Stephen King sold millions of copies of their novels about the supernatural, which commented on social mores. Rice's and King's enormous popularity signaled that most readers were still concerned with primordial questions of love, life, and death.

In 1986 Robert Penn Warren, a Pulitzer Prize winner for both fiction and poetry, was named the first Poet Laureate of the United States, recognition that came at a low point in poetry's commercial viability and popular esteem. Many talented writers embraced the greater opportunities for gaining an audience in the rock arena. Jim Carroll was among the few writers who maintained respectable careers in rock (his 1980 album *Catholic Boy* was well regarded), memoirs (*The Basketball Diaries*, 1978), and poetry (*Living at the Movies*, 1973).

For playwrights, after World War II it was generally conceded that the most adventurous theater productions came from "Off Broadway," and places such as Steppenwolf Theatre in Chicago, which developed contemporary plays and actors who became Hollywood stars. After 1970 the most prolific and successful writers to originate Off Broadway were Sam Shepard and David Mamet. Shepard's *Buried Child* (1978) and *A Lie of the Mind* (1987) were acclaimed for tapping such American imagery as rock stars, gangsters, and cowboys. Mamet became known for eccentric sketches of American life and language such as *Glengarry Glen Ross* (1983). Both playwrights also realized success in Hollywood.

Musical spectacles thrived on Broadway during the 1980s and 1990s, many of them originating on the London stage, especially Andrew Lloyd Webber's *Cats* (1981) and *The Phantom of the Opera* (1986). Movies including *The Lion King* and *Footloose* also became popular stage productions in the 1990s. A shortage of tuneful new songwriting encouraged revivals of the great musicals of the 1940s and 1950s.

As the twentieth century ended, the theater community complained about the increasing cost of producing plays and the difficulty of maintaining a dedicated and discriminating audience. Despite some popular triumphs, many of which relied on technology and visual spectacle, it was not generally considered a great period for new plays. The discouragement aside, even pessimists conceded that the theater remained a powerful medium.

The Cost of Sports

Long an adult pastime, organized sports reached the level of children, who had previously played spontaneously, by their own rules. Some believed that structured play prepared the young for the grown-up world, yet others regretted the loss of joy of unorganized play and complained that children grew up too fast. Most popular was Little League Baseball, which staged a World Series in 1947 and expanded internationally in 1952. By 1990 there were some 16,000 leagues in forty countries with 2.5 million players. For girls, there were the Bobby Sox and American Girl Softball, with 500,000 participants by 1990. The football counterpart to Little League was the Pop Warner League, which grew to 185,000 players in thirty-nine states by the same year. In no sport was the pressure on the young more intense than tennis, in which Jennifer Capriati turned professional at age thirteen and signed product endorsement contracts for $1 million. Girl gymnasts, swimmers, and figure skaters likewise matured young at the Olympic level.

A nostalgic sport for the ever-young, professional baseball was popular with baby boomers, yet it underwent sweeping changes in the Era of Diversity. Major League baseball widened the strike zone to speed the game in the 1960s, then took steps over the next three decades to encourage offense and home runs. Roger Maris's season record of sixty-one home runs, set in 1961 with the New York Yankees, stood until St. Louis Cardinals first baseman Mark McGwire hit seventy in 1998; three years later, San Francisco Giants outfielder Barry Bonds passed McGwire, clubbing seventy-three. An influx of African American, Hispanic, and Asian talent gave the game more power, dazzling speed, and relief pitching. Big market teams grew less dominant because of expanded play-offs, free agency for players, and the amateur draft. Economic imbalances that continued to favor teams in large cities were addressed in a 2002 labor agreement that featured revenue sharing and a "luxury tax" intended to discourage teams from taking on huge player payrolls. There were no dynasties comparable to the Yankees and Dodgers of the 1945–1969 period, although the Yankees and the Atlanta Braves were leading teams in the American League and the National League, respectively.

Football eclipsed baseball as the most popular spectator sport, with its championship, the Super Bowl, becoming a cultural celebration. National Football League (NFL) Commissioner Pete Rozelle promoted the concept of splitting the league's television revenue among all teams, allowing small town franchises such as the Green Bay Packers to survive. Dominating the Era of Diversity, the San Francisco 49ers and Dallas Cowboys won five Super Bowls apiece, the Pittsburgh Steelers four. The "West Coast offense," stressing short, low-risk passes that allowed a team to move down the field efficiently, became the vogue in the 1980s and remained widely used. College football scaled new heights, in part because of television, and became a major source of money and prestige for universities. High school football became a virtual religion, especially in small towns in the South and the Midwest.

Basketball likewise thrived in high schools, colleges, and the professional circuit, probably outdrawing football and baseball in live audiences when all levels of the sport were combined. In college basketball, the greatest dynasty belonged to the University of California, Los Angeles, which won ten national championships, seven consecutively, under coach John Wooden from 1964 to 1975 and featured players such as Lew Alcindor (later Kareem Abdul-Jabbar) and Bill Walton, both of whom went on to stellar careers in the National Basketball Association (NBA). The National Collegiate Athletic Association tournament became one of the most-watched sporting events, so much that CBS-TV paid billions for the right to broadcast it. Other players who electrified fans—Michael Jordan, Larry Bird, and Earvin "Magic" Johnson—catapulted the NBA to global popularity in the 1980s and 1990s. Bird's Boston Celtics and Johnson's Los Angeles Lakers were perennial contenders, but it was Jordan who dominated the 1990s by leading the Chicago Bulls to six league titles. American basketball was humiliated in the 2004 Summer Olympics when the nation's team, composed mostly of NBA stars, was beaten by 19 points by the team representing Puerto Rico and then again by tiny Lithuania.

Professional hockey struggled to gain a wide following outside its limited fan base in the United States, yet the National Hockey League (NHL) benefited from a greater influx of American stars from the college ranks. At the 1980 Winter Olympics in Lake Placid, New York, an unheralded and young U.S. squad stunned the hockey world by upsetting the powerful Soviet Union en route to the gold medal. Another sport that originated outside the United States, soccer, found great popularity among youths, and some forecast that the game would become the most popular sport in the country. Professional soccer did not quite gain the foothold expected in America, though, and predictions of the game's growth as a spectator sport went unfulfilled.

Tennis became one of the fastest-growing games in the 1970s, thanks to stars such as Billie Jean King, Chris Evert, Arthur Ashe, and Jimmy Connors. The sport waned in the 1980s with failures of American men in international competition, then revived in the 1990s, when Pete Sampras, Andre Agassi, and the Williams sisters, Venus and Serena, seized the headlines. Few blacks other than Ashe had left an imprint on the professional game, but the Williamses soon dominated the women's circuit. Golf enjoyed even more growth and overcame its reputation as an exclusively upper-class sport, stimulated by television and players including Arnold Palmer, Jack Nicklaus, the greatest golfer of his generation, and

Tiger Woods, who threatened to shatter Nicklaus's records. Woods helped inspire black youths to take up the game, promising to diversify the sport.

African American participation in sports was pervasive, especially in professional football and basketball. Athletes such as Jordan and Woods reaped the benefits of fame and lucrative contracts, prize money, and endorsement deals. But there were few black head coaches in the NFL or managers in baseball. There were fewer professional opportunities for women, although they made great strides in sports in the Era of Diversity. Feminism was injected into sports as part of the social upheavals of the 1960s and 1970s. Billie Jean King struck a symbolic blow for feminism in 1973 when she defeated tennis hustler Bobby Riggs, who had boasted that he could beat any woman, in a nationally televised match. In 1972, Title IX of the Education Act put the federal government's weight behind this movement, stipulating that colleges or universities that discriminated on the bases of sex, age, or race would lose all their federal funding. Institutions hastened to establish varsity programs for women, paving the way for large increases in the number of women playing intercollegiate sports and in girls playing high school sports. But attendance at women's games lagged, and only a handful of women's sports generated sufficient revenue to sustain themselves; to support the programs, colleges often had to cut spending on men's sports.

The public's taste for sports soured in the 1980s and 1990s as player strikes troubled the major professional leagues, athletes' salaries soared, and fans blamed rising costs for skyrocketing ticket prices. Major league baseball, the NFL, the NBA, and the NHL sought to slow the growth in player wages, but the lure of a big payday enticed more athletes to quit college and turn professional. Rules implemented to curb abuses in college sports and reinforce the importance of academics proved ineffective. Taunting of opposing players increased, especially in the NFL and the NBA, and team-oriented play declined. Many Americans deplored the lack of sportsmanship and questioned whether sports heroes were proper models for the young.

Nor was that former redoubt of amateurism, the Olympics, immune. Permitted by rule changes, the United States sent a team of virtually all professionals to the 1992 Summer Games in Barcelona, Spain, that swept to the gold medal. The Olympic image, however, had become tragic and politicized earlier. Arab terrorists murdered nine Israeli athletes at the 1972 Summer Games in Munich, West Germany. The United States boycotted the 1980 Moscow Summer Games in response to the Soviet invasion of Afghanistan, and the Soviets reciprocated by shunning the 1984 Los

Angeles Summer Games. One tawdry incident involved not drugs but thuggery: figure skater Tonya Harding hired a "hit man" to disable rival Nancy Kerrigan before the 1994 Winter Games in Lillehammer, Norway. Kerrigan recovered and won a medal; Harding did not place.

Big-time sports captivated and entertained countless fans, even if they no longer had the innocence of child's play. Americans nonetheless continued to discover meaning and purpose in sports, which became a metaphor for life, an exercise, and a diversion. Sports was, like many things, a virtue in moderation, a vice in excess.

By 2000 the contours of the first truly global culture were clear, driven by American sports, movies, television, and music and powered by the convergence of media, with the Internet the nexus for TV, radio, films, literature, and most other facets of popular art. Music could be downloaded from the Web, athletic competition watched on television screens in homes. Nonetheless, young people flocked to dance clubs, and sports fans still gathered in arenas and around the electronic campfire of televisions at taverns. The importance of shared experience—part of what it means to be human—endures.

CHAPTER ELEVEN

"Can We All Get Along?": The Soul of the Nation

THE LAST decades of the twentieth century were times of swift growth in population and transition in moral standards. Paradoxically, the nation was more stable than it had been in many such periods. The population was more racially and ethnically diverse than ever, adding versatility in talents. Yet discord shattered peace at home and abroad, yielding, simultaneously, apprehension and a summons for tolerance.

Diversity and Change

Many Americans were proud of their nation's racial and ethnic diversity, yet others considered it a mixed blessing, a source of friction, at best a partial success. The hopes of the civil rights movement had expanded, then fallen short of expectations.

America's population shot upward: 205 million in 1970, 215 million in 1975, 227 million in 1980, 250 million in 1990, 261 million in 1996, and 281 million in 2000. The largest population growth came in the Sunbelt of the South and West; in the Northwest and Midwest growth was slow or stagnant. Offsetting a declining birth rate, life expectancy rose from 67.1 years to 71 for men, from 74.7 to 78.3 for women from 1970 to 1983. Baby boomers began to reach their thirties by the 1970s and middle age by the 1990s. The median age jumped from twenty-eight in 1970, to thirty-one in 1983, to thirty-three in 1992, and to thirty-five in 2000. By the 1990s the United States had one of the oldest populations in the world, and the fastest-growing segment of its population was those older than seventy-five. The rising tide of older Americans, whose political clout increased, stretched the finances of Medicare and Medicaid.

The sexual revolution continued. To some, born late in the century, it no longer seemed a revolution, simply a fact of life. As many people lived alone as lived in nuclear families of husband, wife, and children. The wife often worked; in some cases only the wife worked. Cohabitation was accepted. For many sex started in high school and continued through college, and did not necessarily become monogamous with marriage. Of those aged eighteen to twenty-four, some 90 percent of men and 80 percent of women acknowledged having premarital sex. Junior high and high school girls had unprotected sex and bore children, or aborted them. Sex became an expected part of dating. Affairs among politicians and ministers were common. Bill Clinton was impeached (but acquitted) for lying about sex. Such national leaders as John F. Kennedy, Martin Luther King, and Newt Gingrich had affairs. If Hollywood remained the sex capital of the nation, Washington, D.C., ran it a close second.

The strident rhetoric and noisy demonstrations of the 1960s diminished. In the 1970s some returned to pursuing material rewards, yet others turned inward to "New Age" philosophies. There was a new emphasis on finding meaning to life, dismissed by some at the time as narcissistic, yet in fact based less on selfishness than on the conviction that if the world could change, it would change one person at a time. Increasingly, self-improvement of body and soul became popular. Americans quit smoking, drank diet drinks, walked, and bicycled to keep in shape. Many played golf and tennis, sports increasingly taken up by the middle and lower middle classes. Perhaps most popular among all ages was swimming, which included lessons, leagues, and impromptu dips. The attention to personal health, once largely confined to children, was joined to new concerns with diet, vegetarianism, holistic medicine, and the kind of spirituality that went beyond the walls of churches and synagogues.

Many of the new lifestyles were connected with a bucolic craving for the grass and trees of suburbs and towns rather than the cement of cities. It was also part of the appeal of the Sunbelt, as was its climate. But the main stimulant in the push-pull dynamic that drained the cities was jobs. Just as people once moved to jobs, now jobs moved to people. By 1990 more than 60 percent of jobs were in the suburbs. In fact, many jobs could be done from the home, using computers. The type of jobs changed and with it their locations. Smokestack jobs were giving way to light manufacturing, such as electronics and service jobs. People did not stay in one place as long. Light industry needed workers who were highly educated and mobile. Industrial parks were built outside cities, where traffic and parking were not problems. Some cities outside the Sunbelt had severe financial crises, including

Cleveland, which declared bankruptcy. As whites fled to suburbs, blacks took over as mayors of a number of major cities, winning elections split along racial grounds. Many of the black mayors set about reforming their cities' police departments, which had been mostly white bastions and had mistreated the poor and minorities. Hispanics gained clout, winning elections in several cities in the Sunbelt. In the 1980s cities seemed to be making a comeback, as building surged in downtown areas, especially construction of convention centers and hotels. Many cities boomed despite cuts in their budgets and reductions in urban aid, yet cities never recouped the political and economic dominance they had once enjoyed..

Terrorism took a toll during the Era of Diversity. Sometimes terrorists were inspired by personal frustration, by religious fanaticism, or by grievances directed against the government or American institutions. America's material success and support of the state of Israel also made it a target. Moreover, America was an open society; it was difficult to protect buildings, airports, and other targets without restricting personal liberties. Islamic terrorists exploded a bomb at the World Trade Center in 1993, killing six and injuring one thousand. Radical Muslims bombed American installations abroad. In America, opponents of abortion attacked clinics and assassinated doctors. The site of the 1996 Atlanta Summer Olympics was bombed. Members of an armed cult, the Branch Davidians, perished in a 1993 fire at their compound in Waco, Texas, surrounded by the FBI. The blaze broke out because incendiary devices and ammunition stored inside the compound were ignited, but right-wing groups blamed the government. Vengeance for the Branch Davidians drove Army veteran Timothy McVeigh to bomb the Alfred P. Murrah Federal Building in Oklahoma City in April 1995, killing 168. McVeigh was executed and a coplotter was sentenced to a long prison term. Lashing out against a different target, technology and its allies, the so-called Unabomber, Theodore Kaczynski, mailed bomb packages to his victims from 1978 to 1986, killing three and wounding twenty-two. Not until 1996 did officials arrest Kaczynski, a brilliant math professor but an alienated loner. He pled guilty and was sentenced to life in prison.

In April 1999, a violent tragedy horrified the nation. At Columbine High School in Littleton, Colorado, two high school students shot to death twelve classmates and a teacher before killing themselves. Six years later, a high school student at a Chippewa Indian Reservation school at Red Lake, Minnesota, shot his grandparents to death, drove to his school, murdered seven students, and committed suicide without expressing a motive.

Alienation, perhaps a by-product of the velocity of change, seemed to disturb young people in particular. Some Americans called for gun control,

SCHOOL
SHOOTINGS
A participant at a
memorial service
for the victims of
the Columbine
High School
shootings holds a
"Save Our Kids"
sign in Littleton,
Colorado, in
April 1999.
(AP/Wide World
Photos/Eric Gray)

yet others, such as the National Rifle Association, argued that the right to
bear arms is embedded in the Constitution. Violence at Columbine, Red
Lake, and other schools aroused principals and local police to tighten security. Metal detectors and the presence of policemen in the school hallways
curtailed, but did not end violence. The social and psychological conditions that bred violent behavior, the saturation coverage by the media that
inspired copycat crimes, and the longstanding American culture of homi-
cide, reinforced by action movies, video games, and rock and rap lyrics,
were also held responsible.

Booms and Busts

The United States experienced its greatest boom from 1940 to 1970, then
slipped into stagflation, a decline of industrial jobs, and losses to foreign
competition. Manufacturing began a long decline and was replaced by
lower-paying service jobs. McDonald's and Wal-Mart became the nation's
largest employers. Employers found it difficult to compete with nations
such as Germany and Japan, which rebuilt their industrial plants with newer

★ CESAR CHAVEZ: ORGANIZING THE POOR ★

God writes in exceedingly crooked lines.
—CESAR CHAVEZ

GIVING VOICE TO MIGRANT WORKERS
Farm union leader Caesar Chavez.
(National Archives)

CESAR CHAVEZ was a labor leader, an advocate for the poor, a spokesman for Mexican Americans, and an inspiration for demoralized American liberals whose reform agenda faltered in the late 1960s. In the Era of Diversity, he espoused ethnic consciousness without rejecting the United States or capitalism and wedded an indomitable will to a commitment to nonviolence.

Chavez was born to a middle-class, Roman Catholic, Mexican American family in Arizona. After his father lost the family farm to back taxes, the Chavezes moved to California to become itinerant vegetable and fruit pickers. Educated sporadically, Chavez learned firsthand about the hard lives of the workers and found his mission—to alleviate their suffering. The growers had all the weapons on their side, the government, the law, and economic power. "We herd them like pigs," one grower said of the Mexican workers.

After briefly serving in the Navy, Chavez returned to California, married in 1948, and became an organizer for the Community Service Organization (CSO) in 1952. The CSO, which registered Mexican Americans to vote and provided rudimentary social services, was Chavez's steppingstone to labor organizing. In the 1960s Chavez became a national figure, the Chicano equivalent of Martin Luther King Jr. He founded the United Farm Workers (UFW) and led a series of successful strikes, especially against grape and wine producers. Even more important than work stoppages among Chavez's arsenal of tactics were boycotts and hunger strikes. "We have our own bodies and spirits and the justice of our cause as our weapons," he said. As the leader of a relatively weak group seeking to move the levers of power, Chavez recognized the paradoxes in his situation. He was an individualist, yet he knew his movement must be based on collective action. He witnessed pain and wanted to act to relieve it, yet he knew that success requires patience.

Chavez and his allies aroused the country; the UFW's grape boycott became a national cause in the 1960s. Still, victories were hard earned, and setbacks were numerous. The government, especially California Governor Ronald Reagan and President Richard Nixon, opposed the UFW strikes. But the biggest threat to the union's survival came from a competing union, the Teamsters, which offered easier terms to growers; sometimes growers covertly collaborated with the Teamsters in union elections. And there would be other fights. In the 1970s and 1980s Chavez and the UFW advocated strict enforcement of laws barring illegal immigrants who might compete with UFW workers and campaigned against use of environmentally unsafe pesticides. In the 1990s the UFW unsuccessfully sought to block Senate ratification of the North American Free Trade Agreement, fearing it would cost the union jobs.

By the time Chavez died on April 23, 1993, he had earned an international reputation. Tributes came from the Pope, the Mexican president, and President Bill Clinton. Militant yet mild-mannered, Chavez never lost his courage during more than thirty years of organizing. Most important, Chavez inspired the poor to try to seize control of their own destiny. "History will judge societies and governments—and their institutions—not by how big they are or how well they serve the rich and powerful, but by how effectively they respond to the needs of the poor and the helpless," he predicted.

Sources: Biographies of Chavez and accounts of his movement include Richard Griswold del Castillo and Richard A. Garcia, *Cesar Chavez: A Triumph of Spirit* (1995), and Susan Ferress and Ricardo Sanduval, *The Fight in the Fields: Cesar Chavez* (1997).

technology after World War II. They now produced efficiently such quality goods as electronic equipment and compact automobiles. Still, American cultural products permeated world markets. Perhaps the most memorable American ambassador to the world is Coca-Cola.

The economy began the Reagan years in a grim recession, recovered, and performed well for the remainder of the 1980s. Another decline set in which ended shortly before Bush's defeat in 1992, and thereafter, the 1990s were the most prosperous decade to that time. The stock market soared, and investors and entrepreneurs such as Bill Gates, the chair of the computer software giant Microsoft, became billionaires. Poverty and welfare rolls declined, yet the disparity between rich and poor increased; family income stagnated although hours worked increased. Some manufacturers outsourced work to lower-paying foreign companies or built factories abroad. Unions declined, as did their influence. From 31 percent of nonfarm workers organized in 1960, the percent fell to just 14 by the late 1990s. Unions were less militant about strikes because workers were easier to replace. Presidents of both parties worked to ratify the North American Free Trade Agreement (NAFTA), which won in Senate approval under President Bill Clinton. Union opposition notwithstanding, most economists put their faith in free trade.

The genie of prosperity was technology. It changed home, recreation, and work, making living more comfortable yet also making human beings more replaceable. Government-sponsored research in universities rolled back scientific barriers, yielding theoretical discoveries that were converted into practical applications. Much of the new technology had military and civilian uses. Lasers, powerful light beams, were first employed in the armed forces to direct missiles. By the end of the twentieth century they were being used in medicine to open clogged arteries, destroy tumors, seal capillaries, and cauterize ulcers. Laser eye surgery made it possible to see normally without glasses or contact lenses. Lasers also could sterilize wine without changing its taste and scan the prices of coded products at grocery store checkout counters.

The most important developments were the programmable computer chip and biotechnology. Programmable chips made possible pocket calculators, digital watches, and large, industrial computers. Along with smaller models for offices and homes, the computer revolution harnessed the Internet for worldwide communications. Biotechnology helped scientists understand the genetic basis of diseases, a critical step toward better cures. Biotechnology raised fear, in addition to promise, because of advances in cloning, the production of an individual with the exact genetic blueprint of its parent. Genetic engineering made it possible to create species and to exclude inherited diseases from offspring. Cloning could be used to make healthier or more productive animal species, such as cows who produced more milk, but species might be created that had no natural enemies and could multiply endlessly. Also, cloning of animals and human cells led many to fear that scientists would find a way to clone humans, a development that would pose ethical and religious problems. Embryonic stem cells offered the prospect of replacing diseased cells and generated impassioned debate over whether it was permissible to clone embryos merely to harvest the cells. To some, scientists were dangerously close to playing God. Theologians asked whether a human created by cloning would have a soul.

Almost as miraculous as cloning were advances in medicine. Prozac was developed to treat depression. New therapies alleviated heart disease and cancer. Diagnostic imaging machines eliminated much of the need for exploratory surgery and focused more precisely on the diseased portion of the body. Arthroscopic surgery on joints permitted rapid recovery. Households and hospitals changed because of new inventions and the refinement of older products. Use of microwave ovens soared after 1969, simplifying food preparation, and use of Teflon-coated pans made it easier to clean up after meals.

Moving toward the Right

The ascendance of the right starting in the late 1960s was one of the most significant developments of the era. Conservatives engineered the elections of a host of Republican presidents mitigated only by Watergate: Richard Nixon, Ronald Reagan, George H. W. Bush, and George W. Bush. Opposition to communism, big government, and secularism united them. Some of their books and essays were written by influential neoconservatives, or former liberals. They believed in absolute morality, order in society, and personal responsibility. For the most part, their appeals were directed at individuals rather than groups. Thus they preferred individualism over collectivism, and a marketplace relatively unfettered by government. They appealed to numerous segments of the white middle and lower-middle class who were weary of high taxes, affirmative action, welfare, and busing.

The Era of Diversity also gave birth to a resurgence of evangelicals. Evangelicals and their religious cousins, Fundamentalists, were other worldly. Evangelicalism is permeated by a "born again" experience in which a person recognizes Jesus as Savior and commits to live for God. Their chief mission is to make converts. Perhaps the best-known evangelical of the era was President Jimmy Carter. Fundamentalists espoused the inerrancy of Scripture, the miracles of the Bible, and the second coming of Jesus. Both revered Judeo-Christian morality, yet Fundamentalists were somewhat more militant. Since the Scopes Trial of the 1925, liberal theologians had predicted that evangelicalism and fundamentalism would burn themselves out because they were too passionate and outdated for the modern world. Just the opposite happened. As mainline Protestant churches lost membership, and Catholicism lost vigor, the churches of the Right, such as the Pentecostals and Assemblies of God, grew. Set back by the scandals of the televangelists of the 1970s, they resumed their growth spurt during the 1980s. Relentless foes of abortion, they were joined by Orthodox Jews and Mormons.

Two of the faster-growing evangelical sects were the Southern Baptists and the Pentecostals. Practically all white, the Southern Baptists became the largest Protestant denomination by the late 1980s. Starting from a smaller base, Pentecostals grew even more swiftly in percentage terms. Their largest branch, the Assemblies of God, rose from around a half-million members in 1965 to more than two million by 1985. Pentecostals were fundamentalists who talked of the gift of healing and who spoke in unknown tongues, as had occurred on the day of Pentecost. With Pentecostals, charismatics shared interest in healing and speaking in

LEADING THE MORAL MAJORITY Televangelist Jerry Falwell speaks at a rally on the steps of the Alabama Capitol in August 2003 in support of Alabama Chief Justice Roy Moore. Moore said that he would defy a federal court order to remove his Ten Commandments monument from public display in the State Judicial Building. (AP Wide World Photos/Dave Martin)

unknown tongues. Open to the supernatural, they reached Catholics as well as Protestants. Almost 30 million Americans identified themselves as charismatic Christians.

The Christian right was among the first to merge ideology with technology, allying with conservatives who obtained funds from the grassroots by means of computers, direct mail, television, and market research, as well as from big business. The Christian right's message came into millions of homes on Sunday mornings. With their TV programs, popular "televangelists" such as Oral Roberts, Pat Roberston, Jerry Falwell, Jim and Tammy Faye Bakker, and Jimmy Swaggart raised millions for their ministries. Falwell founded the Moral Majority, a movement that claimed a large share of credit for Reagan's election, and preached a conventional fundamentalism denouncing drug use, permissiveness, and sins of the flesh. He was a formidable political force from the 1980s onward. Swaggart, a skilled musician like his cousin, rock and roll pioneer Jerry Lee Lewis, periodically sat down to pound the piano and spoke emotionally, without notes, delivering fire-and-brimstone sermons. Robertson became the first televangelist to enter politics as a candidate, running in the 1988 Republican presidential primaries. He garnered about 10 percent of the vote in the early contests, but proved unable to expand on his base or break George Bush's hold on the party and eventually withdrew.

In the late 1980s scandals destroyed some televangelists' ministries. Roberts discredited himself by saying that he had received a message from God: if Roberts's followers did not contribute a large amount of money by a deadline, God would kill him. The prophecy failed to materialize. Jim Bakker admitted to having a tawdry affair with a church secretary and was imprisoned for defrauding his adherents. Swaggart, who had been highly critical of Bakker's improprieties, confessed that he had hired a prostitute on several occasions and was briefly suspended by his denomination, the Assemblies of God. Most of the televangelists subsequently retired from the airwaves or kept a lower profile during the rest of the era. Falwell and Robertson remained active, but lost some credibility by making anti-Semitic, anti-gay statements.

Conservative-versus-liberal clashes were not confined to Protestantism. Catholics in the era were still adjusting to the Second Vatican Council that lasted from 1962 to 1965. Now Masses were celebrated in English, not Latin, with the priest facing the congregation, which sang hymns and repeated prayers in English. More time was devoted to sermons that included a moral lesson. The practice of abstaining from eating red meat on Fridays waned. If the reforms of Vatican II brought the Catholic Church up to date, however, they did not restore enthusiasm among the faithful. Some disliked the less formal Masses and the change from Latin to English, finding them undignified. Fewer attended services regularly or went to confession. Many Catholics disagreed with their church. They wanted women ordained as priests; practiced birth control and divorced. Opposition to abortion and homosexuality weakened. Some Catholics considered liberation theology, a doctrine popular in Latin America that attempted to merge Christianity and Marxism to provide a rationale for social revolution. Liberal views were muted, however, after the 1978 papal election of John Paul II, a popular, anticommunist conservative who upheld church traditions.

The more liberal Protestant denominations and Reform Jews allowed women ministers and rabbis and gave women a larger role in services. Gender-inclusive language was introduced in Scriptures and hymns. Roles for gays and lesbians were controversial after a gay liberation movement emerged in the 1970s and 1980s. Because of Scripture and tradition, many Christians and Jews considered homosexuality a sin, but by the 1980s gays had gained some protections against discrimination.

As mainline churches wrestled with questions of diversity, new groups experimented with personal spirituality that borrowed from Eastern and Western religions as well as those of Native Americans. The key to the new spirituality was individual rather than institutional, connecting with the unity of all things through meditation and silence. Some meditators focused their minds by following their breath through their bodies; others chanted a mantra. For some, meditation was primarily a method of relaxation; for others it meant integrating with the universe. Asked the difference between meditation and prayer, one adherent explained: "When you pray, you talk to God; when you meditate, God talks to you. You have to listen closely because God's only voice is silence." Innovators such as Gregory Hoag of Colorado experimented with making meditation tools based on geometric forms, colors, angles and programmed energy which he visualized. Hoag combined a knowledge of ancient texts with engineering and intuition. Other Americans turned to the once-prominent healer and prophet Edgar Cayce, who could diagnose and heal patients thousands of miles away and left tens of thousands of pages of readings based on his observations while in trances. More than three hundred books have been written about Cayce, who died in 1945. Increasingly, Americans, especially young people, turned to mind-body medicine, Eastern rituals, and martial arts in the belief that God is energy or controls a force of energy, such as "the Force" in the *Star Wars* movies.

Other religions were more of the cult variety, frequently variations of Christianity that practiced fanatical commitment, intolerance, separation from society, and worship of an authoritarian leader. The best known was the Unification Church of the Reverend Sun Myung Moon, who believed he was a prophet of God who foretold a heavenly kingdom. Deadlier was the People's Temple under the Reverend Jim Jones, who moved his followers into isolation in Guyana in South America and led them in a mass suicide of nine hundred in November 1978, when he feared the authorities were poised to break up his movement.

Lessons in Education

The consensus of parents, academicians, and school officials in the Era of Diversity was that public schools were failing. Perhaps the schools were failing the students; perhaps the students were not trying; possibly both were true. After billions of dollars poured into city schools, and attempts were made to obtain and retain better-trained teachers, the schools, with some exceptions, were withering within the bureaucracy. The biggest problems seemed lack of discipline, high dropout rates, and lack of morale. The simplest and most effective reform—reducing class size—was often rejected in favor of new equipment and additional brick and mortar. Teacher and administrator burnout is rapid, partly because of low salaries. But most teachers knew salaries would be low when they entered the profession; it is their frustration with the educational process that disturbed them. From the 1950s, when the most serious problem cited by teachers was students chewing gum, the major problem in the 2000s is likely to be drugs or weapons in school, or, worse yet, students who do not think it is important to study.

Some educators and parents believed children might be better educated at private or parochial schools, where discipline was stricter and the learning environment was superior. Milwaukee, Cleveland, and other cities initiated "voucher" systems to pay for the education of some poor children at private schools. Public school officials feared the plans would drain them of money and students; when religious schools were included, they declared vouchers unconstitutional. The results of the programs were marginal; the chief variable in success seemed to be the students, not the schools, the teachers, or the money. Many African Americans began calling for a return to neighborhood schools. Parents would be involved and their children would be spared long trips on buses.

Parents, educators, and religious leaders also clashed over the teaching of evolution in public schools. Fundamentalists wanted to substitute "creation science" for Charles Darwin's theories of natural selection, pitting battles among plants and animals. At least, the religious educators wanted the Genesis account taught as an alternative and Darwin's account designated a theory. At stake was the fear that "secular humanism" was undermining Christianity because it excluded God and ridiculed religious values. Moreover, said fundamentalists, children would be confused if their Christian parents taught them one thing and their secular educators another. Teachers needed freedom of speech but they had no monopoly on truth. Moreover, parents deserved a voice in school curricula. The battle extended to high school textbooks, which temporized by publishing no accounts of creation, watered-down accounts, or both accounts.

In higher education, a vast complex of technical colleges, junior colleges, four-year colleges, and research universities served the nation by the last quarter of the twentieth century. The major universities, including the more prestigious ones, emphasized research, publication, and graduate education. Rarely did a research university reward or promote a professor solely on teaching; research was the key to advancement. On the other hand, many liberal arts schools and some four-year colleges rewarded teaching alone; at some liberal arts colleges, research was even discouraged. The junior colleges and technical schools were feeders to universities and colleges and also offered two-year degrees directed at learning a skill.

Student protests declined after the Vietnam War, although there were a few demonstrations against nuclear weapons, apartheid in South Africa, and the Persian Gulf War. For the most part, college students were pragmatic and materialistic, due to tight job markets. They wanted to earn graduate or business degrees and find well-paying jobs. When the baby boomers graduated from college, the glut in students became a glut of job seekers. From the late 1970s through the end of the century there was an oversupply of Ph.D.s in the humanities. Advertisements for assistant professors in American history, for example, often drew two or three hundred applicants. Some newly minted Ph.D.s found themselves on welfare, at least temporarily.

The racial problems that infected American society did not escape its colleges and universities. Prompted by federal incentives, universities recruited minorities, sometimes employing affirmative action, which included scholarships and favorable admissions standards for certain minorities in order to achieve racial balance. Some white people objected to affirmative action in education, as they did when it was used in the job market. The number of minorities in colleges grew, and those with degrees were highly likely to escape the trap of poverty. Still, ethnic and racial groups often were socially segregated within the college setting, by choice or because they felt unwelcome.

Technology, which permeated society, also grew on campus. Computers were used in libraries, in research, in writing, and in teaching. Colleges offered degrees in computer science, and initially graduates were in high demand. Schools began to teach courses via the Internet so students could take courses at home. There were abuses. Learning became impersonal, as contact with professors and peers was limited, and companies were created to sell term papers over the Internet.

Gender and Society

Feminism continued to evolve. Most disappointing to feminists was defeat of the Equal Rights Amendment three states short of ratification in 1982. Conservative women organized by Phyllis Schlafly and others played a large role in the defeat. Contention mounted over abortion. Women, paradoxically, were both the strongest defenders and the strongest critics of abortion; the voices of potential fathers of fetuses were virtually ignored. The Supreme Court did not overturn *Roe v. Wade* but ruled in *Webster v. Reproductive Health Services* (1989), that it was no longer permissible for tax-supported hospitals to perform abortions unless the woman's health was in danger. In *Planned Parenthood v. Casey* (1992), the Court tried to define what types of restrictions on abortions were acceptable. Militant abortion opponents picketed clinics and blocked the paths of women who wanted to enter them.

In the 1980s women began to take distinctive positions, different from the positions men took on some political issues. More than men, they opposed capital punishment, higher defense spending, military intervention overseas, and nuclear power, while they supported arms control. Ironically, there was little difference between the sexes on so-called women's issues. Men favored the Equal Rights Amendment in slightly higher percentages than women. The most prominent, and most controversial, woman in politics in the era was Hillary Rodham Clinton.

Feminism was not the only current in women's politics or lifestyles. In 1997 just one-quarter of women considered themselves feminists. Among black women, feminism had little appeal, as their problems and priorities differed from those of professional white women. Some women complained that feminism made child-rearing seem unimportant. Cultural feminists agreed that male domination of society was unjust, yet said it was unrealistic to deny the existence of differences between the sexes solely because such differences had been used to exploit women in the past. Instead, cultural feminists celebrated differences and urged women to take pride in talents learned from their experience as mothers. Differences did not imply inferiority, and it was time to use them rather than suppress them, argued Carol Gilligan, a leading advocate of cultural feminism.

Pornography and sexual harassment were battlegrounds in the cultural wars. Some feminists claimed pornography amounted to sexual harassment and should be outlawed. Others, however, believed it was a protected form of free speech. The end of sexual harassment on the job ranked higher on the feminist agenda, and the feminists demanded that damages be paid to women who suffered unwanted advances that created an uncomfortable environment. Several cases of sexual harassment disgraced the armed forces, although the military accepted new roles for women at least as well as society as a whole.

Feminists put a higher priority on education and job fulfillment than on motherhood. Women with graduate degrees married later or not at all. The surge in the divorce rate was striking. From 1960 to 1980 it more than doubled. By the late 1980s nearly one in two first marriages ended in divorce. By 1990 the divorce rate was triple that of 1970. Also striking was the increase in families headed by unmarried mothers. This fact was significant because two-thirds of woman-headed families received child welfare and because two-thirds of the long-term poor were women.

Pluralism and Polarization

For millions of African Americans, the Era of Diversity was a time of progress. Institutionalized racism declined, and many blacks became doctors, lawyers, professors, and businessmen. The condition of African Americans in inner-city ghettos worsened, however, with unemployment averaging 14 or 15 percent, more than double the rate among whites. Among black teens joblessness was as high as 40 or 50 percent. Drug use, crime, delinquency, high dropout rates, teenage pregnancies, and lack of stable families continued to plague the ghetto. By 1999 just 25 percent of black children lived in two-parent families, a statistic linked to the prevalence of poverty among African Americans. The arrival of crack cocaine devastated inner cities during the 1980s, turning them into war zones of feuding gangs and spawning a culture of violence.

At times the frustration boiled over. In 1991, in Los Angeles, police were videotaped beating a black motorist, Rodney King, whom they stopped on suspicion of a traffic violation. A white jury acquitted the four officers despite the videotape, touching off the worst riot of the century. Fifty-three people were killed, thousands were injured, some twelve hundred businesses were destroyed, and $1 billion in property was damaged. Choking back tears, King pleaded for calm on television, saying: "Can we all get along? Can we get along? We've just got to, just got to. We're all stuck here for a while. Let's try to work it out. Let's try to work it out." The four officers were subsequently tried on federal charges of violating King's civil rights, resulting in convictions and short prison terms for two of them.

Further polarizing the races, in 1995 a black former collegiate and professional football star, O. J. Simpson, was acquitted in the Los Angeles murders of his former wife, Nicole Brown Simpson, and her friend, Ronald Goldman, both slashed with a knife. The trial became the most celebrated courtroom drama of the century, attracting more attention than the Sacco-Vanzetti trial or the Scopes trial. Wealthy, Simpson was able to retain the best attorneys and won his case despite convincing circumstantial evidence, including the presence of his DNA at the crime scene. Most white people considered him guilty, but most blacks applauded the outcome, some calling it a payback to the white power structure. So disturbed were the Brown and Goldman families that they sued Simpson for the wrongful deaths of their children and won monetary damages.

Attempts to solve problems that were undermining race relations met with varying degrees of effectiveness. In 1995 Louis Farrakhan, leader of the Nation of Islam, staged a Million Man March in Washington to get black men to take control of their lives and be better husbands, fathers, and providers. The march drew hundreds of thousands, but far less than 1 million, and was controversial because Farrakhan was a notorious anti-Semite. Disturbed at the racial tension, and hoping to gain political capital, President Bill Clinton appointed a commission to study racial issues. Conservatives complained that their views were not represented on the panel. The chair, distinguished black historian John Hope Franklin, responded that conservatives were not included because they had nothing to contribute.

The commission and the controversy surrounding racism degenerated into an ideological skirmish that divided Americans. California banned affirmative action in public employment and college admissions in 1996 through a ballot initiative, and some federal courts prohibited universities from favoring minorities in admissions. Whites remained divided over whether the civil rights revolution had gone too far. The last years of the twentieth century featured more diversity, and probably more equal justice under law, than ever before in the United States. More white people seemed willing to accept laws that afforded equal opportunities, as opposed to laws that tried to guarantee equal outcome.

American Indians faced recurring problems, including alcoholism, diabetes, high rates of school dropouts, illiteracy, youth crime, prejudice, and cultural upheaval. During the latter years of the twentieth century, about half of Native Americans lived in cities and only one-quarter on reservations. Fewer spoke an Indian language as their first tongue, and more Indian children could not speak an Indian language at all.

Indian arts flourished, however. Powwows brought members of diverse tribes together. Novelists such as Louise Erdrich and Gerald Vizenor graced literature, exploring challenges and new dimensions of Indian life. Indian painters offered familiar, realistic works as well as experimental abstractions. By the late 1990s more than two hundred museums and centers of Indian exhibits had been created, many on reservations. Indians demanded the return of relics, such as bones, skulls, or skeletons held by museums or anthropologists, for reburial. Scientists claimed that the relics were too valuable to rebury and had cost them years of work, yet Indians persisted, often winning them back. Indians also found pride in athletic competition, especially basketball, rodeo, and lacrosse.

Another lifeline for Indians, casino gambling on reservations, stirred debate. Indians have the right to sponsor casinos on reservations, even when gambling is otherwise illegal in their states, because of their status as sovereign governments, according to the Supreme Court. The casinos brought economic development but were criticized for profiting from a vice on which Indians have a monopoly. Native Americans defended their prerogative on casinos. Indians also fought sports teams' use of Native American mascots and nicknames and frequently prevailed among colleges.

If Native Americans faced difficulties in the Era of Diversity, so did newcomers. The Immigration and Nationality Act of 1965 unleashed a new torrent of arrivals in the United States, in which women outnumbered men. Forty-five percent of immigrants, mostly Hispanic, came from the Western Hemisphere and 30 percent from Asia. Just 12 percent came from Europe. The Hispanic influx, about 25 percent of it illegal, was so large that Hispanics rose from 2 percent of the population in 1960 to 9 percent in 1990, to 12.5 percent in 2000. Demographers estimated that by 2013 Hispanics would surpass African Americans as the nation's largest minority. Hispanic families were stable, as were Asian families, many of which settled in California. Asian immigrants increased 40 percent in the 1980s. Japanese set a standard for economic achievement, with Japanese American income exceeding the national per capita income by the 1990s.

But because they concentrated in a few states, competed with other Americans for jobs, and required bilingual education and tax increases to support schools, welfare, and medical care, the new immigrants stirred resentment. The 1986 Immigration Reform and Control Act discouraged employers from hiring immigrants by punishing businesses that employed illegal immigrants. California went further: ballot measures halted most state aid to illegal immigrants in 1994 and called for an end to bilingual education in 1998. Nationally, the 1996 federal welfare overhaul cut off many benefits to illegal newcomers, although Clinton persuaded Congress to restore some. Illegal migration and efforts to control it frayed relations with Mexico and inflamed ethnic tension in the Southwest. Politicians from seven states in the region urged the construction of a wall along the border. Meanwhile, immigrants confronted the problems of finding adequate employment and of adjusting to society. Women immigrants were torn between the traditional, submissive roles of their native cultures and the assertiveness of American feminism. For immigrants, as well as for millions of other Americans, Rodney King's question would echo into the twenty-first century.

CHAPTER TWELVE

From George Bush
to George W. Bush

THE ERA OF Diversity culminated with a conservative Republican president and a moderately liberal Democrat, further evidence of the diversity that characterized the nation's highest office after the end of the Second World War. They presided over a nation of technological virtuosity and ideological and racial complexity, one far more diverse than their ancestors had inherited at the dawn of the twentieth century. In 2001 George W. Bush took office, becoming the second half of the only father-and-son presidential tandem since John and John Quincy Adams in the formative years of the Republic. George W. Bush had a sense of adventure and preferred moderate change, not unlike the Republican who became president one hundred years earlier, Theodore Roosevelt. Yet, events, not men, rode the saddle during the tenures of both of these cowboy presidents.

George Bush

Before George W. Bush there was George Herbert Walker Bush. Born to wealth, Bush, who assumed office in 1989, was the son of Prescott Bush, a Wall Street investor and a Republican senator from Connecticut. Bush enlisted in the navy at eighteen, became the service's youngest pilot in World War II, flew fifty-eight combat missions, and was shot down twice. He returned to the United States to attend Yale University, where he was captain of the baseball team that finished second in the nation. Then he invested in the oil business in Texas and entered politics.

Bush ran for the Senate in 1964 as a Goldwater conservative and lost but later won two terms in the House of Representatives, starting in 1966.

After a second unsuccessful Senate race, in 1970, he was appointed ambassador to the United Nations in 1971, and national Republican chair in 1973. In 1974 Bush became envoy to China, then CIA director. His supporters, pointing to his impressive portfolio, plus his experience as Reagan's vice president, said he was the best-qualified politician to succeed the icon of the 1980s. Bush's wife, Barbara, also grew up in a wealthy family, and they had six children, two of whom became the chief executives of major Southern states (Jeb, governor of Florida, and George W., governor of Texas). As first lady, Barbara Bush made literacy her cause and promoted family values and volunteer work. Bush's vice president, Dan Quayle, was a favorite of conservatives.

In temperament, Bush, who led by quiet example, was unlike Reagan, who led by passion and inspiration. Also unlike Reagan, he was not an effective public speaker. In the Era of Diversity, Bush pleased neither political pole; he was neither a reformer nor an ideological conservative. Although he played first base in college, his position in politics was right-center field. He produced a meager domestic record, yet wielded his veto pen to keep liberal Democratic legislation off the books. Congress was a roadblock; Bush faced the largest opposing majorities of any twentieth-century president.

The battle of the budget was central. Deficits had soared under Reagan, yet Bush vowed to avoid new taxes during his campaign. The first budget, in 1989, was accomplished with relative ease. After an economic decline, the 1990 budget became difficult to negotiate. Bush had to back down from his "no new taxes" pledge to compromise with the Democrats. Economic necessity became political calamity, as violation of his pledge haunted Bush in his 1992 reelection campaign. The recession that began in 1990 ended during the campaign of 1992, too late to aid Bush but enough to help his successor's administration enjoy eight years of prosperity. Ironically, the decade of the 1980s, the most prosperous to that time, was followed by an even more prosperous decade.

Bush achieved a modest increase in the minimum wage, stimulated volunteer efforts through a program called "A Thousand Points of Light," encouraged education without significant new funding, and waged a war on drugs. Drug use declined in the 1980s and 1990s largely because 1960s lifestyles were declining as baby boomers aged. Calling for a "kinder, gentler America," the president's main contribution was the Americans with Disabilities Act of 1990. It prohibited employment discrimination against the handicapped and required that buildings and buses be wheelchair accessible. In addition, Bush provided funds for child care, and signed the Clean Air Act of 1990, which restricted emissions from factories and automobiles. An environmental disaster, the enormous oil spill caused by the grounding of the *Exxon Valdez* in Prince William Sound, off the Alaskan coast, on March 24, 1989, alarmed Americans and expedited passage of the bill.

Supreme Court appointments became increasingly politicized in the Era of Diversity, and attempts to obtain ideological and racial diversity often were the focus of the problem. Bush's first nominee, David Souter, an obscure justice of the New Hampshire Supreme Court, breezed through, largely because of a lack of information about Souter's record on controversial issues. In 1991, Thurgood Marshall, the only black Justice, retired. Bush nominated a black conservative, Clarence Thomas, to succeed him. Near the end of the hearings, Anita Hill, who had once worked for Thomas, testified that he had sexually harassed her, telling her dirty jokes and asking her for dates. Thomas was narrowly confirmed, but the affair polarized the country. Thomas went on to become one of the most conservative justices, and a virtual recluse in private life.

Delicate Diplomacy: Warmaking and Peacemaking

Bush will be known to history primarily as a foreign policy president. He preferred policies undergirded by caution and finesse, yet could act decisively. The president appointed an able foreign policy team and relied on world leaders he knew.

In Nicaragua, Bush obtained his objective of containing communism without war. The administration guaranteed $450 million in humanitarian aid, but no military aid, to the anticommunist Contras. With the civil war winding down, the Marxist Sandinistas permitted a free election, which they lost. Violetta Chamorro upset Sandinista President Daniel Ortega, ending Marxist rule.

Americans found a paradox in Panama. The Panamanian dictator, Manuel Noriega, once an American ally and an informer for the CIA, had degenerated into a drug lord. In 1987 American courts indicted Noriega; in 1988 Reagan imposed economic sanctions on Panama; and in 1989 Noriega allowed an election, which his candidate lost. In December 1989 Bush ordered the invasion of Panama and arrest of Noriega, who was captured, tried in the United States, and imprisoned.

Still, turbulence prevailed in many Latin American nations. An election in Haiti, long dominated by the malevolent Jean-Claude Duvalier, placed a reformer in power, Jean-Bertrand Aristide. Yet, reform was short-lived for Haiti. After seven months, the army toppled Aristide. Staying his hand for the time, Bush imposed economic sanctions. Thousands of Haitian refugees tried to reach the Florida coast, only to be turned back. Critics argued that they were rejected on racial grounds, pointing out that

Cuban refugees were accepted. The administration countered that the chief difference was that Cubans were fleeing a Communist regime.

Outside the hemisphere, Bush struggled with an array of problems. The Middle East, which had been the burial ground for many peace initiatives, continued to frustrate. Palestinians insisted that Israelis cease building Jewish settlements in the occupied territories, yet Prime Minister Yitzhak Shamir resisted. After a fruitless peace conference at Madrid in October 1991, Israel elected a more conciliatory prime minister, Shimon Peres. Peres advocated trading land for peace, but opinions were divided: How much land for how much peace?

In Africa, war and famine ravaged Somalia, and tribal battles threatened to destroy United Nations efforts to deliver food and supplies. During the last weeks of the Bush administration, America sent soldiers to protect the mission, hoping that later the U.N. could furnish security. Events had a better ending in South Africa, where years of international pressure against the apartheid regime paid off. In 1990 President F. W. de Klerk reversed the ban on the African National Congress, a leading anti-apartheid group, and black leader Nelson Mandela was freed after decades behind bars. Over the next three years, the country overturned laws that restricted blacks to "homelands," approved a constitution that gave blacks the vote for the first time, and elected Mandela as president.

The currents of history were also running against Soviet President Mikhail Gorbachev, who began contracting his overextended empire to preserve communism. Early in 1989, he began withdrawing tanks and troops from Eastern Europe. In June, he renounced the right to intervene, but events moved on their own momentum. Hungary was the first country to break with the Soviet Union in 1989; its Communist Party renounced Marxism and opened the nation's borders. The party agreed to free elections in 1990 and lost to noncommunists. Also, in 1989, the anticommunist Solidarity trade union, led by Lech Walesa helped draft a new constitution for Poland, won elections, and won control of a coalition government. In October, the new Polish government announced that the country was converting to a market economy. Czechoslovakian lawmakers abolished the communist monopoly on power, and author Vaclav Havel won the presidency. Communism fell elsewhere in the Soviet bloc with little bloodshed, except in Romania, where Dictator Nicolae Ceausescu tried to flee after nearly a quarter-century rule, only to be executed by revolutionaries on Christmas Day, 1989. And, in Yugoslavia, ethnic factions that had been held together under Josip Broz Tito descended into warfare.

In Germany communism's fall was most dramatic. Crowds demonstrated on both sides of the Berlin Wall, then surged over and through the Wall

TEARING DOWN THE WALL
Berliners demolish a symbol of oppression, November 11, 1989.
(AP/Wide World Photos/Lionel Cironneau)

while East German troops refused to fire on their own people. The crowds tore down the Wall with axes, shovels, and bare hands. In 1990, Germany reunified. The heartland of Europe, for one of the few times in its ancient history, was free. Later, Germany and many of the formerly communist Eastern European nations joined NATO.

Ironically, by the time these nations joined NATO, an American-led alliance created to deter communism, there was little communism to deter. Bush did not foresee the collapse of communism in its nerve center and worked with Gorbachev to preserve the Soviet state. Yet, time marched against communism. Not only could the Soviet state no longer compete economically or militarily with the West, but ethnic minorities demanded freedom. Gorbachev went further than any previous Soviet leader in reforming his state, and won a Nobel Peace Prize, yet he only accelerated its destruction. Glasnost and perestroika gave Gorbachev's people only a taste of freedom and Western consumerism without satisfying their pangs of hunger.

In June 1991 Moscow Mayor Boris Yeltsin, an advocate of Russian independence and rapid reform, became the first freely elected president of the Russian republic. Then, Soviet hard-liners staged a coup, placing

Gorbachev under arrest, moves that Bush opposed. Yeltsin climbed atop a hostile tank in Moscow and rallied the people. Much of the army remained loyal to Gorbachev and Yeltsin, and the coup failed. Gorbachev resigned as head of the Communist Party and disbanded its leadership. On December 7, Russia, Ukraine, and Belorussia declared the USSR defunct. Power flowed to Yeltsin, who broke with the party, denied it a role in the government, and confiscated Communist property. On December 25, Gorbachev resigned as president. The following day the members of the rump Parliament acknowledged the dissolution of the Soviet Union. Some of the newly independent states created a weak commonwealth. The Cold War ended suddenly, decisively, and peacefully. The danger of instantaneous nuclear annihilation receded, although terrorist threats remain. Bush shifted his allegiance from Gorbachev to Yeltsin. Yeltsin was unstable, lacked Gorbachev's polish and was unpredictable, but he was a champion of democracy.

Only one major communist power remained, China, though it moved rapidly toward a free market economy. Many Chinese, dissatisfied after seeing they had fewer freedoms and consumer items than people of Western nations, rebelled. In 1989 pro-democracy students gathered in Tiananmen Square, in the heart of Beijing, to protest. Prime Minister Li Peng imposed martial law and demanded that the protesters disperse. Refusing, they erected a "Goddess of Liberty" statue resembling the Statue of Liberty and defied troops. On June 4, troops and tanks moved in to expel the students, killing hundreds, perhaps thousands. Authorities imprisoned protest leaders, closed schools, and disbanded student and worker organizations. Washington imposed sanctions on Beijing, including an end to military sales.

Under Saddam Hussein, Iraq, too, was bottled up by repression. Hussein denied basic freedoms, sponsored terrorism, and threatened his neighbors. Hussein's invasion and conquest of tiny, oil-rich Kuwait in early August 1990, raised moral and geopolitical concerns. He was in position to threaten Israeli security and drive up world oil prices. Bush promised to punish Iraq for its aggression. After economic sanctions failed to persuade Hussein to withdraw, Bush assembled a coalition of forty-eight nations and sent half a million American troops to the Persian Gulf area. Many nations contributed soldiers, including some Arab governments, which also supplied financial aid. Congress authorized the use of force to expel Hussein from Kuwait. Soon afterward, the coalition bombed Iraq for forty-eight days, an unprecedented pounding. With Baghdad still ignoring Bush's ultimatum to withdraw from Kuwait, the president ordered an invasion. Hussein promised "the mother of all battles," but the ground war, like the air war, was so lopsided that the American commander, General H. Norman Schwarzkopf, ridiculed it as "the mother of all retreats" for Iraqi forces. In one hundred hours, the Iraqis were routed, Kuwait was liberated, and Bush terminated hostilities. Although Hussein was not at war with Israel, he attacked the Jewish state with missiles, killing two civilians. Overall, coalition casualties were light, including less than 150 battle deaths for the United States, compared with 300,000 for Iraq. Americans celebrated, yet because coalition forces stopped short of capturing and deposing Hussein, the triumph was incomplete.

From Victory in Iraq to Loss at the Polls

Bush's apparent invulnerability after the victory of Iraq discouraged prominent Democrats from entering the presidential race. New York Governor Mario Cuomo, the potential front-runner for the Democratic nomination, decided not to run, clearing the way for Arkansas Governor Bill Clinton, who was challenged by former Massachusetts Senator Paul Tsongas, Senator Bob Kerry of Nebraska, Virginia Governor Douglas Wilder, and former California Governor "Jerry" Brown. Tsongas upset Clinton in New Hampshire after newspapers reported that Clinton had conducted a twelve-year affair with Arkansas television reporter Jennifer Flowers. Clinton regained the initiative by winning eight primaries (mostly in the South) in

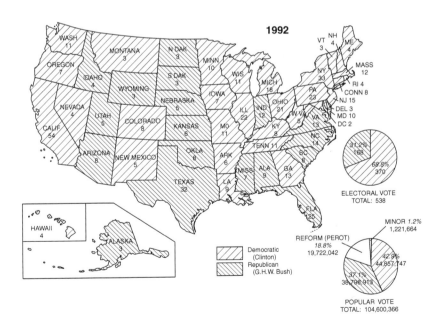

Election of 1992

a single day. Subsequent victories in Michigan, Illinois, and New York later ensured his nomination. Clinton selected a fellow southerner, Senator Al Gore of Tennessee, as his running mate.

Clinton ran as a New Democrat, taking a middle way between anti-government Reaganism and the Democratic tradition that government could solve most problems. He blended liberalism and conservatism, a center-left position similar to Eisenhower's center-right position in the Republican party. Just as Eisenhower had not attempted to roll back the New Deal when he became president in 1953, Clinton accepted some aspects of Reaganism. A fiscal conservative, he believed the government should act, but only when vital.

Clinton's candidacy grew out of the Democratic Leadership Council (DLC), an organization representing New Democratic views, organized in 1984, which gained increased influence after the defeat of Michael Dukakis in 1988. As governor of Arkansas, Clinton had become a leader of the group, which attributed Democratic losses in every presidential election since 1976 to the party straying too far from the political center. To regain the allegiance of the white middle class, necessary to win presidential elections, the DLC believed that Democrats must emphasize personal responsibility and limited government. Clinton's campaign was less ideological than those of previous Democratic candidates.

By the time of the general election, the decline of the economy had drained Bush's support. Clinton shifted the issue from social and foreign policy agenda to the faltering economy. A skilled speaker, highly intelligent, and opportunistic, Clinton attacked Bush's leadership. The president, he charged, lacked vision and neglected the economy while he obsessed over foreign policy.

Actually, Bush's caution at the end of the Cold War might have helped ensure the peaceful demise of the Soviet Union, and his leadership of the coalition that won the Persian Gulf War demonstrated sound leadership. After Reagan set up communism's fall, it collapsed on Bush's watch. Bush's solid record on foreign affairs, however, was not sufficient to dissuade Americans from voting on pocketbook issues, though, ironically, the recession actually ended before the election. In addition, breaking his promise not to raise taxes, although an economic necessity, damaged Bush politically.

A third candidate, Texas billionaire businessman Ross Perot, a conservative, siphoned votes from Bush, a fellow conservative, possibly costing him the election. Clinton won with 44.9 million popular votes (43 percent) and 370 electoral votes to Bush's 39.1 million (37.4 percent) and 168 electoral votes. Perot received 19.7 million popular votes (18.9 percent), the highest proportion ever for a third-party candidate. Democrats won control of Congress. Feminists called 1992 the Year of the Woman, as the

Congress elected in November included fifty-three women in the House and six in the Senate. California became the first state to elect two women to the Senate: Diane Feinstein and Barbara Boxer. Illinois sent the first black woman to the upper house, Carol Moseley Braun.

William "Bill" Jefferson Clinton

Clinton came from a background as humble as Bush's was patrician. Born in the village of Hope, the Arkansan was raised largely by his mother and grandfather, after his father died in a car accident. When he was four, his mother married Roger Clinton, an alcoholic. The family insecurity Clinton endured contributed to a tenacious drive and empathy. Charismatic, Clinton had strains of immaturity and self-destruction. Skilled at compromise, he preferred cutting a deal to standing on principle. Both eloquent and glib, critics termed him "Slick Willie."

An outstanding student, Clinton attended Georgetown University, then Oxford, and earned a law degree at Yale University, where he met his future

THE MAN FROM HOPE, ARKANSAS
Israeli Prime Minister Yitzhak Rabin, President Bill Clinton,
and Palestine Liberation Organization Chairman Yasir Arafat meet
for the signing of the Oslo Accords in September 1993.
(William Jefferson Clinton Presidential Library)

wife, Hillary Rodham. Born to a rich Republican family, she became a Eugene McCarthy Democrat and an antiwar activist in college. A feminist, she started a career before a family (the Clintons had one daughter, Chelsea) and was hard-edged and ambitious. Like her husband, highly intelligent, she possessed even more drive. Initially, Hillary and Al Gore were among the president's closest advisers. The cabinet included moderates and liberals, women and minorities. Two women, Janet Reno and Madeleine Albright, were the first of their sex to serve as attorney general and secretary of state, respectively. Another woman, liberal Ruth Bader Ginsburg, joined the liberal Stephen Breyer as Clinton's Supreme Court appointees.

Economic Laser Beam

Some successes in domestic politics mixed with defeats early in Clinton's first term. A bill Bush had vetoed, the Family and Medical Leave Act, received Clinton's signature in 1993; it permitted workers to take up to twelve weeks' unpaid leave from their jobs to care for a parent, spouse, or child. Clinton's attempt to remove the ban on known homosexuals in the armed forces misfired and he settled for a "don't ask, don't tell" policy. Gays and lesbians would not be asked about their sexual orientation by commanding officers. But, if they volunteered it, or practiced their sexuality openly, they would be dismissed.

Clinton fared even worse with a major initiative, comprehensive health insurance. Such proposals had been advocated by every Democratic president since Harry S Truman, yet Congress, or congressional committees, had been their graveyard. The plan had two objectives: universal coverage and cost control. These aims were difficult to synchronize. First, complete medical coverage was an item of infinite demand and limited supply. It involved competing interests, such as patients, insurance companies, doctors, hospitals, and drug companies. It also involved contrary objectives, such as maximum quality care of the greatest number at the least cost, allowing drug companies incentives to develop wonder drugs while simultaneously regulating drug prices. In addition to wonder drugs, there were wonder machines, that heroically kept patients alive, yet at a high cost. Government operation might create a mammoth bureaucracy vulnerable to political manipulation. Hillary Rodham Clinton headed a task force that worked in secret to shape a comprehensive plan. The president could hardly be objective, critics charged, about a plan developed by his wife. Unpopular even before it reached Congress, Democrats never brought it to a vote. Hillary Rodham Clinton lost status as a policy expert, and the complicated proposal added fuel to Republican charges that the administration was no less mired in a bureaucratic mind-set than previous Democratic presidencies. Clinton salvaged the 1996 Health Insurance and Portability Plan, which enabled workers to retain insurance when they lost jobs or changed work. In addition, the 1997 budget provided health coverage to uninsured children and extended Medicare.

The budget was Clinton's first priority. Vowing to focus "like a laser beam" on the economy, he proposed tax increases on the wealthy to bring down the federal deficit, spending to encourage economic growth and jobs, and retraining of workers whose jobs were threatened by the global economy. Pursuing deficit reduction, Clinton abandoned his campaign pledge to cut middle-class taxes and proposed a modest increase in the gasoline tax. Congress passed his program without the job stimulus, narrowly, in August 1993. The budget squeaked through by two votes in the House and Vice President Gore cast a tie-breaking vote in the Senate. The budget included an Earned Income Tax Credit to help the working poor. The economy gathered momentum. Unemployment plummeted to a four-year low. Inflation remained in check due to the Federal Reserve's high interest rates and tight money policies, and because oil prices stabilized.

By 1994, however, Clinton's approval ratings had slipped because of "character" issues and the public demand for tax cuts and leaner government. Georgia Representative Newt Gingrich proposed a "Contract with America," whereby Republicans pledged themselves to traditional values, balanced budgets, and term limits for Congress. Running on this platform, which resembled "Reaganism without Reagan," the GOP captured both Houses for the first time since 1954.

Electing Gingrich as Speaker, the House majority passed some elements of the "Contract." Clinton regained the momentum when the parties clashed over budgets in 1995 and 1996, causing two brief government shutdowns. The parties temporized by enacting continuing resolutions to keep the government running. Many Americans blamed the Republicans for the shutdowns and supported Clinton's vetoes of steep cuts in spending.

Politically, Clinton outflanked Republicans by borrowing issues from both the Left and Right. Although he professed a belief in personal responsibility, Clinton argued that the Republicans wanted to punish the poor. In 1996, after vetoing two Republican welfare reform measures, Clinton signed a third bill opposed by liberals in his party. The sweeping reform ended six decades of federal aid to indigent mothers and children and transferred major entitlement programs to the states. Recipients could not receive assistance for more than two successive years or five years over a lifetime.

Many whites considered welfare a race problem because of the high percentage of African Americans on welfare. Clinton's belief in a color-blind society clashed with his support for affirmative action, which he wanted to reform, not abolish. Clinton remained popular with blacks, even as he moved right, and a majority of blacks supported him in his election campaign and during his impeachment crisis.

Still, Clinton adopted policies designed to wean the white middle class from allegiance to presidential Republicanism. He supported the death penalty, backed a crime measure that put 100,000 additional policemen on the streets, and steered education measures through Congress, a tax credit for college study, and money to recruit teachers. The National Service Act (1993) provided educational grants in return for community service. Congress provided appropriations for vocational education and increased funds for college loans and scholarships. The Goals 2000 Act of March 1994 set targets for student achievement and teacher standards. Clinton achieved incremental reforms based on modest appropriations rather than blockbuster legislation comparable to the Great Society.

A Prosperous Yet Turbulent Second Term

Prosperity was the engine of Bill Clinton's reelection in 1996 and remains his chief legacy. With the economy performing well and Clinton taking moderate stands on many issues, the Republican nominee, Senator Robert Dole of Kansas, tried to make the campaign a contest of character and patriotism, to no avail. The incumbents defeated Dole, and Ross Perot, running once more. Dole and running mate Jack Kemp, a former House member and ex-Housing and Urban Development secretary, called for a 15 percent tax cut. Clinton countered that a cut this deep would jeopardize economic recovery by feeding the federal deficit, leading to inflation and higher interest rates. Clinton portrayed the Republicans as extremists while he appealed to Democratic core groups by pledging to defend Medicare, education, and the environment. A lackluster campaigner, Dole could not overcome "Clinton prosperity." Winning nearly all of the most populous states and key southern states, Clinton received 47.4 million votes, or 49.2 percent, and 379 electoral votes to Dole's 39.2 million, or 40.7 percent, and 159 electoral votes, the first Democrat since FDR to win two terms. Perot won a much smaller vote in 1996, yet again denied Clinton a majority. Perot received just over 8 million votes, or 8.4 percent, and no electoral votes. The Clinton-Gore ticket did not appreciably help other Democrats; the Republicans retained control of Congress.

In his second term, Clinton proposed relatively minor legislation to appeal to moderates, such as mandatory school uniforms. He moved to regulate tobacco products after the industry became the target of lawsuits by dying smokers and states seeking to regain money spent to care for them. In 1997 the industry approved a $368 billion settlement with states that included curbs on cigarette advertising to youths, but the industry mounted a lavishly-financed lobbying campaign and persuaded Congress to kill the bill. In 1998, cigarette companies reached a smaller court settlement with states, agreeing to pay $200 billion.

The economy continued to command Clinton's attention. In 1997 he signed a GOP measure including selective tax cuts and projecting a balanced budget by 2002, however, prosperity kept running ahead of projections. In his January 1998 State of the Union speech, the president announced the federal budget for 1999 would boast a surplus for the first time. Clinton wanted most of the surplus—which grew to a record $200 billion by the time he left office—devoted to paying off the federal debt and shoring up Social Security so baby-boomers would not bankrupt the system. The forecast of a surplus was just one indicator of how much the fiscal outlook and the economy had improved during the Clinton administration. By the end of his presidency, the United States had recorded its longest economic boom ever, 107 successive months. Wages, corporate profit, home ownership, and the gross national product increased; unemployment dropped below 4 percent for the first time in thirty years; poverty, too, declined. The stock market shot upward, fueled by high-technology firms. Not all was positive: the gap between rich and poor widened, as did the trade deficit; industrial workers' real wages, adjusted for inflation, increased only modestly. On the strength of the boom, large majorities in opinion polls rated Clinton's job performance high.

Although Clinton increasingly strayed beyond the bounds of conventional morality, the Republicans were less effective in exploiting those issues because some of their leaders suffered in moral lapses. Gingrich damaged himself by his arrogance and abrasiveness. After Clinton's reelection, the Speaker found himself investigated by the House Ethics Committee, which fined him $300,000 in 1997 for using a tax-exempt foundation for political aims. Then the Georgian, an exponent of "family values," admitted to an adulterous affair with an aide. Caught in the dual trap of political corruption and hypocrisy, he announced his resignation from Congress three days after the 1998 elections, in which Democrats gained five House seats. Gingrich's designated replacement as speaker, Louisiana Representative Bob Livingston, resigned in December, while the House was considering articles of impeachment against Clinton, after he acknowledged a sexual affair. (One of the paradoxes of the Era of Diversity is that a number of spokesmen of "family values" did not live up to those values in their personal lives.) Eventually, Illinois Representative Dennis Hastert took over as speaker.

A Dangerous World

Initially, Clinton seemed uninterested in foreign affairs, and tried to solve problems piecemeal. The Cold War won, some Americans argued that a large military was no longer necessary. Accordingly, Clinton reduced the armed forces, but the United States retained the world's largest military budget.

Because it affected the domestic scene, Clinton's first priority in foreign affairs was passage of the North American Free Trade Agreement (NAFTA) that Bush had negotiated. One of the Democrats' core constituencies, unions, opposed the agreement, arguing that it would encourage companies to move jobs to Mexico where workers were poorly paid and business regulations were lax. Since the 1970s, Democrats in Congress had become increasingly protectionist. Clinton argued that jobs would be gained by opening Mexican markets. Staking his prestige on ratifying the treaty, Clinton received support from Republicans for the pact, which cleared Congress in 1993.

Just after the 1994 elections, Congress ratified the Uruguay Round of the General Agreement on Tariffs and Trade (GATT), which approved formation of the World Trade Organization (WTO) and reduced tariffs worldwide. There was less opposition to this agreement than to NAFTA. But, the increasing globalization of the economy brought problems, as well as possibilities.

Some problems were more violent than trade. Clinton sent troops and food aid to war-torn Somalia, only to have American soldiers ambushed. Public opinion turned against the mission, yet it helped save some 250,000 Somalis from starvation.

China moved closer to America and free markets, yet, politically, remained totalitarian. Clinton and his successors believed that trade was preferable to isolation, and might in time open China to democratic ideas, as well as consumer goods. In 1999 the administration helped Beijing gain membership in the World Trade Organization. The following year, the United States granted permanent trade concessions to the Chinese. No longer walled off by an edifice of their own construction, the Chinese agreed to treaties that would limit nuclear and chemical weapons. Within and without, America found itself in a more diversifying world.

The newly diverse globe finds the American technological, sexual, and demographic revolutions superimposed upon economic and cultural revolutions that overshadow the vestiges of the Cold War. In fact, America's military prowess might prove less important than its growing status as the world's cultural superpower. Looking at the developing world, some entrepreneurs see an army of potential consumers whereas competition looms as well.

Nations such as China and Vietnam are becoming important trading partners with the United States, even while limiting the political freedoms of their people. Nonetheless, the more prosperous they become, the more they can buy from the United States, and nations whose economies become intertwined are less likely to go to war. What the Chinese most want to buy from the United States, for example, is not heavy machinery or nuclear weapons, but Hollywood films, DVDs, music videos, television sets, sports regalia, and autographed basketballs. Along with these, they embrace fast-food and motel chains as well as tourism in both directions.

Former arch-enemy Vietnam provides another example. After the collapse of the South Vietnamese government to the communists in 1975, the economy backslid, refugees fled, and the Vietnamese army fought wars with China and Cambodia. Yet three decades later Vietnam has adopted the Chinese model of "socialism with market orientation." Its 7.7 percent annual growth rate was second only to China among Asian countries in 2005. Ironically, the country's single largest private employer, with 130,000 workers, was the American firm Nike, which produced $700 million of footwear a year in 2005. Vietnamese who remained abroad after the communist revolution, an estimated 2 million, sent $3.8 billion back to relatives in 2004, fueling economic development. Although doubtless some jobs obtained by foreign workers came at the expense of American workers, what American capitalism needs most is global consumers, who cannot buy American products unless they can earn money. Otherwise, domestic overproduction will outpace domestic purchasing power as it did in the 1930s. In America, older, unskilled workers will suffer most from the changing global economy because the jobs created will be more numerous, but not in the same categories, as the jobs lost. As throughout the Time of Paradox, human dilemmas cannot be uncoupled from economic progress. The ambiguous relationship between Americans and the technology they innovate has been a principal thread in their history. Today, the ambiguity is global.

Yet there are opportunities as well. Many of the new jobs will be reasonably well-paying—airline pilots, cruise ship captains, tourism directors, construction workers, engineers, architects, and theme park designers. Within the coming years it is likely that major league baseball and basketball will expand to countries such as Mexico, Cuba, Japan, and China. The global economy will offer opportunities for Americans who master foreign languages, and for those who want to work and study abroad. In an aesthetic sense, Americans will have the opportunity to learn to appreciate foreign films, books, and music, just as there will be an unprecedented demand abroad for writers and teachers of American history. The information revolution will spill over with demands not simply for programmers and technicians but for researchers and inventors. The problems are real but the possibilities are limited only by the imagination.

Some nations, nonetheless, remain clouded in uncertainty. Clinton was cautious toward America's newly minted friend, Russia, as he watched the difficult transition from long years of communism to capitalism. He met with Yeltsin at a record ten summits and gave America's Cold War enemy billions of dollars in economic aid. Two agreements were signed to reduce nuclear weapons, and America helped supervise their destruction. Yeltsin, in poor health, announced he would not run for reelection in 2000. On December 31, 1999, he resigned and appointed his Prime Minister, Vladimir Putin, to replace him. Putin, a veteran of the Russian secret police, the KGB, won a full term as Yeltsin's successor. Tough and smart, he made no attempt to resocialize the economy, but ethnic tensions and consumer shortages continued.

Clinton's aspirations were high in the Middle East and Northern Ireland, where he hoped to broker lasting peace. With American assistance and Norwegian sponsorship, Israel and the Palestine Liberation Organization signed the Oslo Agreement, in September 1993, at the White House. The accord called for Israel to trade land it had occupied since the 1967 war, culminating in peace and a Palestinian state. Yasir Arafat renounced terror and recognized Israel's right to exist; Israeli Prime Minister Yitzhak Rabin granted self-rule to Palestinians in Jericho and the Gaza Strip. These promises, and other compacts involving Israel and its neighbors, encouraged administration hopes. Agreements in 1995 in Washington and in 1998 near the Wye River in Maryland advanced the land-for-peace formula. But the agreements failed because militant expansionists on both sides, often religious fundamentalists, opposed concessions by their leaders. Rabin paid for his peacemaking attempts with his life, murdered in 1995 by an Israeli opposed to compromise. After a summit called by Clinton at Camp David in 2000 failed to resolve issues, violence flared, leaving Clinton's ambitions as a peacemaker in tatters.

As in the Middle East, nationalism, religion, and history in Northern Ireland made peacemaking treacherous. Catholics, who wanted to affiliate with the Irish Republic, and Protestants, who wanted to retain an attachment to Britain, engaged in guerrilla war. A peace formula brokered by former Senate Majority Leader George Mitchell was announced on Good Friday in April of 1998. The Good Friday agreement provided for election of a provincial assembly representing both factions, yet its future appears dubious.

In Africa, civil wars initiated fratricide and famine. The most heinous occurred in Rwanda, where Hutus slaughtered eight hundred thousand Tutsis until the Tutsis gained the upper hand and killed Hutus. Clinton, still smarting from Somalia, did not send peacekeepers, nor could he devise a plan to end the conflict. Finally, in 1996, the president dispatched several hundred soldiers to protect United Nations relief efforts.

Genocide also tormented Bosnia, Herzegovina, and Kosovo, formerly members of the Yugoslav republic. Under Tito, and for a few years after his death, Yugoslavia managed to hold ethnic rivalries in check, but it broke apart in the wake of the implosion of communism. Hostilities erupted among Serbs, Croats, and Bosnians. In 1992 Bosnian Serbs declared independence and attacked the capital, Sarajevo. Under their leader, Yugoslav President Slobodan Milosevic, the Serbs carried out a campaign of "ethnic cleansing," including murder and torture, to drive Croats and Muslims from Serb areas. Although the Serb brutality sickened the world, President Clinton was unwilling to intervene. Former President Jimmy Carter arranged a December 1994 cease-fire, but it collapsed early the next year, and the White House decided to do more. Late in 1995 Clinton brought together Bosnians, Serbs, and Croats at Dayton, Ohio, and cobbled together a peace plan that preserved the unity of Bosnia-Herzegovina as a nation and divided the country into districts, one controlled by Serbs and one by Muslims and Croats. The United States also pledged to commit troops to help keep the peace.

Next, ethnic hostilities exploded in Kosovo, a Serb province where the Albanian majority demanded independence. In 1998 Serb police began to detain and murder Albanians, prompting Clinton and NATO to stiffen economic sanctions against Milosevic and Yugoslavia. Milosevic massed his army around the province and sent forces surging into Kosovo. NATO responded with eleven weeks of deadly bombing of Serbia. The Serbs surrendered in 1999. Milosevic lost the next election and was turned over to a UN tribunal, which convicted him of war crimes. Not satisfied with their victory, the Kosovars resorted to ethnic cleansing of Serbs in their territory. U.S. and NATO troops remained.

The Middle East continued to be the chief breeding ground for terrorism. Much of it was directed against the State of Israel, and its chief supporter, the United States. Iraq was one of the most anti-Semitic, anti-American hotspots. In 1993 Clinton authorized missile attacks after learning the Iraqi leader, Saddam Hussein, had plotted to assassinate George Bush. Hussein ejected arms inspectors, who wanted to determine whether Hussein was manufacturing chemical and biological weapons, and Clinton responded by placing economic sanctions on Iraq. In December 1998 Clinton ordered a brief bombing campaign against Iraq. Later, Clinton authorized air strikes on suspected terrorist sites in Afghanistan and Sudan, retaliating for bomb attacks against the American Embassies in Nairobi, Kenya, and Dar es Salaam, Tanzania. Sudan claimed a factory destroyed by American air strikes made only pharmaceutical products while the United States charged that it manufactured chemical weapons. In October 2000, a bomb planted by terrorists on a small boat damaged the destroyer *Cole* off Yemen, killing seventeen American sailors.

Earlier in 2000, a six-year-old boy drew Washington into an international dispute. Elian Gonzalez, plucked from the ocean in late 1999 after his mother drowned trying to flee Cuba in a small boat, went to live with relatives in Miami. His father, divorced from Elian's mother and still living in Cuba, demanded his son's return. Cuba's Fidel Castro accused America of kidnapping. Conservatives and anti-Castro Cubans in the United States fought to keep Elian in America. Clinton, Reno, and immigration officials thought Elian should be reunited with his father. Federal agents seized the boy early on April 22 and returned him to his father, who brought him back to Cuba. Castro won a propaganda victory.

Clinton's final two years in office focused increasingly on foreign policy, as the political climate at home deteriorated. The first president to travel to Africa in two decades, he journeyed to Europe and Asia as well.

Sex, Lies, and Impeachment

Paradoxically, a president so skilled at politics and some aspects of policy almost self-destructed. Virtually from the start of Clinton's tenure, the White House was on the defensive due to scandals. Numerous members of the administration became subjects of investigations, and some quit the government. Accusations of illegal political contributions resulted in penalties against a prominent donor and calls for campaign finance reform. Other scandals struck closer to the Clintons. In the "travelgate" affair, Hillary Rodham Clinton was accused of firing members of the travel office to replace them with political cronies. In the Whitewater scandal, a special prosecutor was appointed to investigate a land-development scheme harking back to Arkansas. The Clintons lost money on the deal and were never indicted for wrongdoing, yet there were appearances of influence-peddling and political favoritism. Several Arkansas friends of the Clintons were convicted of crimes.

Kenneth Starr, the special prosecutor with a bloodhound's nose for scandal, then found a salacious episode. A former White House intern, Monica Lewinsky, had a two-year affair with the president, including sex and dirty telephone talk. Worse, the president lied about the affair in a deposition taken by attorneys for an Arkansas woman, Paula Jones, who was suing the president for sexually harassing her while he was governor of Arkansas. Eventually, Lewinsky admitted the affair and Starr sought impeachment of Clinton for perjury and obstruction of justice. Clinton's critics believed the coverup might be grounds for impeachment, although adultery was not.

On December 19, 1998, the House voted along partisan lines to impeach Clinton on four counts. It was the first presidential impeachment (equivalent to indictment) since Andrew Johnson, Abraham Lincoln's successor. Public support for Clinton's economic successes, along with the belief that the gravity of the charges did not justify removal from office, helped save him. On February 12, 1999, the Senate voted to acquit. Clinton, however, suffered public humiliation. He apologized to the public, paid a $25,000 fine for lying in the Paula Jones lawsuit, settled with Jones for $850,000, and had his law license suspended for five years.

The events tarnished Clinton's reputation, though they did not negate his achievements. Many Americans felt ambivalent about Clinton as he left office. Despite the sexual revolution, and the fact that other public figures had strayed, the impeachment demonstrated that large numbers of Americans still took traditional morality seriously and expected potential role models to behave themselves. What most Americans sought in their political leaders was ability coupled with rectitude. Among the presidents of the Era of Diversity, none was more contradictory than Bill Clinton: gifted, human, weak. "He may come to be remembered as the most paradoxical president: an undisciplined man who reformed government and in so doing inspired trust in it, while inspiring none in himself," journalist Jacob Weisberg wrote.

As in the Watergate scandal, the First Family's dirty laundry was washed on national television. Power continued to corrupt. To many, the blood-sport of politics had become vindictive. The special counsel statute was terminated when it came due for renewal later in 1999. Democrats and Republicans agreed that investigations had become obsessively partisan. Every president since Richard Nixon had been investigated.

Since America had awakened to the world as the century dawned, it had made enormous strides economically. Fittingly, the last decade of the century was its most prosperous. Yet, as Clinton left office, his political failures lay in issues that had not been addressed satisfactorily since the time of Theodore Roosevelt and Woodrow Wilson. Is freedom free? Are we our brother's keeper? Both would be addressed by the presidents of the twenty-first century of the third millennium. Although America had won the Cold War on Bush's watch, his successor had failed to define a new role for his nation in the world. Caught between the expediencies of winning elections and holding party interest groups, the president, who had run as a New Democrat, had won tactical victories based on shifting coalitions but had not initiated a new set of priorities for his divided party. Clinton did not inspire idealism and partisanship embittered the nation at century's end. The paradox of opportunities seized and opportunities missed, of how far we had come and how far we still needed to go, reminded us not to take wealth, security, or freedom for granted.

The Era of Diversity provided infinite, chaotic choices. In the century's most prosperous decade, the enigma of poverty and abundance, sundered by class, racial, and gender differences, persisted. Prosperity failed to bring unity and at century's end, the place of the United States in the world was perhaps less clearly defined than it had been in the time of William McKinley. The twentieth century had awakened the nation, guided it through the perils of trials and triumphs, helped it weather uncertainty, and watched it emerge more diverse. The Time of Paradox was one of staggering accomplishments, and festering problems which defied solutions. The twenty-first century beckoned, eager to imprint an identity of its own, one in which the velocity of change would accelerate exponentially. Americans strained to stretch the limits of reality, to reconcile physics and theology, to produce and to conserve, to achieve peace of mind.

The Presidency of
George W. Bush

FOR THE ONLY time in their nation's short history, Americans living in 2000 witnessed the simultaneous turn of the century and turn of the millennium. The fireworks of January 1 were matched by the political fireworks of November as Americans wondered and fought for weeks over who they had elected president.

Vice President Al Gore defeated New Jersey Senator Bill Bradley to win the Democratic nomination and tapped Senator Joseph Lieberman of Connecticut, the first Jew nominated, as his running mate. The Democrats united behind Gore.

In 1997 and 1998 many Republicans had begun urging Texas Governor George W. Bush, the son of former President George H. W. Bush, to seek the Republican nomination. Bush wanted to run, yet he had reservations. With the economy prosperous and the nation at peace, Gore looked unbeatable. Moreover, Bush's wife Laura and his twin daughters valued privacy. Bush had been governor only four years and some Republicans believed he needed more seasoning. On the other hand, the Bush family had a network of political and business friends that could raise enormous sums and produce endorsements. If he entered the race, Bush would be the Republican frontrunner. By early 1999 some prominent Republicans were already in the race, including former Vice President Dan Quayle, Senator John McCain of Arizona, former Tennessee Governor Lamar Alexander, and Elizabeth Dole, ex-Transportation Secretary and wife of the 1996 Republican nominee. McCain won the nation's first primary in New Hampshire. In South Carolina, the next major primary, Bush over-whelmed McCain by waging a negative campaign. South Carolina ended McCain's momentum and Bush coasted to the nomination. Bush wanted an experienced politician for second place on the ticket, one without political ambitions of his own. At his father's suggestion, he appointed Richard Cheney, former Chief of Staff to President Ford, to head the search. Eventually, Bush picked Cheney himself. Bush defined his political philosophy as "compassionate conservatism," a kind of tough love. Two minor party candidates ran, liberal Ralph Nader, the candidate of the Green Party, and conservative Pat Buchanan, of Perot's Reform Party.

Gore won the popular vote yet on election night the electoral count remained close, to be determined by the state of Florida. Florida's popular count see-sawed, swinging initially to Bush, declared the winner by one thousand votes. Yet confusion reigned. A machine recount favored Bush. However, a hand count might favor Gore, some of whose supporters apparently were confused by the nature of the paper ballots. Further, different standards had been used in different counties to determine the counting of partially-detached paper ballots. The race would be decided by the courts. The Florida Supreme Court, with a Democratic majority, ruled for Gore. The climax came at the top. The U.S. Supreme Court, with a conservative majority, supported Bush's election by a 5-4 majority.

The final count showed Gore beating Bush by more than 500,000 ballots in the popular vote. This broke down to 50.9 million for Gore and 50.4 million for Bush, yet Bush narrowly carried the Electoral College, 271 to 266. Nader won 3.5 percent of the Florida vote, which Gore lost by less than 1 percent. Because Nader and Gore were both liberals, it is possible that Nader cost Gore Florida and with it the election. Bush was strong in the South, the Southwest, and the Great Plains while Gore scored well in the large industrial states. The Republicans retained control of Congress by narrow margins, with Vice President Cheney holding the tie-breaking vote in the Senate. One of the new Democratic Senators elected was Hillary Rodham Clinton.

The fourth man to win the presidency despite losing the popular vote, Bush, fifty-four, had graduated from Yale and received a degree in business administration from Harvard. Once a hard-drinking playboy, he changed his lifestyle after an arrest for drunken driving in 1976. George W., as he was known, turned to religion and married a schoolteacher, Laura Welch. He avoided the draft by joining the Air National Guard, and entered the oil supply industry in Texas. Later, he bought and then sold the Texas Rangers major-league baseball team.

Bush differed from his father. In policy, he was more conservative, closer in ideology to Reagan than to the senior Bush. In personality, he was more open and gregarious, more relaxed, with a better sense of humor. He identified with the West and the people of Texas and was less comfortable

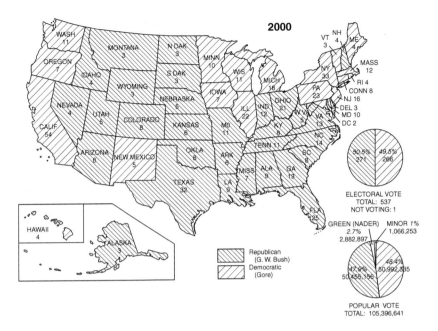

Election of 2000

with the Eastern elite. The father was more skilled at book learning, but the son was better at dealing with people.

Although the new president favored many of Reagan's policies, Bush was more positive about the role of government, although he felt it should be limited. He believed character and hard work, not simply wise economic policies, were necessary for prosperity. The younger Bush was open about his Christianity and the influence it had exerted on his life.

As president, Bush tried to avoid letting the media anger him as it had his father. He was less accessible to the press, preferring to ignore criticism than to confront it. The Washington social scene held less attraction for Bush than it had for his parents. The Bushes escaped Washington frequently for Camp David and their Crawford, Texas, ranch. Bush brought friends and members of the cabinet to Texas. He retired early and jogged daily, exercising to relax.

Bush appointed an experienced cabinet and relied heavily on Cheney. His foreign policy team included Secretary of State Colin Powell, Defense Secretary Donald Rumsfield, and National Security Adviser Condoleeza Rice. The President's major domestic achievement was passage of a $1.35 trillion, ten-year tax cut in May 2001, a measure he hoped would stimulate the economy, which had dipped into recession. From the surpluses of the Clinton era, the Treasury now projected a sea of red ink. Unemployment rose and unions blamed Bush for allowing the loss of jobs to cheap foreign labor. Bush stayed the course and in 2004 the economy began to inch upward.

Terror from the Sky

Bush, unlike his father, did not intend to be a foreign policy president. Fate determined otherwise. Early on September 11, 2001, terrorists on suicide missions hijacked four passenger jets. Two crashed into the Twin Towers of the World Trade Center in New York, killing thousands and destroying symbols of American commercial might. One smashed into the Pentagon, wrecking part of the massive building. The bravery of passengers on the fourth flight, who attacked the hijackers and forced them off course, saved the intended target, possibly the White House. Instead the jet crashed in rural Pennyslvania.

When the September 11 tragedy occurred, most in the administration did not realize the attacks on the Twin Towers had been a deliberate act of terrorism until the second plane slammed into a building. Bush, who was talking to school children in Sarasota, Florida, tried to remain calm yet knew that his administration's priorities had been irrevocably altered. For better or worse, history will largely remember Bush as the president who launched a war on terrorism.

The end of the Cold War did not bring permanent peace and security, only a different type of war in which small, fanatical groups could wreak havoc on their larger, more powerful enemies. In this war military and political intelligence are as important as nuclear might. Rather than waging a defensive war, Bush introduced a controversial new tactic: preemptive strikes at nations believed to be harboring terrorists or preparing weapons of mass destruction. There was little hope of winning a clearcut victory; the best that could be expected was to defuse the threat. However, because terrorism worked undercover, some Americans considered it unwise to fight until it materialized, or feared combating it might jeopardize civil liberties.

Bush saw the issue of terrorism in distinct moral terms. Once he decided to wage war, he planned to do so with maximum force. Although diplomacy would be a tool, he was more willing than his father to initiate action without world approval. In the short run, the attacks on the World Trade Towers united Americans. As time wore on, and the war on terrorism appeared frustrating and interminable, opposition mounted.

The suspected mastermind of the attack was Osama bin Laden, operating from a base in Afghanistan. George Bush senior encouraged his son to rev up the American intelligence system. Instead of a massive assault on Afghanistan, the ex-president suggested a more limited, focused attack directed at overturning the fundamentalist Taliban government by collaborating with their opponents. Bush issued an ultimatum to the Taliban: turn over bin Laden or America would undertake military operations in Afghanistan. CIA operatives working with anti-Taliban forces combined with a precision air campaign to depose the Taliban, who continued limited resistance.

American intelligence believed the chief threat to security lay in chemical and biological weapons, especially the latter. Unlike nuclear weapons they did not require a sophisticated delivery system. Neither did they require years of research and the massive expense of constructing nuclear reactors. The programs could be carried out in small, remote areas, easy to conceal. During the first Persian Gulf War against Iraq Americans feared the Iraqi dictator, Saddam Hussein, possessed and might use chemical and biological weapons. When the war ended with Hussein defeated yet still in power, the Iraqi government was ordered to destroy its stockpiles and terminate its programs. Yet the American government and much of the international community feared Hussein had only concealed, not destroyed his weapons, and the Iraqi dictator contributed to the impression by not allowing international inspectors free access to sites throughout Iraq.

Bush considered Hussein a threat to global security. Moreover, there was personal animosity between the leaders; Hussein had planned to assassinate Bush's father. Bush's ambitions went beyond deposing Hussein. He wanted to plant democracy in the Middle East and ultimately transform the region. On March 6, 2003, Bush offered Hussein a final opportunity to give up power, leave the country, and avoid war. Hussein declined. The president, who believed his father had erred in the first Gulf War by not pushing on to Baghdad and removing Saddam from power, invaded Iraq. The force included some manpower from America's allies, but was less a coalition effort than his father's. The war was won with nearly the ease of the first Iraq war. Saddam, moving from village to village, sometimes living underground, was captured hiding in a hole near a ramshackle "safe house" on December 13, 2003. He was turned over to the new Iraqi government for trial.

Winning the war was the easy part. Saddam's partisans would not give up and directed suicide attacks against Americans, allied soldiers in Iraq, and Iraqi civilian and military officials who supported the United States. Even after the United States officially turned over the government to Iraqi officials in 2004, the attacks continued. Some Iraqis who once feared and detested Saddam and showered with flowers American soldiers who liberated Baghdad, now demanded that Americans leave their country. More important, as U.S. casualties mounted, some Americans turned against the mission, viewing it as a quagmire with no end in sight.

The Political War

The war in Iraq, along with the economy, became major issues in the presidential campaign of 2004. Forty years after Democrat Lyndon Johnson had won the presidency as the peace candidate, Bush found himself locked in rhetorical combat with Democrat Senator John Kerry, who pledged to wage war on war.

Kerry had defeated the early front-runner, ex-Vermont governor Howard Dean, in Iowa and New Hampshire, then vanquished Senator John Edwards of North Carolina, whom he subsequently chose as his running mate. A Vietnam veteran who had renounced the war after returning to America, Kerry offered a liberal critique of Bush's policies, claiming the president had misled the people, and was an inept leader. The election, newsmen agreed, offered a clear distinction between a liberal and conservative vision of America.

The campaign was bitter and intense. Kerry attacked Bush for going to war against Iraq when the real threat was Islamic militant Osama bin Laden and nuclear proliferation. Kerry charged he had a plan to free Americans from the grip of a second Vietnam: ask our allies to carry more of the burden; and train the Iraqis to defend themselves. He pointed out that after the conquest of Iraq, inspectors had found no evidence that Iraq possessed a program to produce weapons of mass destruction. Bush retorted that there was nothing in Kerry's plan that he had not already done. The president further charged that Kerry had supported in the Senate many of the policies he now opposed as a candidate.

The contest was close. The Democrats held the thickly-populated Northeast and the West, with Republican strongholds in the South and Great Plains. This made the Midwest the battleground. The campaign included three debates between the presidential candidates and one between their running mates. In the first, Kerry was assertive, placing the incumbent on the defensive. The others were almost a draw, although Kerry might have emerged with a slight edge. In the vice presidential debate, the exchanges revolved around Vice President Cheney's experience opposed to Edwards's youth and vigor. The campaign was polarizing; there were few voters in the middle, few undecided voters, and few who crossed party lines.

The outcome was determined by Ohio. Bush carried the state and with it the election, winning 286 electoral votes to 251 for Kerry. Bush won the popular vote by a margin of about 3.5 million votes. The turnout was the largest in history and Bush polled the most votes ever won by a presidential candidate. Third party candidate Ralph Nader polled 1 percent of the popular vote and no electoral votes.

Personality played a role in the voting, though the campaign was couched in terms of policy. Although Kerry scored points by his criticism of Bush, many Americans considered Kerry poor leadership timber because of inconsistency that seemed opportunistic. Kerry resonated with intellectuals, yet Bush connected emotionally with ordinary Americans because of his religiosity and open patriotism, even in his cowboy attire and prior part-ownership of a major league baseball team. In the aftermath of the campaign Democrats pondered whether they should turn to secure their left flank or move right to secure the center.

In his second term Bush would have the opportunity to make changes at home and abroad, including the opportunity to restructure the Supreme Court by appointment of a new Chief Justice and an Associate Justice. Although foreign policy continued to dominate the administration, domestic policies provoked debate. Bush's agenda included permanent tax cuts, reform of social security that permitted some of the system's funds to be invested in private accounts, reform of medical care, and protection of businesses and physicians from costly lawsuits. The first budget proposed by Bush in his second term, unveiled in 2005, emphasized tight domestic spending and increases for the military, but at a slower rate than in previous military budgets. Some funds were to be shifted, with an emphasis on domestic security and education reform. Some viewed immigration as a welcoming mat for the poor yet others feared it as an avenue for terrorists. Bush's cabinet was revamped. Rice succeeded Powell as secretary of state, becoming the first black woman to hold that position. The new administration enjoyed majorities in both houses, yet Democrats threatened to filibuster some sensitive issues, including conservative judicial nominees. As with many presidents, Bush's biggest challenges might come not from implementing his platform or keeping his promises but from events not yet on the horizon at the time of his reelection.

Foreign Policy in Bush's Second Term

Bush's second term began in a still dangerous world. On February 10, 2005, North Korea announced it possessed nuclear weapons and Iran moved toward nuclear weapons capability. Some 17,000 American troops remained in Afghanistan, yet casualties were smaller and the media focused on Iraq. Unfortunately, Afghanistan became the world's largest producer of opium. China and Taiwan squabbled, with Taiwan threatening to formally declare independence from the mainland and the People's Republic counterthreatening an invasion if it did.

The Middle East inched toward rapprochement between Israel and the Palestinians after the death of PLO leader Yasser Arafat and the election of Mahmoud Abbas as his successor. The new leader moved to relax tensions, including a crackdown on terrorists. Israel reciprocated by releasing some imprisoned Palestinians and returning some Jewish settlements in Palestinian areas to Palestinian control. Yet militants on both sides did not want peace. In Lebanon the assassination of a former prime minister in March 2005 provoked demonstrations against Syrian occupation of the country and counterdemonstrations by pro-Syrian groups. Syria reluctantly withdrew.

In Iraq, the situation was complex. Terrorist acts continued and American soldiers and larger numbers of Iraqis were killed. Yet Iraqis braved terrorist threats to vote in large numbers on January 30, 2005, and by March they had installed an interim government. Agreement was reached on a more permanent government, charged with writing a new constitution, in April, yet efforts to write a constitution that would satisfy all factions frustrated Iraqis and fueled the insurgency. Key issues included regionalism and the role of Islam. The Iraq war divided America from some of its European allies, yet most decided to deal with Bush in his second term. A few nations, most notably Britain, sent small numbers of troops or medical units to demonstrate support. Russia remained a nominal ally, yet Bush lectured President Vladimir Putin on the need for more democracy during his first trip abroad of the second term. Meanwhile, nations of the former Soviet Union hedged closer to democracy through bloodless revolutions, most notably Ukraine, which elected Viktor Yushchenko president. Many areas of the world seemed in transition to more open, pluralistic, and democratic societies, at least in a relative sense. Throughout what was formally known as the Third World (neither communist nor capitalist) economic growth offered jobs and opportunity, though a tragic tidal wave known as a tsunami killed hundreds of thousands on Pacific islands and on the mainland of Southeast Asia in March 2005 and destroyed cities, villages, livestock, farmland, and industry. Slow to respond, the United States government ultimately provided substantial aid, supplemented by additional donations from millions of individual Americans.

America did not escape national disasters. In late August and September, 2005, hurricane Katrina, followed by hurricane Rita, slammed into the Gulf

Coast. Katrina, the stronger, flooded the historic city of New Orleans and destroyed the Mississippi coastal communities of Gulfport and Biloxi. Before Louisiana had recovered from Katrina, Rita struck, devastating southwestern coastal communities in Louisiana, especially Lake Charles, and southeastern Texas, including Beaumont. The hurricanes temporarily disrupted oil supplies and sent gasoline prices soaring. The cleanup, rebuilding, and human costs ran into the hundreds of billions of dollars.

Earlier, a sad event transpired with the death of Pope John Paul II on April 2, 2005. One of the most influential Popes in the history of the Roman Catholic Church, John Paul's funeral was the largest in world history. He was succeeded by the German Cardinal Joseph Ratzinger, who became Benedict XVI. As has been the case since the end of the Cold War, the United States remains the sole superpower, though China is rapidly moving toward that status, as well as Japan, at least economically. World economic problems are complicated by nationalism and divisive religious wars, especially in Asia and Africa. Indeed with the focus on the Middle East, disease, famine, and war devastate Africa beneath the radar of world scrutiny. Internationally, America is viewed with a mixture of awe, respect, envy, hatred, and gratitude. Americans remained pregnant with hope yet feared the fickleness of fate. In the twenty-first century their world might scale new heights of achievements that had eluded previous generations, or it might topple into the abyss of a new dark age.

Bibliographic Essay

Nixon through Reagan

The best biography of Richard Nixon is Stephen E. Ambrose, *Nixon* (3 vols., 1987–1994). Also see Tom Wicker, *One of Us: Richard Nixon and the American Dream* (1991); Herbert S. Parmet, *Richard Nixon and His America* (1994); and Joan Hoff, *Nixon Reconsidered* (1994). Other sources include John R. Greene, *The Limits of Power: The Nixon and Ford Administrations* (1992), and Melvin Small, *The Presidency of Richard Nixon* (1999). David Greenberg, *Nixon's Shadow: The History of an Image* (2003) is an excellent survey of Nixon stereotypes. Studies on domestic affairs under Nixon include Allen Matusow, *Nixon's Economy: Booms, Busts, Dollars, and Voters* (1998); Robert M. Collins, *People of More: Economic Growth in Postwar America* (2000); and Walter I. Trattner, *From Poor Law to Welfare State: A History of Social Welfare in America* (1994), a thorough general account. The Cold War is discussed in Raymond L. Garthoff, *Detente and Confrontation: American-Soviet Relations from Nixon to Reagan*, rev. ed. (1995); Richard C. Thornton, *The Nixon-Kissinger Years: Reshaping America's Foreign Policy* (1989); and Diane B. Kunz, *Butter and Guns: America's Cold War Economic Diplomacy* (1997). The literature on Watergate is vast. See Stanley I. Kutler, *The Wars of Watergate* (1990), and *Abuse of Power: The New Nixon Tapes* (1997); Fred Emery, *Watergate: The Corruption of American Politics and the Fall of Richard Nixon* (1995); Bob Woodward and Carl Bernstein, *All the President's Men* (1974), and *The Final Days* (1976), journalistic exposes; and Theodore White, *Breach of Faith* (1975), an early yet worthwhile work.

Studies of Nixon's successor include John Robert Greene, *The Presidency of Gerald R. Ford* (1995), the most comprehensive; James Cannon, *Time and Chance: Gerald Ford's Appointment with History* (1994); and Edward Schapsmeier and Frederick Schapsmeier, *Gerald Ford's Date with Destiny: A Political Biography* (1989). On Ford's role in the fall of South Vietnam see Alan Dawson, *55 Days: The Fall of South Vietnam* (1977), and P. Edward Haley, *Congress and the Fall of South Vietnam and Cambodia* (1983). On the *Mayaguez* incident, see Christopher Jon Lamb, *Belief Systems and Decision Making in the Mayaguez Crisis* (1988).

On Jimmy Carter's administration see Burton I. Kaufman, *The Presidency of James Earl Carter* (1993); Peter G. Bourne, *Jimmy Carter: A Comprehensive Biography from Plains to Postpresidency* (1997); Charles O. Jones, *The Trusteeship Presidency: Jimmy Carter and the United States Congress* (1988); and Haynes Johnson, *In the Absence of Power: Governing America* (1980), harshly critical. Aspects of Carter's domestic policies are covered in Anthony S. Campagna, *Economic Policy in the Carter Administration* (1995). More attention has been devoted to Carter's foreign policies than to his domestic policies. Significant studies of the former include Gaddis Smith, *Morality, Reason, and Power: American Diplomacy in the Carter Years* (1986); Alexander Moens, *Foreign Policy under Carter* (1990); Jerel A. Rosati, *The Carter Administration's Quest for Global Community* (1987); A. Glenn Mower Jr., *Human Rights and American Foreign Policy: The Carter and Reagan Experience* (1987); William M. LeoGrande, *Our Own Backyard: The United States in Central America, 1977–1992* (1998); and T. G. Fraser, *The USA and the Middle East since World War II* (1989). Carter's most significant accomplishment is described in William B. Quandt, *Camp David: Peacemaking and Politics* (1986). On Iran, see James A. Bill, *The Eagle and the Lion: The Tragedy of American-Iranian Relations* (1987), and Paul B. Ryan, *The Iranian Rescue Mission and Why It Failed* (1986).

On the ascendance of the right, see Sidney Blumenthal, *The Rise of the Counter-Establishment* (1986); J. David Hoeveler, *Watch on the Right: Conservative Intellectuals in the Reagan Era* (1991); Jerome L. Himmelstein, *To the Right: The Transformation of American Conservatism* (1990); John Ehrman, *The Rise of Neoconservatism: Intellectuals and Foreign Affairs* (1995); John K. White, *The New Politics of Old Values* (1988); Dan T. Carter, *The Politics of Rage: George Wallace, the Origins of the New Conservatism, and the Transformation of American Politics* (1995), critical of Wallace; Paul Gottfried, *The Conservative Movement*, rev. ed. (1993); and Melvin J. Thorne, *American Conservative Thought since World War II: The Core Ideas* (1990). For the New Christian right, see Robert L. Hilliard and Michael C. Keith, *Waves of Rancor: Tuning in the Radical Right*

(1999); Jeffrey K. Hadden and Anson Shupe, *Televangelism: Power and Politics on God's Frontier* (1988); Clyde Wilcox, *God's Warriors: The Christian Right in Twentieth-Century America* (1992); Steve Bruce, *The Rise and Fall of the New Christian Right: Conservative Protestant Politics in America, 1978–1988* (1988); and Michael Lienesch, *Redeeming America: Piety and Politics in the New Christian Right* (1993).

On Ronald Reagan, Edmund Morris had extraordinary access to the president in the White House and used it to help produce *Dutch: A Memoir of Ronald Reagan* (1999), richly detailed but flawed by Morris's insertion of himself as a fictional character who observes Reagan's life. Lou Cannon, *President Reagan: The Role of a Lifetime*, 2nd ed. (2000) is a thorough journalistic account as is Haynes Johnson, *Sleepwalking through History: America in the Reagan Years* (1991). William E. Pemberton, *Exit with Honor: The Life and Presidency of Ronald Reagan* (1997) is succinct, scholarly and fair. More recent is Gil Troy, *Morning in America: How Ronald Reagan Invented the 1980s* (2005).

Among works dealing with Reagan's domestic policy are Joseph J. Minarik, *Making America's Budget Policy: From the 1980s to the 1990s* (1990); David G. Savage, *Turning Right: The Making of the Rehnquist Supreme Court* (1992); and Nicholas Laham, *The Reagan Presidency and the Politics of Race: In Pursuit of Colorblind Justice and Limited Government* (1998). The literature on Reagan's foreign policies is extensive. See Coral Bell, *The Reagan Paradox: American Foreign Policy in the 1980s* (1989); Richard A. Melanson, *Reconstructing Consensus: American Foreign Policy since the Vietnam War* (1991); Warren I. Cohen, *America in the Age of Soviet Power, 1945–1991* (1993); Steve Crawshaw, *Goodbye to the USSR: The Collapse of Soviet Power* (1992); Richard Crockatt, *The Fifty Years War: The United States and the Soviet Union in World Politics, 1941–1991* (1995); John Lewis Gaddis, *The United States and the End of the Cold War: Implications, Reconsiderations, Provocations* (1992); Daniel Wirls, *Buildup: The Politics of Defense in the Reagan Era* (1992); Don Oberdorfer, *The Turn: From the Cold War to a New Era, the United States and the Soviet Union* (1991); and Thomas W. Simons Jr., *The End of the Cold War* (1990). Reagan and Central America are discussed in Roy Gutman, *Banana Diplomacy: The Making of American Policy in Nicaragua, 1981–1987* (1988). On the Iran-Contra scandal, see Don Lawson, *America Held Hostage: The Iran Hostage Crisis and the Iran-Contra Affair* (1991), and Theodore Draper, *A Very Thin Line: The Iran-Contra Affairs* (1991). On the Middle East, see Charles D. Smith, *Palestine and the Arab-Israeli Conflict*, 2nd ed. (1992).

Culture and Society

Norman F. Cantor, *The American Century: Varieties of Culture in Modern Times* (1997), is an excellent overview. Robert Hughes, *The Culture of Complaint: The Fraying of America* (1993), is a penetrating analysis of late twentieth-century art and its opponents. Also see James Davison Hunter, *Culture Wars: The Struggle to Define America* (1991). Although ostensibly a study of Bob Dylan, Greil Marcus, *Invisible Republic: Bob Dylan's Basement Tapes* (1997), is valuable for its analysis of themes in culture. Dylan's memoir, *Chronicles* (2004) is spellbinding, yet episodic. Gregor Ehrlich and Dmitri Ehrlich, *Crowd: Voices and Faces of the Hip-Hop Nation* (1999), is a study of hip-hop and rap music, complemented by Nelson George, *Hip Hop America* (1998). Ronald L. Davis, *Celluloid Mirrors: Hollywood and American Society since 1945* (1997), is a brief survey. Among studies of the media are David Halberstam, *The Powers That Be* (1979); Herbert J. Gans, *Deciding What's News: A Study of CBS Evening News, NBC Nightly News, Newsweek and Time* (1979); and Daniel J. Czitrom, *Media and the American Mind: From Morse to McLuhan* (1982).

General histories of the 1970s are Bruce J. Schulman, *The Seventies* (2001), and Peter Carroll, *It Seemed Like Nothing Happened* (1982). On the 1980s, see John Ehrman, *The Eighties: America in the Age of Reagan* (2005). On technology and business, see James Cortada, *Making the Information Society* (2002), an account of the computer revolution. For the 1990s, consult Alan Wolfe, *One Nation after All: What Middle-Class America Really Thinks About* (1998), and Michael Sandel, *Democracy's Discontent: America in Search of a Public Philosophy* (1996), which focuses on political ideas. Useful on economic change, are Haynes Johnson, *The Best of Times: The Boom and Bust Years of America before and after Everything Changed* (2002), and David Gordon, *Fat and Mean: The Corporate Squeezing of Working Americans* (1996).

Religion is examined in Thomas C. Reeves, *The Empty Church: Does Organized Religion Matter Anymore?* (1996); George Marsden, *Religion and American Culture* (1990); Robert Wuthnow, *The Restructuring of American Religion: Society and Faith Since World War II* (1988); and Howard M. Sachar, *A History of the Jews in America* (1992). Among the many books on abortion are Kristin Luker, *Abortion and the Politics of Motherhood* (1984), and Rosalind Petchesky, *Abortion and Women's Choice* (1984). A medical scourge that became an emotional issue in politics and religion is described in Randy Shilts, *And the Band Played On: Politics, People, and the AIDS Epidemic* (1987), and *AIDS: The Making of a Chronic Disease* (1992).

Books on race include William Julius Wilson, *When Work Disappears: The World of the New Urban Poor* (1996); Orlando Patterson, *The Ordeal of Integration: Progress and Resentment in America's "Racial" Crisis* (1997); Abigail Thernstrom and Stephan Thernstrom, *America in Black and White, Indivisible* (1996), an interpretation of race relations since the 1940s, Andrew Hacker, *Two Nations: Black and White, Separate, Hostile, Unequal* (1992), and Thomas Byrne Edsall and Mary D. Edsall, *Chain Reaction: The Impact of Race, Rights, and Taxes on American Politics* (1991). Debates over welfare, race, and class are discussed in Michael Katz, *The Undeserving Poor: From the War on Poverty to the War on Welfare* (1989). Valuable works on civil rights include Leon E. Panetta and Peter Gall, *"Bring Us Together": The Nixon Team and the Civil Rights Retreat* (1971), and Steven A. Shull, *A Kinder, Gentler Racism? The Reagan-Bush Civil Rights Legacy* (1993). On Chicanos, see Rodolfo Acuna, *Occupied America: A History of Chicanos*, 3rd ed. (1988), and Jorge Ramos, *The Other Face of America: Chronicles of Immigrants Shaping Our Future* (2002). On Indians, see Stephen Cornell, *The Return of the Native: Indian Political Resurgence* (1988); Wilcomb E. Washburn, *The Indian in America* (1975); and Vine Deloria Jr., *American Indian Policy in the Twentieth Century* (1985).

Books on ethnicity and immigration include David M. Reimers, *Still the Golden Door: The Third World Comes to America* (1985); John Crewdson, *The Tarnished Door: The New Immigrants and the Transformation of America* (1983); Patrick H. Buchanan, *The Death of the West: How Dying Populations and Immigrant Invasions Imperil Our Country and Civilization* (2001); Vernon Briggs, *Mass Immigration: The National Interest* (1994); James S. Olson, *The Ethnic Dimension in American History* (1994); Jose A. Hernandez, *Mutual Aid for Survival: The Case of the Mexican American* (1985); Henry Tsai Shi-shan, *The Chinese Experience in America* (1986); Gail P. Kelly, *From Vietnam to America: A Chronicle of the Vietnamese Immigration to the USA* (1977); and Paul Rutledge, *The Vietnamese Experience in America* (1992).

Women's history is the subject of Marian Faux, *Roe v. Wade* (1988); David Garrow, *Liberty and Sexuality: The Right to Privacy and the Making of Roe v. Wade* (1994); Winifred D. Wandersee, *On the Move: American Women in the 1970s* (1988); Susan M. Hartmann, *From Margin to Mainstream: Women in American Politics since 1960* (1989); Mary Francis Berry, *Why ERA Failed* (1986); and Nancy Caraway, *Segregated Sisterhood: Racism and the Politics of American Feminism* (1991). Jean Bethke Elshtain, *Women and War* (1987), is the best work on the subject.

The Bush and Clinton Presidencies

Studies of George H. W. Bush include John Robert Greene, *The Presidency of George Bush* (2000); Herbert S. Parmet, *George Bush: The Life of a Lone Star Yankee* (1997); and Michael Duffy, *Marching in Place: The Status Quo Presidency of George Bush* (1992). Among books dealing with politics and domestic policy are Haynes Johnson, *Divided We Fall: Gambling with History in the Nineties* (1994), and Kevin Phillips, *The Politics of Rich and Poor: Wealth and the American Electorate in the Reagan Aftermath* (1990). Much has been written about Bush's diplomacy and the end of the Cold War. David Halberstam, *War in a Time of Peace: Bush, Clinton and the Generals* (2002), is a good general work. For American relations with the Soviet Union, see Joseph G. Whelan, *Soviet Diplomacy and Negotiating Behavior, 1988–1990: Gorbachev-Reagan-Bush Meetings at the Summit* (1991). On the collapse of the Soviet empire, see Marshall Goldman, *What Went Wrong with Perestroika?* (1992), and Jack F. Matlock's massive but readable *Autopsy of an Empire* (1995). Also useful are Bernard Gwertzman and Michael T. Kaufman, eds., *The Collapse of Communism* (1990); Paul Kennedy, *The Rise and Fall of the Great Powers* (1987); and Robert Kuttner, *The End of Laissez-Faire: National Purpose and the Global Economy after the Cold War* (1991). Bush's chief foreign policy accomplishment is the subject of Alberto Bin, Richard Hill, and Archer Jones, *Desert Storm: A Forgotten War* (1998).

Bill Clinton has been the subject of several journalistic studies, including David Maraniss, *First in His Class: A Biography of Bill Clinton* (1995), which traces his prepresidential career; R. Emmett Tyrrell Jr., *Boy Clinton: The Political Biography* (1996), and Nigel Hamilton, *Bill Clinton: An American Journey* (2003). James MacGregor Burns and Georgia J. Sorenson, *Dead Center: Clinton-Gore Leadership and the Perils of Moderation* (1999) is more policy oriented. Alex Wadden, *Clinton's Legacy: A New Democrat in Governance*, is strong on Clinton's economic policies. Sidney Blumenthal, *The Clinton Wars* (2003), is an insider's dissection of the scandals that nearly ended the Clinton presidency. Richard A. Posner, *An Affair of State: The Investigation, Impeachment, and Trial of President Clinton* (1999), is a legal study. Roger Morris, *Partners in Power: The Clintons and Their America* (1996), a joint biography of the presidential couple, includes valuable insights. The Clintons published separate memoirs, Bill Clinton, *My Life* (2004), and Hillary Rodham Clinton, *Living History* (2003).

Studies involving politics and change include Theda Skocpol, *Boomerang: Clinton's Health Security Effort and the Turn against Government in U.S.*

Politics (1996); John F. Bibby, *Return of Divided Party Government* (1995); Felice D. Perlmutter, *From Welfare to Work: Corporate Initiatives and Welfare Reform* (1997); Robert M. Solow, *Work and Welfare* (1998), and Gwendolyn Mink, *Welfare's End* (1998). On terrorism in the 1990s, see Stephen Jones and Peter Israel, *Others Unknown: The Oklahoma City Bombing Case* (1998), an account by the defense attorneys in the case; David Thibodeau, *A Place Called Waco: A Survivor's Story of Life and Death at Mt. Carmel* (1999); and Michael D. Kelleher, *When Good Kids Kill* (1998). For treatments of foreign affairs, consult Robert J. Myers, *U.S. Foreign Policy in the Twenty-First Century* (1999); and Gerald B. Solomon, *The NATO Enlargment Debate, 1990–1997* (1998), are helpful.

Postlude

For developments after Clinton, see the Political Staff of the *Washington Post, Deadlock: The Inside Story of America's Closest Election* (2001), on the 2000 presidential election, and Bob Woodward, *Bush at War* (2002), which examines steps that President George W. Bush and the other major players in foreign policy took in the early months after the 2001 terror attacks. Steve Coll, *Ghost Wars: The Secret History of the CIA, Afghanistan, and Bin Laden from the Soviet Invasion to September 10, 2001* (2005), is useful.

Peter Schweizer and Rochele Schweizer, *The Bushes: Portrait of a Dynasty* (2004), is a favorable portrait of the family. Three books of essays also contribute to an early assessment of George W. Bush: Steven E. Schier, ed. *High Risk and Big Ambition: The Presidency of George W. Bush* (2004); Jon Kraus, Kevin J. McMahon, and David M. Rankin, eds. *Transformed by Crisis: The Presidency of George W. Bush and American Politics* (2004); and Bryan Hilliard, Tom Lansford, and Robert P. Watson, *George W. Bush: Evaluating the President at Midterm* (2004).

"It was the best of times, it was the worst of times, it was the age of wisdom, it was the age of foolishness, it was the epoch of belief, it was the epoch of incredulity, it was the season of Darkness, it was the spring of hope, it was the winter of despair, we had everything before us, we had nothing before us, we were all going direct to Heaven, we were all going direct the other way—in short, the period was so far like the present period, that some of its noisiest authorities insisted on its being received, for good or evil, in the superlative degree of comparison only."

—Charles Dickens, *A Tale of Two Cities* (1859)

THE POST–WORLD WAR II period was America's golden age. The United States reached the apogee of world power. Yet like many who prospect for gold, Americans often came up empty-handed. Like the time described by Charles Dickens, the era represents a glass half-empty, half-full. It was a time where the light side of humanity battled the dark side nearly to a draw. It was an epoch when the unexpected was commonplace, riven by contractions that can be considered paradoxes in a metaphorical, if not in a literal sense. We conquered Hitler and polio, and gathered rocks on the surface of the moon. Yet we were humiliated in the steamy jungles of Vietnam, found poverty intractable, and failed to cure the common cold. We were the world's leaders. We set examples, good and bad.

The sexual revolution marched on. In the postwar era sexuality was the chief weapon in the arsenal of youthful rebellion and carved the deepest canyon in the generation gap. It was intertwined with music, dance, drinking, smoking, and drugs. Woodstock was as much known for good sex as for good music. Freer sex found support in science: in the psychiatry of Sigmund Freud, in the anthropology of Margaret Mead, reaching back to the evolutionary theories of Charles Darwin. In America its most important spokesman was Alfred Kinsey who both preached and practiced free love. But the sexual revolution, like all revolutions, had a dark side. It was partly responsible for the dismantling of nuclear families and the prolifer-ation of dysfunctional families. There were sexually transmitted diseases, particularly AIDS, which is incurable and deadly.

Sexuality is also related to religion. Sexual energy and religious excite-ment have been linked in fiction, in motion pictures, and in real life. Yet for much of American history, religion has served to restrain sexuality, as an incentive to remain faithful to one's spouse, to avoid divorce, and to abstain from per-marital sex or promiscuity. Though many of these restraints have been swept away, religion continues as a major force in American society, helping to reinforce morality, to bolster morale, and to ponder questions about the enigma of death and the reasons for life, as well as the place of humanity in the cosmos.

In the period from the Cold War to the Third Millennium, Americans increasingly found fulfillment in non-traditional religions. Since the 1960s there has been an enormous increase in spiritual mysticism, an interest in Eastern religions such as Hinduism and Buddhism, as well as Japanese and Chinese martial arts, in meditation and mind-body medicine. Once on the fringes of American society, these practices are now mainstream, coupled with alternative medicine with employs yoga, biofeedback, acupuncture, the use of herbs and spiritual energy in healing, as well as prayer. The argu-ment that they are unscientific seems irrelevant to their practitioners, who point out that many human decisions, such as whom to marry or vote for, are more intuitive than scientific. Since the human brain has two lobes we might as well use both of them.

The pace of change exploded exponentially in the period, driven by technology, the information revolution, the global economy, and our com-mon concern about diminishing resources and the fouling of the environ-ment. America was particularly dependent on foreign oil, which is expensive, and other resources declined in supply, yet we refused to change our lifestyles because it involved sacrifice.

Much of the time of the baby-boom generation was spent parked before television sets or computers. We crowded around TVs to watch Joseph McCarthy destroy himself with his excesses in the Army-McCarthy hearings, Richard Nixon save his career in the Checkers Speech of 1952, then destroy it by lying about Watergate. We watched Friday Night Fights and Monday Night Football, the Super Bowl, and Roger Maris pursue Babe Ruth. TV broke our hearts as we saw live the assassinations of John and Robert Kennedy—replayed endlessly. It lifted our spirits when Neil Armstrong set foot upon the moon and brought them crashing to earth with the Challenger exploded. We saw war live in Vietnam and Iraq. We saw the people of the Eastern Bloc dismantle the Red Empire, the people of Russia pull down statues of Lenin and Stalin, and students in Tiananmen Square taunt tanks.

Computers are indispensable in modern America. They run every big business and most small business. They make airline reservations and point planes in the right direction. Strike up Google and a world of information is at your disposal, much of it wonderful, much of it that belongs in the recycle bin. There is even computer dating. Perhaps more bad blind dates have been set up by computers than by another other method—yet some people find happiness in cyberspace. Computers have their dark side, as I discovered when I deleted the first draft of this epilogue. When they do things better than people do, they take jobs that people used to do. Moreover, computers are no better than their programmers. The rule of thumb is: garbage in—garbage out.

As the millennium changed, Americans were in the process of re-seg-regating their schools and communities, and they were operating in a post-industrial, post-urban society. Small towns offered a livable alternative to cities and suburbs and they continued to produce presidents. Those who longed for smokestacks and pavement were overtaken by those who preferred grass, trees, lakes, and private lawns. Cities were still important, but their day of dominance was done. This had nothing to do with moral failure any more than the shift from farm to city in the nineteenth century had. It was based more on individual convenience and personal choice than on government policies.

The politics of the period from the Cold War through the Third Millennium became increasingly partisan, small-minded, and testy. Every politician proclaimed the necessity for budget-cutting, especially in the military, and a balanced budget, yet even the most dovish of Congressmen howled like hyenas at the prospect of closing of a military base in their district. The all-volunteer army introduced in the wake of Vietnam seemed to work fine until we had a war to fight.

For all this, the world was a better place in 2000 than it had been in 1945. Nazism and fascism, once considered portents of the future, lay discredited, along with racism, in the rubble of the Third Reich. Racism became unacceptable in public discourse. The shifting intellectual and moral position cleared the path for the Civil Rights movement, and influenced the reasoning behind some of the Supreme Court's decisions on discrimination.

By the end of the twentieth century, other ideas that once enjoyed significant currency had been devalued. Marxism was already in sharp decline following the publication of Aleksander Solzhenitsyn's *The Gulag Archipelgo*, revelations of Cambodian genocide under the Khmer Rouge, and the degragadation of China's Cultural Revolution. Even more important were the stark comparisons of countries divided between capitalist and communist economies, such as North Korea and South Korea, East Germany and West Germany, or Communist China and Taiwan. Most of the communist countries, including the Soviet Union itself, struggled to feed themselves. Many smaller countries found it easier to win revolutions or conquer their neighbors than to collect the garbage on time.

In aesthetics, modernists found themselves challenged by a horde of postmodernists who advocated cultural changes as diverse as a return to historical styles in architecture to the idea that reality was virtually unknowable. Paradoxically, modernism no longer seemed modern.

Some intellectuals perceived the end of the century as a time when orthodoxies had collapsed and nothing had risen in their place. But it was apparent that a society based on free markets and unregulated commerce and consumerism had become the governing ideology of a global economy.

Reviewers and critics complained about unimaginative redundancy in music and movies, the decline of significant fiction in an era when fact was often fantastic, and the isolation of the visual and performing arts from the main currents of culture. However, culture became a lure for local boosters in American cities hoping to lure young professionals. More books and sound recordings were published in the 1990s than ever before in an era in which niche marketing assumed importance. The glut of cultural offerings made it difficult for anyone to pay close attention to specific things. Paradoxically, a large segment of curious youth embraced the music of the 1960s and 1970s, preferring it to the sounds of their own generation.

In the 1990s it was argued that rock, once he bellwether of youth rebellion, had become old-fashioned, its role supplanted by rap, the newest music to spring from African-American culture. Yet rock bands continued to play, record, and attract fans, even as rap and its seeming antithesis, country music, battled pop for control of the charts.

Sports still fascinated Americans. Yet some were alienated by the big salaries, big egos, and arrogance of professional athletes. Moreover, teams shifted cities and athletes switched teams with the frequency of musical chairs. The team aspect of professional sports was diminished; owners now sought to buy a few big stars. Players strutted after scoring, talked trash, and taunted opponents. Athletes used drugs to enhance performance, then lied about it. Other athletes, at the professional and college levels, were arrested for use of recreational drugs, public intoxication, and beating up their girl friends or wives. Many thought that money had become too important a factor in sports, and that the number of games on television represented overkill.

Yet every summer hope emerged anew in Mudville as Little Leaguers took the field, and as the leaves began to fall, Pop Warner coaches told their young players that maybe someday they could play at Notre Dame. And on tennis and basketball courts all across America people played for fun. Despite their dark side, college and professional sports served as a source of identity for cities and universities, a way of bonding for alumni, and a focus of pride. The effect of sports was paradoxical; it could be inspiring and uplifting, yet like an overcooked turkey it might spoil Thanksgiving.

The period from the Cold War to the Third Millennium piled paradoxes as high as the national debt:

The paradox that despite the status of the U.S. as the world's sole superpower, the wealthiest, and most generous nation, it was the chief source of resentment as well as envy. People throw rocks up, not down.

The paradox that despite the growth of terrorism in the twenty-first century, America was actually a safer place than in the late 1960s, when thousands of nuclear warheads were aimed at the hearts of the U.S. and the Soviet Union, capable of destroying the world at a moment's notice, possibly by simple miscalculation.

The paradox that despite the trials and triumphs and sacrifices of the civil rights movement, America's big-city schools are re-segregated and chronically underachieving, problems that no amount of money or good will seem capable of solving.

The paradox that the nation, having survived adolescence and grown to middle age, has not mellowed but has become cynical—that it craves security and a return to its own ideals.

The paradox that America's greatest impact worldwide is not its economy or military might or even its democratic ideals but its popular culture, which intrudes where soldiers dare not tread.

The paradox that interest group politics, a source of succor for the underprivileged, has degenerated into a dog-eat-dog squabble for spoils.

The paradox that, as a nation of perfectionists, we can never be perfect enough to satisfy our own expectations. The world's most successful nation is the world's most doubting.

The paradox that some of the brightest presidents, such as Jimmy Carter, have been among the least effective.

The paradox that trying to do too much good, at home and abroad, results in the opposite of our intentions.

The paradox that sometimes the more generous we are, the more resented we are.

The paradox that many traits that are virtues in individuals are vices in nations.

The paradox that we are the world's biggest complainers and have the least to complain about.

The third millennium and the fourth American century beckon with opportunity and loom with catastrophe. We might not repeat the wisdom of the twentieth century in avoiding self-destruction. We might plant democracy in the Middle East or shatter what little stability exists. We might celebrate our finer qualities or turn upon ourselves in hate and vengeance. We have opportunities open to no great civilization of the past: to mitigate, if not eliminate, poverty, disease, and discrimination; to open our hearts and minds to each other and to new ideas; to explore the universe without and the universe within; to bring hope, not despair, to the world; to survive another century as the world's longest-lasting democracy; to justify the faith of the Founding fathers; to renew our faith in ourselves and our ideals; to turn consistently to our better natures; to conquer realms and dimensions invisible as we write.

Index

About the Author

GLEN JEANSONNE has taught twentieth-century American history at the University of Louisiana–Lafayette, Williams College, and the University of Wisconsin–Milwaukee. *A Time of Paradox* is his ninth book, which include *Leander Perez* (1977), *Gerald L. K. Smith* (1988), *Huey Long* (1993), *Transformation and Reaction* (1994), and *Women of the Far Right* (1997). Jeansonne received his B.A. in history from the University of Louisiana–Lafayette, where he graduated salutatorian in 1968, and his Ph.D. from Florida State University in 1973.

DAVID LUHRSSEN has lectured at Marquette University, Beloit College, and the Milwaukee Institute of Art and Design. He has written extensively on music, film, and culture.